'Warning of threats to the Republic before they occu[r is one of] the many intelligence duties—and the main reason w[hy we spend] each year trying to understand where dangers lurk i[n today's] world. The warning responsibility places an understanding of intelligence failure directly at the heart of U.S. national security considerations. Only a handful of people in the world can address this subject with authority and deep insight; James J. Wirtz is one of them. In this gracefully written and absorbing volume, he makes a strong case for a greater synergism and integration of this nation's intelligence efforts as a means for reducing the likelihood of failure. This book is one of the "must reads" for anyone interested in intelligence and national security as we enter an era of growing nuclear threats and ongoing global terrorism.'

Loch K. Johnson, University of Georgia, USA

'This characteristically erudite and thought-provoking volume from one of the leading figures in both Intelligence Studies and Strategic Studies is required reading for those seeking to understand, and minimise the occurrence of, strategic surprise.'

Mark Phythian, University of Leicester, UK

'This book, a premier in the field, distinguishes itself by skillfully merging theory of strategic surprise with theory of coercion. Wirtz diagnoses the main pathologies in the art of intelligence, and offers the most innovative doctrinal solution to deal with them, for the age of uncertainty and instability. As such, the book takes theoreticians and practitioners of intelligence and strategy a quantum leap forward.'

Dima Adamsky, Interdisciplinary Center (IDC) Herzliya, Israel

'In this fascinating and absorbing account Professor Wirtz masterfully explores the interconnectedness between risk, intelligence, and warning. His clear analysis and identification of the lessons of the past make this essential reading for scholars, analysts and policy-makers alike.'

Michael S. Goodman, King's College London, UK

'Intelligence failure and surprise attacks are flip sides of the same coin, though all too frequently studied separately. In *Understanding Intelligence Failure: Warning, response and deterrence* James J. Wirtz effectively integrates the two sides together by exploring how knowledge and power interact to improve our understanding of surprise in international affairs. In doing so, he makes a significant contribution to both intelligence studies and security studies by providing a holistic theory of surprise which explains the planning and implementation of surprise attacks as well as practical suggestions for what can be done to prevent them. Written in an easily digestible fashion, this insightful exposition of the dynamics that underlie surprise attack will provide much knowledge and insight for those interested in intelligence and security.'

Stephen Marrin, James Madison University, USA

UNDERSTANDING INTELLIGENCE FAILURE

This collection, comprising key works by James J. Wirtz, explains how different threat perceptions can lead to strategic surprise attack, intelligence failure and the failure of deterrence.

This volume adopts a strategist's view of the issue of surprise and intelligence failure by placing these phenomena in the context of conflict between strong and weak actors in world affairs. A two-level theory explains the incentives and perceptions of both parties when significant imbalances of military power exist between potential combatants, and how this situation sets the stage for strategic surprise and intelligence failure to occur. The volume illustrates this theory by applying it to the Kargil Crisis, attacks launched by non-state actors, and by offering a comparison of Pearl Harbor and the September 11, 2001 attacks. It explores the phenomenon of deterrence failure; specifically, how weaker parties in an enduring or nascent conflict come to believe that deterrent threats posed by militarily stronger antagonists will be undermined by various constraints, increasing the attractiveness of utilising surprise attack to achieve their objectives. This work also offers strategies that could mitigate the occurrence of intelligence failure, strategic surprise and the failure of deterrence.

This book will be of much interest to students of intelligence studies, security studies and International Relations.

James J. Wirtz is Professor and Dean of the School of International Graduate Studies at the Naval Postgraduate School Monterey, California, USA, and author/editor of numerous books, including, most recently, *Intelligence: The Secret World of Spies*, 4th edition (ed., with Loch Johnson, 2015).

Studies in Intelligence
General Editors: Richard J. Aldrich and Christopher Andrew

Understanding the Intelligence Cycle
Edited by Mark Phythian

Propaganda and Intelligence in the Cold War
The NATO information service
Linda Risso

The Future of Intelligence
Challenges in the 21st century
Isabelle Duyvesteyn, Ben de Jong and Joop van Reijn

The Ethics of Intelligence
A new framework
Ross W. Bellaby

An International History of the Cuban Missile Crisis
A 50-year retrospective
Edited by David Gioe, Len Scott and Christopher Andrew

Interrogation in War and Conflict
A comparative and interdisciplinary analysis
Edited by Christopher Andrew and Simona Tobia

Ethics and the Future of Spying
Technology, national security and intelligence collection
Edited by Jai Galliott and Warren Reed

Intelligence Governance and Democratisation
A comparative analysis of the limits of reform
Peter Gill

The CIA and the Congress for Cultural Freedom in the Early Cold War
The limits of making common cause
Sarah Miller Harris

Understanding Intelligence Failure
Warning, response and deterrence
James J. Wirtz

UNDERSTANDING INTELLIGENCE FAILURE

Warning, response and deterrence

James J. Wirtz

Routledge
Taylor & Francis Group

LONDON AND NEW YORK

First published 2017
by Routledge
2 Park Square, Milton Park, Abingdon, Oxon OX14 4RN

and by Routledge
711 Third Avenue, New York, NY 10017

Routledge is an imprint of the Taylor & Francis Group, an informa business

© 2017 James J. Wirtz

The right of James J. Wirtz to be identified as author of this work has been asserted by him/her in accordance with sections 77 and 78 of the Copyright, Designs and Patents Act 1988.

All rights reserved. No part of this book may be reprinted or reproduced or utilised in any form or by any electronic, mechanical, or other means, now known or hereafter invented, including photocopying and recording, or in any information storage or retrieval system, without permission in writing from the publishers.

Trademark notice: Product or corporate names may be trademarks or registered trademarks, and are used only for identification and explanation without intent to infringe.

British Library Cataloguing-in-Publication Data
A catalogue record for this book is available from the British Library

Library of Congress Cataloging-in-Publication Data
Names: Wirtz, James J., 1958- author.
Title: Understanding intelligence failure : warning, response and deterrence / James J. Wirtz.
Description: New York, NY : Routledge, 2016. | Series: Studies in intelligence | Includes bibliographical references and index.
Identifiers: LCCN 2016025047| ISBN 9781138942134 (hardback) | ISBN 9781138942141 (pbk.) | ISBN 9781315673295 (ebook)
Subjects: LCSH: Intelligence service—Methodology. | Surprise (Military science) | Asymmetric warfare. | Deterrence (Strategy)
Classification: LCC JF1525.I6 W55 2016 | DDC 327.12—dc23
LC record available at https://lccn.loc.gov/2016025047

ISBN: 978-1-138-94213-4 (hbk)
ISBN: 978-1-138-94214-1 (pbk)
ISBN: 978-1-315-67329-5 (ebk)

Typeset in Bembo
by Fish Books Ltd.
Printed in Great Britain by Ashford Colour Press Ltd.

To Robert Jervis, Robert Art, James R. Soles,
James A. Nathan, James K. Oliver, Richard K. Betts,
Samuel Huntington, Warner R. Schilling, Jack Snyder and
Michael J. Handel, scholars who believed that political
science advances one graduate student at a time.

CONTENTS

Preface		xi
Acknowledgments		xv
	Introduction	1
1	Theory of surprise	9

PART I
The theory of surprise applied   25

2	Surprise at the top of the world	27
3	Surprise and the non-state actor	46
4	Déjà vu? Comparing Pearl Harbor and 9/11	56

PART II
Surprise and deterrence failure   63

5	The balance of power paradox	65
6	Deterring the weak: problems and prospects	83

PART III
Avoiding surprise: toward a new intelligence doctrine — 101

7 Red teaming surprise — 103

8 Indications and warning in an age of uncertainty — 113

9 From combined arms to combined intelligence: philosophy, doctrine and operations — 124

10 Conclusion — 142

Index — 153

PREFACE

I was not immune to the magical attraction of the City. For my seventh birthday, I asked for a trip to New York and to my astonishment my parents took me across the river for my first day in Manhattan. It culminated in a show at Radio City Music Hall. In the 8th grade, our class trip found its way to the Big Apple. There also was a clandestine junior high adventure to the City. Without parental permission or knowledge, Gerry Cafaro, Bob Wolf and I rode the commuter trains to spend a day wandering the streets of midtown Manhattan like suburban Huck Finns. I will never forget the doorman who said "you kids must be from the country, you look healthy." Unlike many high-school students in Northern New Jersey, however, I didn't spend much time hanging out in the Village. Trips to New York were mostly undertaken for Broadway matinees, visits to museums or Christmas shopping trips along Fifth Avenue. I had my favorite restaurants in Little Italy, Chinatown and there was Jeremy's Ale House, but many of my friends from back East knew the City much better than I did.

My first real memories of the World Trade Center are from the mid-1970s. The Towers were visible from the third floor of my high school and I remember spending fall afternoons staring off into the distance wondering about what was going on in the City at that moment, the fortunes being made, the millions of people going about their business, the excitement of the place. The skyline off in the distance was like the future, like the gateway to the real world. It led me to wonder what life had in store for me. I think I once took a college girlfriend to the top of the Trade Center. I guess there is no going back there now.

One of my friends from graduate school used to throw great parties in his Jersey City apartment that had a panoramic view of the City. My girlfriend Janet and I liked to go to his Fourth of July and New Year's parties because his rooftop, where most of the festivities took place, was dominated by the Trade Center. You almost had to look straight up to see the top of the Towers from across the river and the skyline really lit up the party. It was the perfect vantage point to appreciate the true dimensions of the Towers, to look at the skyline, and to watch the fireworks over the lower Hudson. Years later, I had to laugh when I heard a news reporter speculate about how Islamic terrorists living in Jersey City got the idea to try to blow up the World Trade Center in 1993. Obviously, the reporter had never been to Jersey City.

I think the first night's sleep I got after my son Daniel was born was in the City. I had been on the East Coast for a couple of days and I had driven up from Washington, DC to attend the American Political Science Association Convention. Although I must have looked the worse for wear, I received an upgrade at the Hilton on 53rd Street. When the doors to the elevator opened at the concierge level, a maid asked me if I was on the correct floor. I assured her that yes, indeed, I had finally arrived where I belonged. That was a lively convention, with plenty of extraordinary conversations until the wee hours of the morning about the meaning of life, especially scholarly life. Anyway, the City has been having that affect on people for years. My colleague Pete even popped the question to his girlfriend over a dinner at Puglias. I wonder if he was overwhelmed by the garlic?

For my son Daniel's seventh birthday, we went on a transatlantic voyage to New York via London, Southampton and Le Havre aboard the Queen Elizabeth II. Although I asked him on the flight from San Francisco to London to get some sleep, he remained awake all night (day?) with two Indian boys who were on their way to New Delhi. They played their Game Boys all the way across the Atlantic, leaving me to ponder the meaning of globalization. Clearly, discussion of various cheats or boasting about the level achieved in some Japanese video game would be the icebreaker at future diplomatic receptions. For the first time, I obtained my tickets and hotel reservations online and watched as the ATM at Heathrow produced British pounds from my bank account back in Monterey. I was amazed how the information revolution was eliminating the seams in the world, making it so easy to move people, money and data across continents and oceans. Alas, this was no great insight in the summer of 2001; others had noticed more diabolical opportunities created by globalization.

It was a wonderfully warm and calm summer crossing, and Daniel, along with the more than three hundred other children who were running around the ship, thoroughly enjoyed themselves as we steamed across the Atlantic. I remember chatting up the US immigration officers we carried on board, telling them how they were increasingly becoming the first line of America's defense and listening to how they had intercepted some hapless Romanian with a badly forged Italian passport. They listened politely, but I got the impression that they believed that I was making too big a deal about the incident, which after all just involved some hapless Romanian who could not produce legitimate documents.

We picked up the pilot on a glorious morning and crossed under the Verrazano-Narrows Bridge to a Manhattan skyline that turned golden in the sunrise. All I could think of was how different this was from Southampton or Le Havre, and how proud I was to be associated with a people who could build such a place. Most of the passengers moved to the port side to watch the Statue of Liberty pass by, but I stood on the starboard side, pointing out the highlights of the City to Daniel who was not amused that his father had dragged him out of bed to take his picture. Nevertheless, I thought it would be a good souvenir of his seventh birthday. Little did I know it would be so much more, a souvenir of that wonderful time before the surprise.

ACKNOWLEDGMENTS

This volume consists of previously published essays and the author would like to acknowledge the permissions granted to reprint these articles and book chapters.

Chapter 1 was first published as James J. Wirtz, "Theory of Surprise," in Richard K. Betts and Thomas G. Mahnken (eds), *Paradoxes of Strategic Intelligence* (London: Frank Cass, 2003). Reprinted by permission of Routledge.

Chapter 2 was first published as "Surprise at the Top of the World: India's Systemic Intelligence Failure," in Peter R. Lavoy (ed.), *Asymmetric Warfare in South Asia* (2009). Copyright © 2009 by Cambridge University Press. All rights reserved. Reprinted by permission of the publisher, Cambridge University Press.

Chapter 3 was first published as James J. Wirtz, "Hiding in Plain Sight: Denial, Deception, and the Non-State Actor," in *The SAIS Review of International Affairs* Vol. 27, No 1 (Winter-Spring 2008), 55–63. Copyright © 2008 Johns Hopkins University Press. Reprinted by permission of Johns Hopkins University Press.

Chapter 4 was first published as James J. Wirtz, "Deja Vu? Comparing Pearl Harbor and Sepember 11," *Harvard International Review* Vol. 24, No 3 (Fall 2002). Reprinted by permission of the Harvard International Review.

Chapter 5 was first published as "The Balance of Power Paradox," in T.V. Paul, James J. Wirtz and Michele Fortmann (eds), *Balance of Power: Theory and Practice in the 21st Century* (2004). Copyright © 2004 by the Board of Trustees of the Leland Stanford Jr. University. All rights reserved. Reprinted by permission of the publisher, Stanford University Press, sup. org.

Chapter 6 was first published as James J. Wirtz, "Deterring the Weak: Problems and Prospects," *Proliferation Papers* No. 43, Fall 2012. Reprinted by permission of the Insitut Francais des Relations Internationales.

Chapter 7 was first published as James J. Wirtz, "Red Teaming Surprise," Defense Adaptive Red Team Working Paper (Hicks & Associates September 2002). Reprinted by permission of SAIC.

Chapter 8 was first published as James J. Wirtz (2013) "Indications and Warning in an Age of Uncertainty," *International Journal of Intelligence and CounterIntelligence* Vol. 26, No 3, 550–562. Reprinted by permission of Taylor and Francis.

Chapter 9 was first published as James J. Wirtz & Jon J. Rosenwasser (2010) "From Combined Arms to Combined Intelligence: Philosophy, Doctrine and Operations," *Intelligence and National Security* Vol. 25, No 6, 725–743. Reprinted by permission of Taylor and Francis.

INTRODUCTION

To understand intelligence failure, one would have to be able to answer a series of questions. Why do states or non-state actors attempt to surprise their opponents to achieve strategic effect? Why do they often succeed? How does surprise affect the outcomes of strategic interactions, competitions in which the behavior of both sides determines the outcome? Why do some surprise initiatives succeed spectacularly, only to end in disaster for the side that initially benefited from surprise? Why do instances of intelligence failure and "strategic surprise" seem so closely linked not only to deterrence failure, but overall strategic failure from the victim's perspective? If we can explain surprise, can we prevent it from occurring?

To answer these questions, one would have to develop a theory of surprise—a unifying explanation of why states, for example, attempt to surprise their opponents with diplomatic or military initiatives, why they succeed, and how surprise helps them to achieve their objectives. One would also expect that the theory would explain why some states fall victim to surprise, despite the fact that accurate indications of what is about to happen are usually available to intelligence analysts and policymakers. Some might protest, however, that such a powerful (in the sense that it would apply to state and non-state actors) and parsimonious (thrifty in the number of causal factors it highlights) explanation would be impossible to construct because of the many problems that often bedevil those wishing to avoid surprise. Yet, instances of strategic surprise—one side's effort to present their competitor with a fait accompli by basing an extraordinarily ambitious initiative on the achievement of surprise—have occurred repeatedly throughout history, suggesting that it can addressed by a unifying theory. Strategic surprises share many similarities despite differences in the culture and history of the participants, a shifting technological and diplomatic setting, and the varied nature of the disputes that animate conflicts in the first place. Instances of strategic surprise also share one additional similarity: they tend to defeat or render superfluous a victim's deterrent strategy at the very outset of a conflict. In other words, it is the destruction of an opponent's deterrent *strategy*, not necessarily the battlefield impact of a surprise attack, that makes strategic surprise such a devastating and consequential event in international relations. Indeed, it might be useful to think of intelligence failure, strategic surprise and deterrence failure as three phases of a single phenomenon. Surprise is strategic when it destroys an opponent's strategy—usually a deterrent strategy—at the instant when hostilities commence.

Strategic surprise attacks can change the course of world history. On a grand scale, they can shift the trajectory of the nations that are the victims or the agents of surprise. The Japanese attack on Pearl Harbor, for instance, compelled the United States to abandon isolationism to defend democracy, a mission it has embraced throughout the Cold War to the present day. Despite the fact that Pearl Harbor was a brilliant military success for the Japanese, the daring attack ended in the disaster of nuclear war and humiliating defeat. For entire societies, surprise attacks create generational effects as victims internalize the shock and dismay that often accompanies the human and material toll of a devastating attack or diplomatic fait accompli. "Where we you on 9/11?" is a question that will always receive a prompt answer as long as that tragic morning exists in living memory. Strategic surprise is bound to shift the status quo, but in ways that are often unpredictable, unintended and far beyond the control of the parties involved. Strategic surprise is one of the most dangerous, risky and unpredictable phenomena in international relations because it combines the rapid destruction of the diplomatic or military status quo with an outpouring of human emotions. What might be politically or militarily unthinkable—war, domestic surveillance, shifting alliances—becomes politically compelling in the aftermath of strategic surprise.

Surprise also is a key factor in the failure of defense strategies and planning and efforts to deter specific attacks or general security challenges. Surprise provides attackers with an apparent way to achieve their objectives without having to confront opponents' military capabilities or deterrent threats. In that sense, surprise is an extraordinarily dangerous phenomenon in international relations because it can temporarily render superfluous significant military capability and what are often considered *ex ante* to be credible deterrent threats. Intelligence failure and surprise attack generate an immediate strategic defeat for the victim because they literally destroy the victim's national defense strategy. Surprise creates unnecessary wars, wars that should have been avoided because a credible deterrent had been created by the side victimized by surprise. Paradoxically, as the theory of surprise will demonstrate, it is the very existence of a significant asymmetry in military capability that sets the stage for surprise to occur. The perception that surprise can provide immediate and significant advantages over militarily stronger opponents acts as an enabler of war.

Why is surprise under theorized?

Despite these similarities among instances of surprise attacks and faits accomplis, the great impact surprise can have on world events, its link to the outbreak of war, and the presence of an extraordinarily rich and sophisticated literature on surprise and intelligence failure, no unified theory has emerged to explain the phenomenon of strategic surprise. Several reasons can probably account for why surprise is "under theorized." One reason is that most official inquiries into surprise focus on identifying the causes of a specific intelligence failure. In the aftermath of the Japanese attack on Pearl Harbor and the September 11, 2001 terrorist attacks on the World Trade Center and the Pentagon, for example, blue-ribbon commissions provided highly detailed reports on why the United States fell victim to surprise by identifying shortcomings that were specific to the case at hand.[1] In the aftermath of strategic surprise, intelligence failure is treated as an isolated political or public policy issue that can be overcome by appropriate reforms.

A second reason is that scholars tend to focus on devising explanations of intelligence failure, not the overarching phenomenon of surprise in world politics. This literature is both rich and highly sophisticated and clusters around four levels of analysis: idiosyncratic factors, cognitive limitations, bureaucratic culture and imperatives, and the costs of responding to warning.[2] Idiosyncratic factors inherent in the process of producing intelligence complicate institutional efforts at intelligence analysis and the production of finished estimates. The "Ultra syndrome," for example, is the tendency for analysts and policymakers to rely too heavily on sources of information that are accurate, trusted and timely. Named for the "ultra secret" Allied decrypts of German military messages during World War II, the syndrome can lead to trouble if generally reliable sources fail to provide warning because analysts will be slow to develop new or creative ways to gather and assess information. The "cry-wolf syndrome" is the tendency for repeated false warnings to desensitize a target audience to future alerts. Analysts also face the problem of "information overload," especially as the information revolution provides them with ever increasing amounts of data. The fact that signals—accurate and timely information about an opponent's future activities—is surrounded by noise—irrelevant or inaccurate information—at every point in the intelligence cycle suggests that supplying analysts with more information is not a panacea when it comes to avoiding surprise.[3] Al Qaeda operatives responsible for the September 11, 2001 terrorist attacks against the United States understood that American Signals Intelligence (SIGINT) capabilities could monitor their communications, but they might have also realized that it would take US analysts days to sift through the information at their disposal to identify specific phone calls.[4]

Many scholars see humans themselves as the fundamental hurdle when it comes to avoiding surprise. At the heart of the problem are the limits to human cognition that constrain our ability to anticipate the unexpected or novel, especially if the future fails to match our existing analytical concepts, beliefs or assumptions.[5] If analysts happen to hold an accurate image of the opponent's intentions, they stand a greater chance of recognizing signals and producing an accurate assessment of what is about to unfold. In the absence of this accurate cognitive framework, data is fit into inaccurate cognitive schema or unproductive biases that shape analyses. For example, mirror imaging is the tendency to project one's own way of doing business onto the opponent, despite differences in history, culture, objectives and government and military institutions. Analysts also tend to see the opponents' behavior as more centralized, planned and coordinated than it is, attributing exquisite rationality to the opponent that flies in the face of readily apparent organizational behavior and pathology.[6] Before the 2003 invasion of Iraq, for example, the US intelligence community hotly debated whether or not aluminum tubes purchased by Iraqi agents were to be used in a gas centrifuge, for producing fissile material, or a multiple-launch rocket system (MLRS), a conventional weapon of minimal consequences to American security. Because the tubes exceeded the design specification for the MLRS, many argued (incorrectly) that they had to be destined for use in a gas centrifuge. Analysts never thought that the Iraqis might have been engaged in an "irrational" bit of "gold-plating," despite the fact that the practice is not unheard of within the US defense establishment.[7] Analysts who suffer from the "not-invented-here syndrome" fail to recognize an opponent's ability to solve known problems in unique ways. Most often, however, inaccurate beliefs are tied to specific contexts and conflicts. Prior to the 1973 Arab–Israeli war, for instance, Israeli analysts dismissed indications that Egypt was preparing to attack because their image of Egyptian strategy (which they referred to as "The Concept") held that Egypt would not strike unless it could cripple the Israeli Air Force and attack Israel itself.[8] More rarely, events that are about to transpire are literally inconceivable to analysts and observers, who simply lack a cognitive framework needed to recognize what is about to unfold even when they are presented with compelling data. Some students of the Holocaust, for example, suggest that both its victims and some allied officials could simply not fathom the depravity and extent of the crimes that were about to be committed by fellow human beings until it was too late.[9]

Bureaucracy itself can impede efforts to avoid surprise. Bureaucracies have their own organizational interests that often cause their rank and file to pay attention to threats and issues that support programmatic and budgetary priorities and to ignore issues that cannot be used to further bureaucratic interests. This "mission-specific myopia" not only prevents organizations from monitoring the entire strategic horizon, it can also make defense of bureaucratic turf an organizational priority.[10] Efforts to pool information and analysis, necessary in the creations of formal, all-source, finished intelligence, can serve as a forum for intense bureaucratic battles. Often turning on highly esoteric matters of scientific, professional or analytic judgments, these battles cause the analysts and organizations involved to lose sight of the "big picture."[11] When analysts from the State Department and Central Intelligence Agency hotly debated whether or not aluminum tubes imported by Iraq could be used to build gas centrifuges they failed to realize that this inconclusive technical debate was an extraordinarily weak reed to use as a basis for suggesting that Iraq might have restarted its nuclear weapons program. Intelligence bureaucracies also are notorious for exploiting the principle of compartmentalization—the restriction of information on a "need to know basis"—as a source of power and influence within government. Investigators determined that compartmentalization, however, was a primary source of intelligence failure in the weeks leading up to the Japanese attack on Pearl Harbor. Signals were available within the "intelligence pipeline" prior to the Japanese attack, but intelligence information failed to flow to a central location where it could be analyzed to create a compelling and accurate depiction of Japanese intentions in December 1941.

Even if intelligence organizations manage to produce accurate warnings of what is about to unfold, there are enormous economic, political and military costs entailed in responding to warning of potential surprise attacks or faits accomplis. These *real* costs of taking action loom large in the minds of officials as they contemplate responding to warnings of *possible* enemy initiatives. In the summer of 1990, for instance, the intelligence community warned President George H.W. Bush that Saddam Hussein's forces were poised to invade Kuwait at any moment, but he was also asked by friendly Arab leaders in the Gulf to take a backseat in the looming crisis to allow Arabs to settle their problems themselves. Bush decided to show restraint; in any event, the United States was not in a position to back up strenuous deterrent threats with prompt and significant military action and there was a belief that major movement of US forces to the region could exacerbate the situation.[12] In this case, acting on the *known costs* of response trumped acting on the *potential costs* of inaction. Moreover, when analysts produce relevant analyses that have an impact on political and policy issues of their day by highlighting an emerging threat or undermining a politician's pet theory or favorite project, they are likely to be accused of politicization, i.e., allowing political pressure or their own political biases to skew their intelligence estimates.[13] Responding to warning will always create real dilemmas for policymakers because the costs of response are certain, while the costs of not responding to warning remain hypothetical until it is too late.

The third reason for the failure to make much progress in developing a unified theory of surprise is that a consensus exists among scholars and practitioners alike that intelligence failures are more or less inevitable. Richard Betts best explained this consensus nearly forty years ago.[14] According to Betts, it is difficult to anticipate future challenges, so reformers can never be certain exactly what changes are needed to meet future threats. Even more troubling is the fact that organizational reforms intended to solve specific problems tend to create problems elsewhere in the intelligence production process, which in turn lays the seeds of future intelligence failures. In the aftermath of the September 11, 2001 terrorist attacks, for instance, intelligence analysts were criticized for "failing to connect the dots" and for a lack of creativity when it came to predicting the nefarious activities of Al-Qaeda. But in their determination to avoid repeating this Type I error (failure to develop an accurate estimate of a real attack), they later suffered a Type II error (overestimating a potential threat) when it came time to assess Iraq's weapons of mass destruction program. It is extremely difficult to strike the exact balance between prudence and vigilance necessary to prevent Type I and Type II mistakes, and errors of omission and commission can creep anywhere into the intelligence cycle (i.e., setting intelligence requirements, collecting information, analyzing information, getting policymakers to act on warning, and disseminating warning). Providing analysts with more information also is no panacea. Increasing the flow of information to analysts can lead to information overload, preventing analysts from sifting through noise (extraneous information) to concentrate on signals (accurate indications of what is about to unfold). Intelligence reform itself can actually set the stage for future intelligence failure.

The theory of surprise

There are plenty of reasons why avoiding surprise is difficult and why intelligence failures are inevitable. What adds insult to injury, however, is the fact that the road to disaster becomes clear in the aftermath of surprise. Bill Clinton, on hearing that the World Trade Center and Pentagon had been attacked, said without hesitation "Bin Laden did this." In a blink of an eye, intelligence pathologies, cognitive biases and bureaucratic nightmares lose their efficacy as impediments to accurate analysis. If we could be equipped with this ex-post cognitive framework before surprise befalls us, then the chances of suffering a military disaster or diplomatic fait accompli would be diminished. Although some observers have suggested that surprise occurs because analysts simply fail to receive signals of what is about to transpire in time to prevent a fait accompli,[15] signals of what was about to happen can always be found in the intelligence pipeline. In the nine months before the Al-Qaeda attacks on the Pentagon and World Trade Center, 40 articles in the highly classified President's Daily Brief (PDB) discussed the increasing threat posed by Osama bin Ladin and his followers. On 30 June 2001, for instance, the CIA warned that bin Laden was planning a high profile attack and that his network expected that the strike would produce catastrophic consequences.[16] What needs to be explained is why events, which are so easy to recognize in hindsight, are so difficult to understand and recognize before they completely unfold.

The purpose of this volume is to explain the relationship among surprise, intelligence failure, warning, response and failures of deterrence. It adopts a strategist's view of the issue of surprise and intelligence failure by placing these phenomena in an overall strategic context. In the first chapter, the "Theory of Surprise" is presented, which is a two-level theory that links the cognitive framework of both the attacker and the victim in an instance of strategic surprise and intelligence failure to their structural position in a conflict dyad. In other words, it explains the incentives and perceptions of both parties when significant imbalances of military power exist between potential combatants, and how this situation sets the stage for strategic surprise and intelligence failure to occur. Part I then illustrates the theory by applying it to the Kargil Crisis, by examining the role of asymmetric attacks launched by non-state actors, and by offering a comparison between the Pearl Harbor and the September 11, 2001 attacks. Part I demonstrates how the Theory of Surprise can explain the general phenomenon of strategic surprise and intelligence failure and can be used to illustrate commonalities in specific instances of strategic surprise attack.

In Part II, the volume explores the phenomenon of deterrence failure; specifically, how weaker parties in an enduring or nascent conflict come to believe that deterrent threats posed by militarily stronger antagonists will be undermined by various constraints. Although the chapters in this section highlight the role strategic surprise attack plays in these failures of deterrence, they also illustrate how weaker parties in these asymmetric conflicts are highly attuned not to their military weakness, but to the many factors that can temper their opponent's response to some sort of fait accompli. The section explains how the interaction of the competing strategies adopted by strong and weak parties creates a nexus that is sometimes populated by strategic surprise attack and intelligence failure. It also illustrates how surprise becomes strategic when it causes an opponent's deterrent strategy to fail promptly.

Part III applies the Theory of Surprise more directly to the issues facing intelligence analysts. It explores the issue of war gaming to suggest ways that the phenomenon of surprise attack should be framed when exploring the consequences of various scenarios. It also revisits the concept of indications and warning analysis, demonstrating how this concept can reduce the likelihood of intelligence failure, especially by providing a method to frame potential responses to a threatening situation in ways that will be salient to policymakers. The section also borrows the concept of "combined arms operations" from military doctrine to suggest a potential method to better integrate multi-phenomena intelligence collections capabilities into the intelligence enterprise, thereby increasing the possibility of detecting an opponent's denial and deception initiatives before they contribute to failures of intelligence.

The final chapter revisits the issues of surprise attack, intelligence failure, warning, response and failures of deterrence from a *strategist's* perspective. It suggests that intelligence failure and surprise attack are best understood as a phenomenon that manifests in a specific strategic setting in which the structure of a conflict produces fundamentally different perspectives on what can be achieved in war. It depicts intelligence failure and surprise as a product of competing strategies, one intended to deter war, the other intended to circumvent deterrence. It also offers strategies that could mitigate the occurrence of intelligence failure, strategic surprise and the failure of deterrence.

Notes

1 *Investigation of the Pearl Harbor Attack: Report of the Joint Committee on the Investigation of the Pearl Harbor Attack*, Congress of the United States 79th Congress, Senate 2nd Session Document No. 244 (Washington, DC: United States Government Printing Office 1946); and, *The 9/11 Commission Report* (New York: W.W. Norton, 2004).
2 Ephraim Kam, *Surprise Attack: The Victim's Perspective* (Cambridge, MA: Harvard University Press, 1988); and James J. Wirtz, "The Intelligence Paradigm," *Intelligence and National Security* Vol. 4, No. 4 (October 1989), pp. 829–837.
3 This theme is the centerpiece of the classic study of Pearl Harbor, Roberta Wohlstetter, *Pearl Harbor: Warning and Decision* (Stanford, CA: Stanford University Press, 1962).

4 George Friedman, *America's Secret War* (New York: Doubleday, 2004), p. 2.
5 Robert Jervis, *Perception and Misperception in World Politics* (Princeton, NJ: Princeton University Press, 1976); and Richards J. Heuer, Jr., *Psychology of Intelligence Analysis* (Center for the Study of Intelligence, Government Printing Office, 1999).
6 Jervis, *Perception and Misperception*, pp. 319–321.
7 Tim Weiner, *Blank Check: The Pentagon's Black Budget* (New York: Warner Books, 1990).
8 Eliot Cohen and John Gooch, *Military Misfortunes* (New York: Vintage, 1991), pp. 114–115; and Ephraim Kahana, "Early Warning versus Concept: The Case of the Yom Kippur War, 1973," *Intelligence and National Security* Vol. 17 (Summer 2002), pp. 81–104.
9 Richard Rhodes, *Masters of Death* (New York: Alfred A. Knopf, 2002), pp. 251–252; Walter Laqueur, *The Terrible Secret* (Boston, MA: Little Brown, 1980).
10 Michael Turner, *Why Secret Intelligence Fails* (Dulles, VA, Potomac Books, 2005), pp. 42–43.
11 James J. Wirtz, "Intelligence to Please? The Order of Battle Controversy during the Vietnam War," *Political Science Quarterly* Vol. 106 (Summer 1991), pp. 239–263.
12 Richard Russell, "CIA's Strategic Intelligence in Iraq," *Political Science Quarterly*, 117 (Summer 2002), pp. 191–207.
13 Richard K. Betts, "Politicization of Intelligence: Costs and Benefits," in Richard K. Betts and Thomas Mahnken (eds), *Paradoxes of Strategic Intelligence: Essays in Honor of Michael I. Handel* (London: Frank Cass, 2003), pp. 59–79.
14 Richard K. Betts, "Analysis War and Decision: Why Intelligence Failures are Inevitable," *World Politics* Vol. 31 (October 1978), pp. 61–89.
15 Ariel Levite, *Intelligence and Strategic Surprise* (New York: Columbia University Press, 1987); and Erik J. Dahl, *Intelligence and Surprise Attack: Failure and Success from Pearl Harbor to 9/11 and Beyond* (Washington, DC: Georgetown University Press, 2013).
16 *The 9/11 Commission Report*, pp. 254–259.

1
THEORY OF SURPRISE

Why do states, non-state actors or individuals attempt to surprise their opponents? Why do they often succeed? How does surprise affect strategic interactions, competitions in which the behavior of both sides determine the outcome? Why do some surprise initiatives succeed spectacularly, only to end in disaster for the side that initially benefited from surprise? If we can explain surprise, can we prevent it from occurring?

To answer these questions, one would have to develop a theory of surprise—a unifying explanation of why states, for example, attempt to surprise their opponents with diplomatic or military initiatives, why they succeed and how surprise helps them to achieve their objectives. Some might protest, however, that such a powerful (in the sense that it would apply to people, businesses, bureaucracies and states) and parsimonious (thrifty in the number of causal factors it highlights) explanation would be impossible to construct because of the many challenges that often bedevil those wishing to avoid surprise.[1] At the heart of the problem are the limits to human cognition that constrain our ability to anticipate the unexpected or novel, especially if the future fails to match our existing analytical concepts, beliefs or assumptions.[2] Idiosyncratic factors—the "Ultra syndrome," the "cry-wolf syndrome," denial and deception or an unfavorable signal-to-noise ratio—complicate institutional efforts at intelligence analysis and the production of finished estimates.[3] Compartmentalization, hierarchy, "group think," a deference to organizational preferences or an organizational culture that creates "intelligence to please," in other words, bureaucracy itself, can impede efforts to avoid surprise.[4] Historians also might note that each instance of surprise is wedded to a unique set of circumstances, institutions and personalities. They would suggest that efforts to surprise an opponent have been present throughout history, but attaining and benefiting from surprise really is embedded in a specific technical, political or military context.

Given this Pandora's Box of cognitive weaknesses, intelligence pathologies and bureaucratic nightmares, it is impossible to say exactly which combination of shortcomings will conspire to assist cunning opponents in surprising their victims. Nevertheless, it is possible to predict when and why that Pandora's Box opens and why its consequences can be devastating for the victim. It also is possible to explain why the side that achieved surprise can suffer a devastating setback when the box snaps shut. Additionally, the key role played by surprise in asymmetric attacks and special operations can be identified. There are discernible patterns in the history of surprise in warfare and diplomacy, suggesting that surprise is a general phenomenon that can be explained with a general theory.[5]

To the best of my knowledge, the theory of surprise has never been fully articulated elsewhere. The theory is derived largely from Michael Handel's writings, especially his early philosophical musings about the nature of intelligence and surprise. It is no coincidence, therefore, that the theory of surprise is based on Clausewitz's concept of strategy and war—Handel was a devoted student of Clausewitz's *On War*. The theory relies on this Clausewitzian vision of war to explain why surprise is attractive to a specific party in a conflict, although it diverges sharply from the great Prussian philosopher's judgment that surprise was overrated as a strategic instrument in war. It then turns to Handel's insights about actors' incentives to base their strategy on the element of surprise and how this inherently risky enterprise increases the likelihood that efforts to achieve surprise will succeed. These insights, what I call "Handel's risk paradox," provide an important link between the structure of conflict and the psychology of surprise. The theory then explains why those who rely on surprise might win a battle, but rarely achieve overall victory in war. The theory also identifies a way at least to mitigate the threat of being victimized by surprise in the future.

War as administration

Surprise is often described as a force multiplier, something that increases the effectiveness of one's forces in combat. Across cultures and history, military doctrines have encouraged soldiers to incorporate surprise, along with other force multipliers such as the use of cover or maneuver, into their military operations because they increase the prospects for success and reduce casualties. In 1984, Handel summarized the battlefield advantages derived from surprise:

> A successful unanticipated attack will facilitate the destruction of a sizable portion of the enemy's forces at a lower cost to the attacker by throwing the inherently stronger defense psychologically off balance, and hence temporarily reducing his resistance … the numerically inferior side is able to take the initiative by concentrating superior forces at the time and place of its choosing, thereby vastly improving the likelihood of achieving a decisive victory.[6]

Clearly, surprise serves as a force multiplier or, as Handel notes, it allows one side to achieve the temporary numerical superiority needed to launch offensive operations. Nevertheless, Handel only alludes to how surprise produces this force multiplier effect. Upon reflection, the impact of surprise can be explained succinctly. Surprise temporarily suspends the dialectical nature of warfare (or any other strategic contest) by eliminating an active opponent from the battlefield. Surprise turns war into a stochastic exercise in which the probability of some event can be determined with a degree of certainty or, more rarely, an event in which the outcome can be not only known in advance, but also controlled by one side in the conflict.

Surprise literally transforms war from a strategic interaction into a matter of accounting and logistics. Probability and chance still influence administrative matters and friction still can bedevil any evolution, whether it is conducted in peacetime or in war. But surprise eliminates war's dialectic: achieving a military objective no longer is impeded by an opponent who can be expected to do everything in their power to make one's life miserable. This has a profound effect on military operations.[7] For example, the amount of time it might take to arrive at and seize a destination can be derived from simple calculations about how fast a unit can drive down some autobahn. (Of course, those gifted in mathematics might use more elegant algorithms to determine the effects of equipment breakdowns, road conditions or crew fatigue to estimate probabilities of likely arrival times.) No account need be made for delays caused by roadblocks, blown bridges, pre-registered artillery or major enemy units astride one's path. "Without a reacting enemy," according to Edward Luttwak, "or rather to the extent and degree that surprise is achieved, the conduct of war becomes mere administration."[8]

Doctrine and planning guides universally encourage officers to incorporate surprise and other force multipliers into military operations. Even when surprise is virtually nonexistent, military planners appear compelled to explain that they have attained a degree of surprise. US planners, for example, prior to the start of air strikes against Iraq in 1991 and Afghanistan in 2001, claimed they surprised their opponents, even though the attacks were preceded by very public force deployments and diplomacy.[9] But all of the lip service paid to the desirability of utilizing force multipliers hides the fact that surprise really offers a "silver bullet" in war. Whether it occurs at the tactical, theater, or strategic level of operations, surprise allows weak adversaries to contemplate operations that are simply beyond their capability in wartime.[10] Although surprise usually is a matter of degree,[11] when it approximates its ideal type, surprise literally makes war go away.

For a theory that is avowedly based on Clausewitz's work, it might at first appear a bit odd to reach a conclusion about the potential utility of surprise that diverges completely from the judgment of the great philosopher of war.[12] From a dialectical perspective, there is a cost to everything in war: operational security can prevent proper planning and briefing; diversionary attacks and deception operations can take on a life of their own or draw resources away from the main battle. Even spectacular successes like the September 11, 2001 attacks on the Pentagon and the

World Trade Center operate on the narrowest margins of success. For instance, there simply were too few Al-Qaeda operatives aboard hijacked aircraft to maintain control in the face of determined opposition from the passengers and crew. Increasing the number of hijackers assigned to each aircraft would create a different set of liabilities—inserting more operatives into the United States only would have increased the chances of detection and overall failure of the terrorist attacks.[13] Clausewitz estimated that the costs of obtaining surprise generally outweighed the benefits that surprise provided. Clausewitz, however, was more concerned with explaining war's dialectic and the way it shaped the nature, course and outcome of battle. What the theory of surprise posits is that, under ideal circumstances that occasionally can be achieved in practice, war's dialectic can be eliminated. In other words, it identifies a way to eliminate one's opposition by pre-empting the "dual" that is war. When surprise occurs at the onset of hostilities it can produce a strategic effect by delivering a strategic defeat to an opponent by destroying deterrence strategies intended to prevent the eruption of war itself.

Surprise makes extraordinary kinds of military activity in warfare possible because it eliminates an active opponent from the battlefield. Special Operations or commando raids, for instance, are a good example of a type of activity that is made possible by the element of surprise. Despite their cultivated reputation for ferocity, combat skill and daring, commandos and other types of Special Forces are lightly armed, poorly supplied and generally outnumbered by their adversaries. In a pitched battle against competent conventional units, they would be quickly surrounded and outgunned. To achieve their objectives, they have become experts in unconventional modes of transportation and operations to enable them to appear and disappear in unexpected ways and at unanticipated times and places. Surprise is the key enabler of all types of unconventional operations because it allows commandos to achieve some objective or attack some target without significant opposition or no opposition at all. Surprise also creates the opportunity for special operations to produce strategic effects. A dozen or so operatives appearing at a crucial command center deep behind enemy lines can affect the course of some battle. Yet, the same commandos would have no discernible impact on the course of a conflict if they joined a divisional engagement on the front line.[14]

Unless it produces complete victory, the ability of surprise to transform conflict is fleeting. Enjoying the benefits of complete surprise, the first wave of Japanese aircraft that attacked Pearl Harbor on 7 December 1941 apparently suffered few casualties. Nevertheless, by the time the second wave left the airspace over Oahu about two hours later, twenty-nine aircraft had been lost, even though the island's defenses had been damaged by the first wave of attacks.[15] When the Japanese returned in June 1942 to ambush the US Navy near Midway, it had become extremely difficult to surprise Americans with a carrier air strike in the waters around Hawaii. After all, the concept was no longer novel after the attack on Pearl Harbor. An outstanding American intelligence effort denied Japan the element of surprise that was crucial to their success in the engagement. The US Navy then delivered a stunning defeat to the Japanese, making Midway the beginning of the end for Imperial Japan. Similarly, surprise was the crucial element in the September 11, 2001 terrorist attacks against the World Trade Center and the Pentagon. When passengers aboard a fourth hijacked airliner learned of their probable fate in cell phone conversations with loved ones, they stopped the terrorists from completing their mission. Without the surprise needed to prevent the passengers from realizing that they were engaged in a conflict, the terrorists lacked the forces necessary to maintain control of the aircraft.

Surprise is extraordinarily attractive because it allows actors to achieve objectives that would normally be well beyond their reach if they faced an alert and determined opponent. Surprise allows one side to operate with virtually no opposition. Relying on the element of surprise, however, is extraordinarily risky. It is impossible ex ante to guarantee that surprise will occur, or for that matter, exactly when the effects of surprise will begin to wear off, and the inability to achieve surprise will doom the operation to failure. Stronger adversaries always can rely on more predictable attrition strategies to wear down weaker opponents.[16] In fact, stronger adversaries generally do not want to surprise their opponents. They prefer to intimidate them into surrender by announcing clearly their intention to fight if the adversary does not comply with their demands or to use their superior strength to deter potential adversaries in the first place. US officials for example, made clear their intention to attack Afghanistan if the Taliban did not hand over the Al-Qaeda ringleaders responsible for the September 11 attacks. The Taliban might have been surprised by the way the US campaign unfolded and by the speed with which their forces collapsed, but they were not really surprised by the war itself.

The risk paradox and surprise

Surprise is attractive to the weaker party in a conflict because it allows it to contemplate decisive actions against a stronger adversary.[17] Because achieving surprise is a risky proposition and because it allows actors to consider initiatives that are beyond their capabilities, however, the victim of surprise often will dismiss potential surprise scenarios as harebrained. In other words, even if the victims of surprise detect the beginnings of an initiative, they will have to overcome their existing assumption that the unfolding initiative is beyond the capability of their adversary or will prove to be suicidal. This asymmetry in the perception of what is prudent and what is reckless creates a paradox, identified by Handel, which lies at the heart of the theory of surprise: "The greater the risk, the less likely it seems, and the less risky it becomes. In fact, the greater the risk, the smaller it becomes."[18]

Handel is suggesting that there is a direct link between the weaker party's incentive to use surprise and the stronger party's propensity actually to be surprised by the initiative. He offered this insight, however, without fully outlining the causal linkages he was suggesting. Elsewhere, for example, he wrote: "The powerful stronger side conversely lacks the incentive to resort to surprise and thus not only sacrifices an important military advantage but also plays into his enemy's hands."[19]

From this passage it would appear that Handel believes that weakness is a necessary condition for one side to gamble an entire operation on surprise. In this sense, he is probably correct; stronger parties lack the incentive to risk everything on an effort to gain surprise. Stronger parties, however, often hope to achieve and benefit from surprise. American officials thought that the technological surprise suffered by Japan over Hiroshima and Nagasaki would shock the Japanese into surrender, but they did not stop their preparations to launch a bloody attritional invasion of the home islands to force a surrender. They did not risk everything on gaining and benefiting from surprise. In other words, the causal claims made by Handel required some refinement (e.g., the weaker party in a conflict is more likely than the stronger side to attempt operations or strategies that *require* the element of surprise to succeed). Similarly, Handel never really explains how victims of surprise contribute to their own demise. In this sense, he missed an opportunity to offer an important advance in the theory of surprise.

From a political scientist's perspective, what is especially elegant about Handel's risk paradox is that it provides a link between explanatory levels of analysis.[20] The incentives to seek surprise are located at a systemic level of analysis, or in the very structure of the situation we find ourselves in. Without parties in competition, without surprise becoming a priority for the weaker party in its quest for victory, there would be no deliberate efforts to risk everything on strategies that require surprise for success. But surprise is not a systemic or a structural phenomenon; it exists in the mind of the victim. Surprise is about human cognition, perception and psychology. In other words, the different perceptions of risk between the stronger and weaker opponent link the *structural setting*, which creates the incentive for surprise, with the *cognitive setting*, which creates the opportunity to surprise an opponent. The weaker party has a stronger interest in basing its plans on the element of surprise, while the more powerful side has reason to overlook the danger of enemy attack.

The ex ante divergence in perceptions of risk and opportunity sets the stage for human cognition and psychology to create the phenomenon of surprise. The weaker side becomes mesmerized by the potential opportunity created by surprise (i.e., suspending the dialectic of war), while the stronger side fails to consider possible courses of enemy action based on stochastic estimates because it becomes focused on estimates of the enemy's *wartime* capabilities. This cognitive divergence, for example, sets the stage for the use of denial and deception. It is relatively easy for the weaker side to hide (deny) information from opponents who are not looking for it, or to mislead opponents by feeding them information that confirms their more realistic expectations of what is possible in war. A leading student of denial and deception has even gone so far as to claim that "deception operations usually have substantial payoffs and never backfire."[21] Moreover, if accurate information reaches the victim concerning what is about to transpire, it is likely to be dismissed as fantastic or implausible based on the real facts of the situation. In planning surprise, the weaker side, out of desperation, is likely to grasp at straws and to believe that they have opportunities that really do not exist with or without the element of surprise. Prior to the Tet offensive, most American analysts dismissed information that the North Vietnamese and their Viet Cong allies were planning to instigate a revolt among the South Vietnamese population because they accurately perceived that southerners would not rebel against the regime in Saigon.[22] Opponents who are desperate enough to gamble everything on surprise also can be expected to ignore data that complicates their planning or calls into question their predictions about how their victims will respond to surprise.[23] Nikita Khrushchev was warned repeatedly by various advisors that even if he surprised Americans with his plan to deploy nuclear weapons and associated delivery vehicles to Cuba, the US reaction to the deployment would erase any gains the Soviets might obtain from the gambit. (The Central Intelligence Agency's Special National Intelligence Estimate [SNIE] 85-3-62 that was published in September 1962 also predicted that the Soviets would not place missiles in Cuba because it would be too risky.)[24] The side that is planning surprise is prone to make mistakes because it walks an extraordinarily fine line between success and failure. This fact creates a real challenge for intelligence analysts: they often have to convince their chain of command that the opponent is about to launch an operation that appears ex ante to suffer from a fundamental flaw, or to be extraordinarily reckless or to be strategically incoherent, perceptions that are likely to undermine the plausibility of their warning.

To prevent surprise the victim must overcome several challenges. It must overcome efforts at denial and deception. It must anticipate how weaker opponents might expect to achieve wildly ambitious objectives aided by surprise. It must anticipate that its opponent's strategy might be riddled with errors of omission or commission, or at least an overly optimistic view of its prospects of success. All of this must occur, however, as analysts and policymakers are blinded by their own assumptions and theories about how the conflict should unfold, perceptions colored by their conservative, attritional, view of the battlefield. The possibility that the opponent will launch asymmetrical attacks is hard to imagine because of the inherent difficulty in discovering weaknesses in one's own forces or strategies. In the absence of compelling data, mirror imaging—or the use of one's own preferences, culture and strategy to explain an opponent's behavior—is likely to occur. This tendency to understand the opponent's behavior in light of one's own perception of the situation really constitutes the heart of the surprise problem from the victim's perspective. This is the point at which a host of cognitive biases, intelligence pathologies or bureaucratic weaknesses will conspire to hide the possibilities for surprise from potential victims.[25] Even more troubling is the fact that evidence of what is about to transpire, or an eerily prophetic analysis, generally can be identified somewhere in the intelligence pipeline in the aftermath of surprise.[26] What is missing from the victim's perspective is the analytical context necessary to use accurate data to generate a useful and timely warning.

The fundamental divergence in the perception of what is possible and what is foolish creates a paradox that leaves open the possibility for surprise to occur. Extraordinarily ambitious initiatives are not only planned, but are often brilliantly executed against opponents who fail to recognize what is happening before it is too late. They succeed because extraordinarily risky operations that require an acquiescent opponent to be sucessful appear implausible ex ante to the victim. This plausibility assumption will lead the victim to place impending signals of an opponent's unfolding initiative in an analytic context that is likely to be flawed.

The failure of surprise

Much is written about intelligence failure, but little is written about the failure of surprise. Scholars have focused on successful surprise at the operational level of war, not on the effect of surprise in achieving overall victory. Surprise attacks often produce spectacular results temporarily or locally, but surprise rarely wins wars. Successful operational surprise may even hasten defeat by mobilizing the victim (e.g., the American response to the Japanese attack on Pearl Harbor) or by expending scarce assets without achieving a decisive victory (e.g., the fate of the Nazi offensive through the Ardennes forest in the winter of 1944). Even when surprise produces positive strategic consequences, the price can be extraordinarily high. The shock of the Tet attacks or the Egyptian surprise attack at the outset of the 1973 Yom Kippur war can be said to have produced victory in the very important sense that they altered the political balance between the combatants, but from the North Vietnamese or Egyptian perspective, events on the battlefield did not unfold according to plan. In that sense, the shock of surprise itself, not the temporary suspension of war's dialectic, helped to deliver victory. Nevertheless, this massive political shock effect is rare and in the previously mentioned cases it was an unanticipated, albeit not unwelcome, positive effect produced by a failed military attack. Because they can alter the political balance in a conflict, the consequences of surprise are often unanticipated and unintended by the side launching the initiative. If surprise is an *immediate force multiplier*, then over time it can act as a *resistance multiplier*.[27] The side that achieves surprise may reach the culminating point of attack, thereby achieving some fantastic local victory, without ever reaching the culminating point of victory, thereby hastening its defeat in war.

Surprise attacks often fail disastrously because the side undertaking the initiative miscalculates in several ways. Those contemplating surprise might correctly estimate that surprise is needed to achieve their military objectives, only to find that a successful surprise attack undermines the political or moral basis of their campaign. The Japanese attack on Pearl Harbor was a military tour de force, a feat of professional skill that will be remembered for a thousand years. Yet, the successful surprise attack was a political disaster for Japan because it eliminated the basis of its grand strategy in the Pacific: a "casualty averse" American public that would negotiate rather than fight over relatively unknown and unwanted territory. The Japanese failed to understand that the military force multiplier they needed to succeed—surprise—would destroy the political basis of their quest for empire. Those launching an attack often fail to understand that surprise can maximize the impact of a specific blow, but that even the most successful surprise attack needs to be integrated into an overall strategy to win the war. Surprise can worsen the weaker side's position once the dialectic of war is re-established because it can elicit a heightened response from the stronger victim. Successful surprise can make it impossible for the attacker to reach the culminating point of victory in war because it causes the more powerful victim to engage fully in battle.

Failures also occur because of a mismatch between the weaker side's objectives and the degree, duration or scope of the paralysis induced in the stronger opponent. The attacker might achieve surprise, but not across a large enough front or for a sufficient enough time, allowing the opponent to muster its superior forces to crush the attack. Indeed, when the effects of surprise begin to dissipate, the weaker side risks being caught overextended without the combat power needed to manage even a decent fighting withdrawal. This is what happened to the Nazi counter-attack through the Ardennes forest. Nazi forces achieved surprise and punched through the Allied line, but the Allies had sufficient forces to absorb the attack and launch their own counter-attack against the exposed Nazi flanks and lines of communication. If surprise is not linked to some sort of knockout blow or an overall strategy to win the conflict, it often worsens the weaker party's position and accelerates its loss of the war.[28] Ironically, the history of strategic surprise is generally characterized by attackers who fail to develop a robust theory of victory; instead they entertain politically, strategically or militarily unrealistic expectations of what might happen once the opponent recovers from the paralysis produced by surprise.

The failure of surprise is related to Handel's risk paradox in the sense that it vindicates the stronger side's judgment that a possible operation is extraordinarily risky or simply irrational. It made no sense for the Japanese to attack Pearl Harbor because they lacked the resources to defeat the United States; the sneak attack on December 7, 1941 simply guaranteed that superior American resources would be brought to bear against them. Even aided by the element of surprise, operations that appear harebrained ex ante can actually turn out to be harebrained. The analysts who predicted in SNIE 85-3-62 that the Soviets would not place missiles in Cuba because it would be too dangerous stated in the aftermath of the Cuban Missile Crisis that their analysis was at least partially vindicated by events. In other words, the Soviets should not have placed missiles in Cuba because the gambit risked superpower war for what were at best marginal benefits. CIA analysts were not alone in this judgment. When Secretary of State Dean Rusk called on Soviet Ambassador Anatoly Dobrynin to inform him that the United States had detected missiles in Cuba, he surprised the Soviet official with the news (Dobrynin had not been privy to the decisions made in Moscow). Rusk stated informally that it was incomprehensible to him how leaders in Moscow could make such a gross error of judgment about what was acceptable to the United States.[29] Years later, he noted that Dobrynin was so shaken by the news that he aged ten years right before his eyes.[30]

Surprise fails because it leads the weaker side in the conflict to reach for goals that are truly beyond their grasp or to forget that, when the effects of surprise dissipate, the dialectic of war returns with a vengeance. Indeed, the ultimate paradox of surprise is that it often amounts to a "Lose–Lose" proposition: it creates a disastrous initial loss for the victim, including the destruction of its peacetime deterrence strategy, and a painful loss of the war for the attacker. Surprise is an extremely dangerous phenomenon in international relations because it is an enabler of war. Ironically, the outcome of the war often confirms both sides estimate of the pre-war balance of power as the stronger power defeats the weaker side in the conflict. The theory of surprise thus offers an important caveat to Geoffrey Blainey's argument that war is more likely as states near parity.[31] Even though the leaders of the weaker side in a conflict might recognize the disparity in power between them and their opponent, the prospect of surprise can prompt them to believe that they can nullify that disparity and achieve their objectives.

The future of surprise

In the aftermath of September 11, 2001, the idea that the United States, its allies, military forces or interests are likely targets of surprise attacks or initiatives would not stir much controversy. But this prediction is not based solely on recent events. Instead, the theory of surprise suggests that America's opponents must somehow circumvent its diplomatic, economic or military might to achieve goals that Washington opposes. The United States' relative strength creates incentives for its opponents to launch surprise initiatives or asymmetric attacks to achieve their objectives before America and its allies can bring their full power to bear. This relative strength also creates an attritional mindset that blinds Americans to the possibility that enemies will use surprise to attempt to achieve objectives that in war would be beyond their reach.

Evidence exists to support the idea that the problem of surprise is especially acute for the United States. Thomas Christensen, for example, notes that the American academic and policy debate about the potential threat created by the emergence of China as a peer competitor (i.e., a state capable of challenging the United States in a battle of attrition), ignores a more likely road to war. Chinese leaders' perceptions of their own weakness have led them to a search for methods to distract, deter, or bloody the United States.[32] What is particularly chilling is that the thinking emerging in China is eerily similar to Japanese strategy on the eve of Pearl Harbor: a casualty-averse America will seek a negotiated settlement following some military setback. The fact that many American observers fail to realize that China might gamble on surprise rather than work for decades to match US military capabilities also is disturbing. Additionally, the nearly two decades of terrorism that followed Al-Qaeda's success in the skies over New York and Washington demonstrates that terrorists, fanatics or syndicates might find the element of surprise attractive because it affords them a way to attack an infinitely more powerful United States. As the information and communication revolution continues to empower individuals, the US intelligence community increasingly faces non-state actors attempting to capitalize on surprise to achieve their objectives. The stage is set for surprise to occur.

Michael Handel was a pessimist when it came to the future of surprise, agreeing with his colleague Richard Betts that intelligence failures are inevitable.[33] Handel came to this conclusion in his early writings, and the advent of advanced data processing and reconnaissance capabilities did little to alter his judgment. Indeed, what is especially vexing to Handel, Betts and a host of other scholars is that victims of surprise often had a chance to avert disaster, but cognitive, bureaucratic or political constraints or pathologies prevented them from capitalizing on these opportunities. Accurate signals of impending attack generally can be discovered in the intelligence pipeline after surprise occurs. Some people even manage to recognize these signals. Intelligence "dissenters"—individuals who swim against the analytical or policy tide—often issue accurate warnings before disaster strikes only to be ignored by fellow intelligence analysts or policymakers. Prior to the Tet offensive, for instance, civilian analysts in Saigon developed an accurate estimate of North Vietnamese and Viet Cong intentions, only to have their analysis dismissed as far-fetched by analysts at the headquarters of the Central Intelligence Agency.[34] Occasionally intelligence analysts might even get things right: US intelligence analysts surprised the Japanese Navy at Midway. Nevertheless, the American miracle at Midway was made possible by the American disaster at Pearl Harbor. According to Handel:

> Arrogance and a sense of invincibility blinded the Japanese, who did not consider their opponent worthy of much attention. On the other hand, the Americans, who had been humbled early in the war and who lacked both confidence and ships, knew that learning as much as possible about their enemy was imperative. There is no stronger incentive to encourage the appreciation of intelligence than fear and weakness (whether actual or perceived); conversely, victory and power reduce one's motivation to learn about the enemy, thus bringing about the conditions that may eventually cause defeat.[35]

What changed in the months following Pearl Harbor was that the Japanese had adopted the attritional mindset characteristic of the strong while US analysts and officers recognized that they needed force multipliers to overcome their disadvantage in numbers, equipment, morale and experience.

The American experience at Midway thus offers some insights into possible ways of avoiding future surprise that American policymakers and analysts might use to great benefit. The outcome of the Battle of Midway raises an important question: why did the same analysts and intelligence organizations fail so badly in their task prior to Pearl Harbor yet succeed so well in its aftermath? Was it war alone that concentrated their minds? In the past, most observers have identified cognitive, bureaucratic or political problems as a source of intelligence failure. Nevertheless, the pathologies and bureaucratic and cognitive limits to analysis often identified as the source of intelligence failure might simply be consequences of a more fundamental causal force. The theory of surprise suggests that it is the initial cognitive framework created by the relative power position of the parties in conflict that sets the stage for surprise to occur. In other words, if strong parties began to view conflict from the weaker party's perspective, while weak actors kept war's dialectic in mind, then surprise would become less likely. Christensen's analysis of the potential Chinese threat ends on a similar note: Chinese officers and officials should be encouraged to visit Pearl Harbor to take note of the fact that it is a mistake to count on a lack of American resolve in war.[36] One might also think about modifying the tour to include the surrender deck of the battleship *Missouri* to suggest that, once the effect of surprise fades, the dialectic of war returns.

Clearly, reversing the cognitive predisposition that accompanies one's position in a conflict is no small or simple matter. Midway suggests that it might be possible to alter this fundamental bias quickly, although it is not apparent if this change in mindset can be accomplished quickly enough or completely before disaster strikes. The theory of surprise suggests, however, that at least a "theoretical" path to reducing the likelihood that surprise will be attempted or succeed is available.

Conclusion

Handel began his 1977 article in *International Studies Quarterly* with the observation that the theory of surprise would be better at explaining, rather than preventing, disaster. He turned to Hegel's famous passage to capture this shortcoming: "The owl of Minerva begins its flight when dusk is falling ... man can perceive the conception of actuality ... only when the actuality has already been fully unfolded and has indeed become cut and dried."[37] One can only add the observation that things in fact did become pretty cut and dried on the morning of September 11, when the old bird returned home to roost. Millions of people in real time experienced surprise, which was accompanied by an inability on the part of nearly all concerned to interfere with the airplane hijackers. War, for a moment, became a matter of administration, a phenomenon in which it was possible for a few people to destroy the World Trade Center with the aid of a box cutter in just two hours. The very brilliance of such an audacious surprise attack showed that the assumption that people, groups or states would not dare do such a thing was flawed, if not downright stupid. Osama bin Ladin, after all, had established a track record of attacking American interests and targets and made no effort to hide the fact that he intended to attack Americans in the future.[38] The fact that we could have seen the attack coming simply adds insult to injury. Handel would of course suggest that this sort of thing is inevitable, that this is what it means to be a victim of surprise.

It is too much to expect that surprise can be prevented in the future. Nevertheless, the theory of surprise can identify when it is likely to occur, who is likely to find the element of surprise attractive as a basis of policy or strategy and who is likely to be its victim. It also explains why the beginning of the end for Al-Qaeda came when the first New Yorker noticed an aircraft heading toward the World Trade Center. The trick now lies in making operational use of the theory of surprise.

Notes

1 A host of factors also bedevils those wishing to achieve surprise. For efforts to organize the body of theory related to intelligence and surprise see Michael Handel, "The Politics of Intelligence," *Intelligence and National Security* Vol. 2, No. 4 (October 1987), pp. 5–46; and James J. Wirtz, "The Intelligence Paradigm," *Intelligence and National Security* Vol. 4, No. 4 (October 1989), pp. 829–837.
2 Robert Jervis, *Perception and Misperception in World Politics* (Princeton, NJ: Princeton University Press, 1976); and Richards J. Heuer, Jr., *Psychology of Intelligence Analysis* (Center for the Study of Intelligence, Government Printing Office, 1999).
3 The "Ultra Syndrome" is the tendency to become overly reliant on a clandestine source of information that has proven to be useful in the past, while the "cry-wolf syndrome" is the tendency for repeated false warnings to desensitize an audience to subsequent alarms Ephraim Kam, *Surprise Attack: The Victim's Perspective* (Cambridge, MA: Harvard University Press, 1988).
4 Walter Laqueur, *A World of Secrets: The Uses and Limits of Intelligence* (New York: Basic Books, 1985).
5 For a similar argument about the prospects for a theory of deception see Barton Whaley and Jeffrey Busby, "Detecting Deception: Practice, Practitioners, and Theory," in Roy Godson and James J. Wirtz (eds), *Strategic Denial and Deception* (New Brunswick, NJ: Transaction, 2002), pp. 181–221.
6 Michael Handel, "Intelligence and the Problem of Strategic Surprise," *The Journal of Strategic Studies* Vol. 7, No. 3 (September 1984), pp. 229–230.
7 Surprise, however, cannot overcome gross incompetence (troops that cannot conduct basic maneuvers), or negligence (weapons that will not work or vehicles that will not run) on the part of the attacker.
8 Edward Luttwak, *Strategy: The Logic of War and Peace* (Cambridge, MA: Harvard University Press, 1987), p. 8.
9 Although in both instances US forces can be said to have benefited from technological surprise. On that phenomenon see Michael Handel, "Technological Surprise in War," *Intelligence and National Security* Vol. 2, No 1 (January 1987), pp. 1–53.
10 Handel often made the similar point that "the weaker side has a very strong incentive to compensate for his weakness by resorting to the use of stratagem and surprise as a force multiplier." Michael Handel, "Crisis and Surprise in Three Arab-Israeli Wars," in Klaus Knorr and Patrick Morgan (eds), *Strategic Military Surprise* (New Brunswick, NJ: Transaction Books, 1983), p. 113.
11 Richard Betts, *Surprise Attack: Lessons for Defense Planning* (Washington, DC: The Brookings Institution, 1982), especially pp. 88–92.
12 In his writings Handel often stated that Clausewitz was no fan of intelligence, deception and surprise, but he also often noted that since the early 19th century, changes in technology, logistics, and communications increased the attractiveness of surprise in war. In 1996, for instance, he wrote: "While for Clausewitz, surprise was rarely achievable on the strategic level but was more feasible on the operational or strategic levels, today the opposite is true ... the development of radars and other sensors have made operational and tactical surprise easier to prevent." Michael Handel, *Masters of War*, 2nd rev edn (London: Frank Cass 1996), p. 131.
13 After all, one of the would-be hijackers apparently was already in police custody prior to September 11, 2001.
14 William McRaven, *Spec Ops Case Studies in Special Operations Warfare: Theory and Practice* (Novato, CA: Presidio Press, 1998).

15 Samuel Eliot Morison, *The Two-Ocean War: A Short History of the United States Navy in the Second World War* (Boston, MA: Little, Brown & Co., 1963), p. 67.
16 In the revised edition of his seminal volume, Luttwak makes the same point: "... military leaders whose forces are altogether superior may be quite justified in spurning surprise, for the sake of ample preparations to use their full strength with the simplest methods, to minimize organizational risk." Edward Luttwak, *Strategy: The Logic of War and Peace*, rev edn (Cambridge, MA: Harvard University Press, 2001), p. 13.
17 According to Luttwak "In a manner itself paradoxical, it is those who are materially weaker, and therefore have good reason to fear a straightforward clash of strength against strength, who can most benefit by self-weakening paradoxical conduct—if it obtains the advantage of surprise, which may yet offer victory." Luttwak, *Strategy Revised Edition*, p. 14.
18 Michael Handel, "The Yom Kippur War and the Inevitability of Surprise," *International Studies Quarterly* Vol. 21, No. 3 (September 1977), p. 468.
19 Handel, "Crisis and Surprise in Three Arab-Israeli Wars," p. 113.
20 Another important effort to link levels of analysis is Robert Putnam, "The Logic of Two-Level Games," *International Organization* Vol. 42, No. 2 (Spring 1988), pp. 427–460.
21 Barton Whaley, "Conditions Making for Success and Failure of D&D: Authoritarian and Transition Regimes," in Roy Godson and James J. Wirtz (eds), *Strategic Denial and Deception: The 21st Century Challenge* (New Brunswick, NJ: Transaction, 2001), p. 67.
22 James J. Wirtz, *The Tet Offensive: Intelligence Failure in War* (Ithaca, NY: Cornell University Press, 1991).
23 According to Jervis, "A person is less apt to reorganize evidence into a new theory or image if he is deeply committed to the established view." Jervis, *Perception and Misperception*, p. 196.
24 Special National Intelligence Estimate 85-3-62, *The Military Buildup in Cuba* (September 1962), pp. 1–2, 8–9; and James J. Wirtz, "Organizing for Crisis Intelligence: Lessons from the Cuban Missile Crisis," in James G. Blight and David Welch (eds), *Intelligence and the Cuban Missile Crisis* (London: Frank Cass, 1998).
25 Betts, *Surprise Attack*, pp. 87–149. This also is the point at which the theory of surprise can integrate the existing literature and competing theories of surprise into a unified explanation of the phenomenon.
26 Richard Betts, "Surprise Despite Warning," *Political Science Quarterly* Vol. 95, No. 4, pp. 551–572; and Michael Handel, *The Diplomacy of Surprise: Hitler, Nixon, Sadat* (Cambridge, MA: Center for the Study of International Affairs, 1981), p. 144. Roberta Wohlstetter's use of a metaphorical "signal to noise" ratio was an effort to show how accurate "signals" could always be found in an intelligence system, along with extraneous information described as "noise." Signals would have to grow stronger than this background noise before they could be perceived accurately. Ariel Levite offered a dissenting opinion on the issue, that surprise often occurred because of a lack of accurate warning, if not raw data, in an intelligence bureaucracy. See Ariel Levite, *Intelligence and Strategic Surprises* (New York: Columbia University Press, 1987).
27 Surprise can make war go away, but it rarely can prevent it from returning.
28 Stalin offered a similar judgment about the effectiveness of surprise, which provided him with an excuse for the denigration of the disaster of June 1941. For Stalin, surprise was a transient influence in war, not a permanently operating factor that could determine the outcome of a conflict. I would like to thank Dick Betts for offering this observation.
29 "State Department Cable on Secretary of State Dean Rusk Meeting with Soviet Ambassador Dobrynin to Give Kennedy's Letter to Premier Khrushchev, Announcing

30 Discovery of Missiles in Cuba," contained in Laurence Chang and Peter Kornbluh (eds), *The Cuban Missile Crisis, 1962* (New York, The New Press, 1982), pp. 146–147.
30 James Blight's interview with Dean Rusk, May 18, 1987, in James G. Blight and David Welch, *On the Brink: Americans and Soviets Reexamine the Cuban Missile Crisis* (New York: Hill and Wang, 1989), p. 185.
31 Geoffrey Blainey, *The Causes of War* (New York: The Free Press, 1988).
32 Thomas J. Christensen, "Posing Problems without Catching Up: China's Rise and Challenges for U.S. Security Policy," *International Security* Vol. 23, No. 4 (Spring 2001), pp. 5–40.
33 Handel, "The Yom Kippur War," pp. 461–462; and Richard Betts, "Analysis, War and Decision: Why Intelligence Failures are Inevitable," *World Politics* Vol. 31 (October 1977).
34 Wirtz, *The Tet Offensive*, pp. 172–177.
35 Michael Handel, "Intelligence and Military Operations," in Michael Handel (ed.), *Intelligence and Military Operations* (London: Frank Cass, 1990), p. 39.
36 Christensen, "Posing Problems," p. 36.
37 Handel, "The Yom Kippur War and the Inevitability of Surprise," p. 462.
38 Kenneth Katzman, "Terrorism: Near Eastern Groups and State Sponsors" (CRS Report to Congress, September 10, 2001), pp. 9–13.

PART I
The theory of surprise applied

2
SURPRISE AT THE TOP OF THE WORLD

Although there is much unique about the Pakistani effort to present their Indian rivals with a fait accompli along the frozen ridges and mountain outposts near Kargil, the incident is a textbook case of both the *success and failure* of military surprise. The Pakistani armed forces succeeded in infiltrating members of the Northern Light Infantry (NLI) undetected into disputed territory, but initial tactical success led to an overall strategic humiliation that culminated in the coup against Pakistani Prime Minister Nawaz Sharif. Much like the Japanese Navy at Pearl Harbor or the German attack through the Ardennes forest in December 1944, Pakistani officials and soldiers were unable to turn operational success into a strategic victory against a vastly superior opponent. This Pakistani success, however, still haunts Indian intelligence analysts, officials, and officers. Indian and Pakistani forces had been exchanging fire in Jammu and Kashmir for years. Both sides had a clear idea about the other's intentions. Nevertheless, Indian officers and intelligence analysts were surprised by Pakistan. Much in the same way the surprise suffered by Israel in the October 1973 war produced a major reassessment of what went wrong and lingering doubts about future intelligence,[1] Kargil shook the entire Indian defense establishment and led to several official inquiries into the sources of the intelligence failure.[2]

What is unusual about the Kargil incident is the fact that a relatively inconsequential military move posed potentially horrific consequences for all concerned. Not since the Cuban Missile Crisis had a nuclear-armed country attempted to surprise a similarly equipped opponent with a military fait accompli. There was a clear sense of nuclear danger in the air once this enduring rivalry erupted into open hostilities. Surprise under these circumstances is extraordinarily dangerous because it can prompt the victim to react with emotion, which amplifies the victim's military imperative to escalate the conflict to overturn the fait accompli.[3] Exploring the Pakistani motivations for attempting to achieve a fait accompli and the Indian response to surprise can generate important insight into the stability of the nuclear balance in South Asia and, for that matter, other situations in which nuclear powers find themselves in an asymmetric military rivalry.[4] Kargil also highlights an important observation about the phenomenon of surprise: despite variations in culture, history, geography, and the issues under dispute, instances of strategic surprise are fundamentally the same phenomenon and produce similar military results.[5] Kargil, Pearl Harbor, and the September 11 terrorist attacks contain striking similarities.

To illustrate the similarities that exist in all instances of strategic surprise, to explain the Pakistani decision to present India with a fait accompli, and to explain the surprise suffered by Indian analysts and officers, the chapter elaborates a theory of surprise. The theory is a structural explanation that links both actors' positions in a strategic interaction with their perceptions of information about what the opponent is likely to do under a given set of circumstances. It deals primarily with major instances of surprise, events that suspend the dialectic of war, thereby turning combat into a matter of mere administration by removing an active opponent from the battlefield. Kargil is unusual in the history of warfare because the stronger party was surprised when the weaker party occupied positions that the former had abandoned due to weather and altitude conditions that barely permitted human habitation.[6] In other words, India inadvertently suspended the dialectic of war on the Kargil heights: Pakistani officers saw India's inattentiveness as an opportunity worth exploiting.

Because the theory does not deal with the use of surprise as a force multiplier at the operational or tactical level of warfare, those who see Kargil as a minor tactical operation that escalated out of control might object to the idea that those behind the operation intended it to have strategic consequences. Nevertheless, the theory can explain why the weaker party in a conflict often becomes mesmerized by a specific operation at the expense of making realistic strategic calculations about its prospects in the overall campaign. As the theory would predict, Pakistan's military leadership, which represented the weaker side in the conflict, was attracted to surprise because it would allow Pakistani troops to achieve immediate objectives that could be expected to lead to major gains at the expense of India, its far stronger opponent. The theory also would predict that India, as the stronger side in the conflict, not only would be surprised by the fait accompli, but also would go on to redouble its efforts, regain the initiative, and eventual victory.

The chapter begins by briefly describing the theory of surprise. It then applies the theory to explain the Pakistani decision to present India with a fait accompli at Kargil. It then explains the reasons for the failure of Indian intelligence. The chapter concludes by offering some observations about the impact of surprise on the stability of enduring rivalries given the incentives and perceptions involved in asymmetric conflict.

The theory of surprise

The theory of surprise does not seek to explain all instances of military surprise, but it does explain the events that alter history by punctuating the beginning of conflicts, or events that can inflict catastrophic damage. Kargil thus represents a somewhat muted instance of surprise in the sense that the fait accompli Pakistan achieved did not provoke large-scale conventional combat or a nuclear exchange. Outside diplomatic intervention on the part of the United States and the failure of China to take sides with Pakistan in the conflict—exogenous factors in terms of the theory—helped to prevent escalation of the conflict. The Pakistani officers who planned the operation, however, apparently expected that the fait accompli would produce great results by altering the military balance in the theater of operations by cutting the ability of India to re-supply its forces to the Ladakh region.

Three key propositions make up the theory of surprise.

Proposition 1: Surprise temporarily suspends the dialectical nature of warfare by eliminating an active opponent from the battlefield

Surprise transforms war from a situation in which the outcome is determined by an interaction between two combatants into a matter of accounting and logistics, an event whose outcome can be controlled by one side. Probability and chance still influence administrative matters and friction still can bedevil any evolution, whether it is conducted in peacetime or in war. But surprise eliminates war's dialectic: achieving a military objective no longer is impeded by opponents who can be expected to make one's life miserable. This has a profound effect on military operations. For example, the amount of time it might take to arrive at and seize an objective can be derived from simple calculations about how fast a unit can drive down some highway. (Of course, more sophisticated analyses might be undertaken to determine the effects of equipment breakdowns, road conditions or crew fatigue to estimate probabilities of likely arrival times.) No account need be made for delays caused by roadblocks, blown bridges, pre-registered artillery or major enemy units astride one's path. Needless to say, the fact that Pakistani forces encountered no opposition as they occupied positions that Indian units had abandoned greatly facilitated their movement into mountaintop positions in Kargil, even though weather and terrain remained major obstacles.

Although surprise often is described as a force multiplier, something that increases the effectiveness of one's forces in combat, it can transform war as it approaches its ideal type. Surprise, and the asymmetric attacks it facilitates, thus can yield spectacular results. In other words, by placing combatants in critical places where they face no opposition, strategic outcomes can be achieved at an extraordinarily low price in blood and treasure. Weaker parties in a conflict thus become mesmerized by the prospect of suspending war's dialectic because it allows them to contemplate operations that are beyond their reach in wartime. By avoiding the military forces of their opponent, weaker parties use surprise to avoid the attrition and opposition that is inevitable in war to inflict some sort of setback on their stronger opponents. Stronger parties prefer more predictable and less risky strategies based on attrition to achieve their objectives; they are extremely unlikely to risk a battle, to say nothing of an entire campaign, on achieving surprise.

Proposition 2: The weaker party in a conflict is far more likely than the stronger party to adopt strategies that require the element of surprise to succeed

Proposition two applies to actors that rely on surprise for success, not as a mundane force multiplier. This is an important qualification because strategists everywhere recognize the benefits of surprise. Across cultures and history, military doctrines have encouraged soldiers to incorporate surprise, along with other force multipliers such as the use of cover or maneuver, into their military planning and operations. In ritualistic fashion, for instance, US officials and officers often report that some attack has achieved surprise, even though the United States rarely attempts to surprise opponents in a significant way. As the stronger party in the conflict, it generally seeks to intimidate, coerce, or deter its opponents without fighting by telegraphing its intentions to fight and the general size and severity of the blow that is about to land.[7] Prior to the Second Gulf War, for instance, US Defense Department officials provided many details about the "shock and awe" campaign that would unfold if Saddam Hussein failed to cooperate with UN mandates to disarm.

The weaker party in a conflict, by contrast, generally cannot engage in coercive strategies to intimidate its opponent into complying with its wishes or in attritional combat to eliminate the stronger party from the field. In fact, even the potential threat that the weaker party poses is often not recognized by the stronger opponent. Japan had been engaged in a war in Asia for nearly a decade prior to Pearl Harbor. It had abandoned the international arms control regime governing naval deployments and had joined the original "axis of evil" with Germany and Italy. Yet, US officers and officials never really took the Japanese threat seriously, although they believed that it was likely that the Japanese might attack someone else. Similarly, Indian officers and analysts probably believed that the advent of open nuclear competition as well as Prime Minister Vajpayee's Lahore initiative signaled an improvement in relations between India and Pakistan, but not a final settlement of the enduring rivalry between the two countries. What is clear to Indian officials in *hindsight*, however, is that the Pakistanis remained willing to exploit any opportunity that came their way to deliver a military or political setback to New Delhi.

The leaders of the weaker side in a conflict are more likely to risk all in attacks that depend on surprise to succeed because they lack credible alternatives to defeat their stronger opponents. They cannot win force-on-force engagements so they become preoccupied with using surprise to deliver a devastating blow to an unsuspecting enemy. The weaker party begins to focus on what might be possible in war if military operations could unfold without opposition. By contrast, the stronger party in the conflict remains focused on the attritional nature of warfare and thus fails to perceive the opportunities created by surprise. Moreover, even if the stronger party detects evidence of the weaker party's initiative, it will dismiss the threat as extraordinarily reckless or simply too fantastic to be taken seriously.

Proposition 3: Strategies based on surprise appear to all concerned as extremely risky ex ante and often turn out to be reckless and ill advised.

A paradox inherent in surprise is that both sides generally share the same perception of the risk inherent in relying on surprise in some sort of war-winning strategy. For example, Roberta Wohlstetter, in her classic study of Pearl Harbor, noted; "Japanese and American estimates of the risks to the Japanese were identical for the large-scale war they had planned, as well as for individual operations. What we miscalculated was the ability of the willingness of the Japanese to accept such risks."[8] Because the stronger party assesses any potential threat of surprise attack as doomed to eventual failure, it tends to dismiss evidence of an impending threat. Michael Handel captured this phenomenon in the "risk paradox" that is at the core of the theory of surprise: "The greater the risk, the less likely it seems, and the less risky it becomes. In fact, the greater the risk, the smaller it becomes."[9] At this point the structure of the conflict becomes linked to the perceptual biases of the parties involved. The weaker party plays down the extreme risks inherent in the effort to benefit from surprise because of the prospect of achieving gains that otherwise are beyond its grasp. The stronger party, armed with an attritional perspective, focuses on the real impediments—the balance of military capabilities—that the weaker party faces in achieving any gain at all. Both parties' perceptions of risk also are validated. The weaker party generally succeeds in surprising its more capable opponent; while the more capable opponent usually goes on to defeat the weaker party.

Propositions two and three thus link the structure of the conflict that two opponents find themselves in to the perceptual biases they embrace in assessing their preferred strategy and likely outcomes of a potential conflict. When combined, these propositions do not bode well for those whose job it is to detect denial and deception. What it suggests is that weak opponents perceive great incentives to surprise their stronger opponents using asymmetric attacks and that the stronger opponents will probably dismiss evidence of these emerging threats as harebrained. The stronger party views a potential conflict through the lens of war's dialectic: conflict will involve a clash of wills and combat on some battlefield. This attritional view of war shapes the stronger side's evaluation of information about potential initiatives by the weaker side. By contrast, the weaker side focuses on what might be possible if the opposition turns out to be a "no show." The strategic planning undertaken by weaker opponents, however, also shares another common attribute: it often becomes extremely vague when it comes time to explain how initial tactical or operational success will produce overall success in some campaign or even victory in the overall conflict. Japanese plans for the Pearl Harbor attack itself, for example, were extraordinarily precise, but their plans for the rest of the war were fuzzy.[10] Wishful thinking tends to intrude on the weaker side's estimates of its stronger opponent's response to surprise and the way the entire operation eventually will produce a favorable outcome. The ex post debate among Pakistani officials and officers about the objectives behind Kargil, for example, probably reflects the lack of strategic clarity that bedeviled the operation from its inception.

The fait accompli at Kargil

Although the Pakistani government had supported an insurgency in Kashmir since 1990, it had failed to spark a mass movement that could be exploited to settle the Kashmir issue in its favor. Given India's military superiority, an all-out military offensive in Kashmir would have ended in disaster for Pakistan. To overcome this stalemate, which was shifting increasingly in India's favor, Pakistani military leaders devised a plan to surprise the Indian military with a fait accompli that, in their thinking, would rejuvenate the waning insurgency in Kashmir and provide them strategic leverage against the Indian army's deployment along the so-called Line of Control (LoC) in Kashmir.[11] Because of its preoccupation with the Kashmir insurgency, India's defense and intelligence establishment did not believe that the Pakistani army was capable of significant offensive activity in the region, especially in light of the earlier failed Pakistani attempts to capture Indian territory in Siachen. Since India had secured the Saltaro ridgeline in 1984, its strong defensive positions and longer-range artillery—most notably the Bofors gun—had been consistently able to defeat Pakistani offensives.[12] When local operatives working for the Jammu and Kashmir government intelligence agencies reported in early May 1999 that the Kargil heights were being occupied by Pakistani regulars and not by a few stray militants, Indian army officials scoffed at the idea that the Pakistani army was on the move in Kargil.[13]

Planning the fait accompli: The view from Pakistan

Pakistani military officials grew increasingly frustrated in the mid-1980s with their inability to respond to the Indian occupation of the Siachen Glacier, its capture of a string of Pakistani posts along the LoC in the Northern Areas, and its artillery harassment of the Neelum Valley area. The idea of launching a "Kargil-like" operation in response to India's activities had been floating around for over a decade, but Pakistani leaders had rejected this kind of gambit as too risky. For their part, Indian intelligence agencies had no prior knowledge of any such plans.[14] The idea of launching an operation during the winter months was probably championed by the Headquarters of the Force Commander Northern Areas (FCNA) and the Headquarters of 10 Corps, the commands respectively charged with conduct of military operations in the Siachen region and the LoC in Kashmir.[15]

The operation probably had the immediate tactical objectives of infiltrating through the gaps in Indian defenses that were created by winter redeployment, and seizing dominating terrain features.[16] Pakistani officials apparently calculated that due to difficulties imposed by terrain and weather, the positions once occupied would be extremely difficult to recapture. If they could be held until the following winter, when large-scale military operations would become impossible, these limited gains might become permanent. Pakistani officers might have hoped that Kargil would deliver a shock to Indian officials, enable Pakistan to garner international support for its position, and permit Pakistani officials to enter into negotiations with India from a position of strength.[17]

Even in hindsight, however, these goals appear ill defined and far-fetched. Why would China, the United States, or the European Union, for instance, intervene in a dispute over some mountaintop outposts? Some have suggested that the operation was intended to generate the threat of nuclear escalation, which would have prompted an international response to the crisis.[18] But if one wanted to gain international notoriety, why stage the operation in such a remote and harsh location? This type of failure to link tactical or operational success to victory in a given campaign is actually quite common in the history of surprise and constitutes a phenomenon that transcends history, culture, and the specific points in dispute in a given conflict. Much like Nikita Khrushchev believed that the Americans simply would learn to live with the deployment of nuclear-armed surface-to-surface missiles in Cuba, Pakistani officers simply believed that Kargil would generate significant international support from the great powers in their enduring rivalry with India.[19] From the perspective of the Pakistani officials, apparently only positive consequences would flow from the effort to surprise India in Kargil.

Exactly how the planning for the operation unfolded remains somewhat obscure. The planning initially was limited to four senior officers: Lieutenant General Javed Hasan, (FCNA); Lieutenant General Mahmud Ahmad, Commander 10 Corps; Lieutenant General Aziz Khan; Chief of General Staff, and Chief of the Army Staff (COAS), General Pervez Musharraf. Lieutenant General Mahmud Ahmed briefed it to General Musharraf, in mid-November 1998. Prime Minister Nawaz Sharif probably was informed about the operation sometime between January and March 1999.[20] The planners' preoccupation with secrecy resulted in centralized decision making, which prevented the plan from being vetted and staffed before a larger group of offices and analysts.

Although the secrecy surrounding the operation probably was justified in terms of operational security (if Indian intelligence organizations had detected the operation, they could have scuttled it before it started by reoccupying the mountain positions) and not as a necessary requirement of some sort of conspiracy, the internal security surrounding the operation had unintended consequences. By preventing individuals not involved with devising the Kargil operation from testing its assumptions and estimating its likely consequences, the handful of planners cut themselves off from an honest appraisal of the risks they were about to undertake. Once again, this failure on the side contemplating a surprise attack against a vastly superior opponent is quite common in the history of surprise and is a phenomenon that transcends culture. Planners at the Central Intelligence Agency, for instance, relied on émigré reports when they estimated that the Cuban people would simply revolt at the first news that a few hundred liberators had landed at the Bay of Pigs. They ignored a fact that might have been readily apparent to those with fewer vested interests in the operation: the émigrés themselves had a keen hatred for the Castro regime and a profound interest in seeing the operation go forward.

The secrecy surrounding the planning of the Kargil fait accompli might have interfered in the execution of the operation. The movement of Pakistani forces initially was directed to four areas on the Indian side of the LoC that made a good deal of strategic sense: Mushkoh, Dras, Kaksar, and Batalik. The most important positions were located in the Dras sector because they allowed direct observation of National Highway 1A, permitting Pakistani artillery to target the road and surrounding Indian facilities. The Dras positions also could serve as a base for patrols and raids to supplement artillery interdiction of the road. But Zafar Iqbal Cheema has recently noted that the overall scope of the operation might have doomed it to failure—by late spring 1999 Pakistani forces had occupied over one hundred outposts covering an expanse of 130 square kilometers in depth ranging from seven to fifteen kilometers inside Indian-held Kashmir.[21] It was impossible for Pakistan to meet the logistical needs of such a large and far-flung force once Indian units responded to the incursion. Also, to achieve surprise, Pakistani planners used local, Northern Light Infantry troops for the operation, rather than moving additional troops from outside the region. As a result, the Pakistan army limited its options for reacting to India's offensive response when the element of surprise was lost.[22] It is impossible to determine if this oversight was the product of bad planning or overzealous implementation on the part of local commanders or militants. But from an operational perspective, Pakistani forces never severed National Highway 1A, thereby isolating Indian forces in the Leh Garrison.

Ripe for surprise: The view from India

Although several elements are unique about the surprise suffered by India at Kargil, from the Indian perspective, many phenomena common to strategic surprise can be identified in the incident. The fact that Indian officers themselves created the opportunity for surprise by abandoning their positions in winter is somewhat unique. The fact that they set a pattern of activity that was recognized and exploited by Pakistan (i.e., generally rotating units out of fixed positions in winter) is more common to instances of intelligence failure. The fact that the gambit adopted by Pakistan had similarities to the Indian military occupation of the Siachen Glacier in 1984 should have sensitized them to the possibility that Pakistan might try to avenge Siachen.[23] The inability of Indian analysts to recognize their vulnerability, however, is not surprising, given their apparently low opinion of their opponent. If Indian forces found it too difficult to garrison mountain top positions in the dead of winter, it was deemed unlikely that Pakistani forces would be willing or able to occupy the same positions.[24]

Indian intelligence officials, whose analyses of possible Pakistani moves seemed to reflect classic cost-benefit calculations, believed that political circumstances did not support a hostile move by Pakistan.[25] The Lahore initiative suggested that political relations between India and Pakistan were improving and it made little sense to upset the diplomatic apple cart. Pakistani efforts to stir up unrest in Indian territory adjacent to Kargil also had met with little success.[26] As for the strategic logic behind the move, it might be possible to occupy the mountain positions, but significant military activity in the mountains in the dead of winter was extremely problematic.[27] Indeed, the severity of the conditions along the ridgelines slowly wore down Indian troops and officers who were supposed to patrol the mountains vigorously once positions were vacated for the winter. These patrols were supposed to detect signs of Pakistani activity in the mountains so that aerial reconnaissance could be undertaken at the first sign of trouble.

Problems with India's intelligence organizations

India's civilian and military intelligence organizations were tasked with detecting and analyzing Pakistan's military movements along the LoC. The Intelligence Bureau (IB), which had its origins in British police efforts to combat thuggery at the start of the twentieth century, is the oldest civilian intelligence organization in India.[28] The IB focuses its efforts on internal security and is at the center of the Indian intelligence community. It is staffed primarily by police officers. Its international affairs divisions are staffed by active-duty or retired military officers. The Army, Air Force, and Navy each maintain their own independent intelligence agencies. The IB tracks terrorist or insurgency-related activities, conducts counter-espionage, detects economic crimes, and helps solve serious violent crimes. The IB also is required to gather information on the issues having long-term national security implications, such as demographic changes and ethnic or communal tensions. IB officials are posted in all Indian states and stations are located along the border with Pakistan. IB officials work in close cooperation with the respective state police and other law enforcement agencies. The IB also possesses its own communications intelligence (COMINT) collection capability.[29]

A second agency, the Research and Analysis Wing (R&AW) was created in September 1968 as an external intelligence division of the IB. It was placed under the control of the Cabinet Secretariat of India. The R&AW is staffed by active duty and retired military officers, police personnel, and civilian professionals with expertise in the fields of economics and information technology. Over time, the R&AW expanded its military intelligence capability by strengthening its coverage of technical and aviation intelligence and by creating a military intelligence group, which is headed by a senior army officer. The R&AW monitors foreign developments using a variety of sources: human intelligence (HUMINT) gathered from Field Intelligence Posts (situated along the border with China, Pakistan, Nepal,

Bangladesh, Bhutan, and Burma) and officials posted in the foreign diplomatic missions; imagery intelligence (IMINT) using aerial and satellite assets; electronic intelligence (ELINT) generated by monitoring electromagnetic emissions; and communications intelligence (COMINT) produced from intercepted signals communications. The main consumers of the intelligence products provided by R&AW are the Ministry of External Affairs (MEA), the Home Ministry (including the IB, and the Border Security Force), the Defense Ministry, the National Security Council Secretariat and the intelligence organizations maintained by the three military services.

Several smaller organizations also form part of the Indian intelligence community. The Border Security Force (BSF) is charged with policing the border during peacetime and with collecting information using HUMINT, ELINT, and COMINT networks. The Directorate General of Military Intelligence (DGMI) gathers intelligence relevant to army operations from divisional and brigade intelligence units. The Joint Intelligence Center of the National Security Council Secretariat serves as the central intelligence organization for senior government officials. It gathers relevant inputs from all national and state intelligence agencies for review by representatives of all intelligence agencies and concerned ministries during fortnightly meetings.[30]

Collection failures

A proximate cause of the surprise suffered by India at Kargil was the failure of reconnaissance efforts to collect information about the movement of Pakistani units. Between November 1998 and April 1999, Indian and Pakistani forces adopted a winter posture in the Kargil region and vacated some mountain posts.[31] For India, however, winter deployments were purely an administrative matter, not an operational imperative. To keep watch over areas controlled by border outposts, units were required to send winter reconnaissance patrols to areas vacated during the winter.[32] Reconnaissance patrols were not sent to Mushkoh from January 10 to March 30, Yaldor from February 1 to April 5, and Kaksar from March 3 to April 11, 1999.[33] Even though Brigadier Surinder Singh, the commander of the 121 Independent Brigade (the unit responsible for the defense of Kargil), is said to have visualized a serious Pakistani threat in his areas of responsibility, he did not organize reconnaissance patrols during the winter because he feared that he would be held responsible if these patrols suffered weather casualties.[34] The Kargil Review Committee absolved Singh by saying that under these conditions of uncertainty, his decision not to risk his troops was rational. The decision by unit commanders not to send ground patrols during winter months had been approved by higher authority.

In hindsight, the failure to mount ground patrols carried its own risks. Pakistani Army planners apparently had identified patterns in the Indian army's operations, and sent troops into the very areas that were not kept under ground surveillance by the Indian Army. Pakistan had begun to move units into the region in

December 1998, and by March 1999, the Pakistani military had established 132 posts inside Indian territory covering an area of 100 kilometers in width and 7 to 15 kilometers in depth.[35] It is difficult to explain why even the limited ground and aerial reconnaissance carried out by India that winter failed to detect such large-scale intrusions. It is possible that Indian army personnel deployed on these reconnaissance missions did not venture out of their immediate winter locations and instead chose to send false reports indicating that "patrols" had detected no activity.

The Indian army's aviation corps carried out Winter Air Surveillance Operations (WASO) to supplement ground reconnaissance during the winter. Local commanders often fly in the aviation corps helicopter sorties under WASO to reconnoiter their areas of responsibility. The aviation corps' Leh squadron was charged with undertaking WASO operations in the Kargil and Mushkoh sectors. Records show that six WASO sorties flew between November 10, 1998 to May 4, 1999 over the area occupied by Pakistani units. Brigadier Surinder Singh was on board during four of the six sorties, and the remaining two sorties carried the Commander of the Leh Division, Major General V. Budhwar. During the same period, five additional operational sorties were undertaken for ground observation missions and thirteen training sorties also flew over the same area. Of all the sorties flown, only the personnel of the WASO mission on March 31, 1999 observed some footprints in the snow within the Mashkoh sector.[36] Subsequent sorties flown over this area did not detect evidence of any activity.

The Kargil Review Committee report noted that WASO patrols suffered from several shortcomings. The sound of approaching helicopters warned of their movement and allowed ground forces to move into camouflaged positions before the helicopters arrived on the scene. In-flight vibrations made it difficult for crews to use binoculars for observation. Additionally, peacetime restrictions prevented low altitude operations and over flight of the LoC.

The Review Committee's explanations, however, do not stand up to close scrutiny. Operational experience suggests that in the rugged, mountainous terrain found in Mushkoh and Kargil, individuals on the ground will be able to hear an approaching helicopter when it is about seven miles away. A helicopter flying at 90–120 miles per hour covers that distance in less than five minutes, not enough time for personnel to hide extensive operations or large amounts of equipment and supplies. During winter, operations are even easier to detect because activity makes distinctive disturbances on the snow-covered terrain. Even though Pakistani personnel wore white clothes to camouflage themselves against the snow covered background, they were supported by large columns of load-carrying mules, which could not have remained hidden from aerial observation.[37]

In contrast to the Review Committee's report, a more compelling reason can be suggested for the failure of WASO operations. Without contact reports forwarded by ground patrols, WASO observers lacked the data needed to direct them towards areas of interest. An analysis of WASO flight activity thus suggests that most sorties were being used to ferry commanders from one location to another, not to search for insurgent activity. Even if one of these transportation sorties flew close to the LoC, observers were probably scanning Pakistani territory, not looking for signs of activity on the Indian side of the LoC.

The Review Committee also placed blame on the intelligence community's collection capabilities. It noted that if India had a half-meter-resolution satellite imagery capability, unmanned aerial vehicles (UAVs), and better HUMINT, then the Kargil intrusion might have been detected earlier. The Review Committee reported that the R&AW had reduced the assets it targeted against Pakistan in the Kargil region due to the Indian government's general budgetary cut imposed in 1978, and those cutbacks continued to affect its surveillance capabilities in the region over twenty years later.[38] These deficiencies noted by the Review Committee, however, are rooted in something other than strategic culture, bureaucratic inertia, or the limitations of existing collection systems. These shortcomings could have been remedied quickly if only the R&AW or the Indian army identified Kargil as a region of immediate strategic importance. But without the strategic and analytical decision to focus intelligence assets on Kargil, satellite imagery, HUMINT, or UAVs would not have detected activity in the region because they probably would have been focused on some other target. Indian intelligence and military organization had ruled out a Pakistani threat in the Kargil region, and once this was done, it was unlikely that significant collection assets would be targeted against this region.

Institutional failures and failures of analysis

The official and semi-official inquiries into the failure of the Indian intelligence community to foresee the fait accompli at Kargil often suggest that the intelligence failure could have been avoided. The Kargil Review Committee suggested that a series of war games conducted by officers, diplomats, and intelligence specialists who study Pakistan might have anticipated Kargil.[39] But this observation fails to reflect the realities of India's defense and foreign policy formulation process. War gaming is common in the Indian army, but national defense strategy and consideration of fundamental strategic issues lie within the exclusive domain of elected officials and civilian administrators. Rarely are outside academic experts asked to participate in policy deliberations.

Army intelligence analysts were attuned to the prospect of a large-scale conventional operation in the Kargil region. To detect a conventional offensive, army intelligence would be on the alert for various "indications and warning." These include: mobilization of infantry and artillery units; an increase in logistical activity (e.g., creation and replenishment of ammunition dumps); the construction of roads, bridges helipads or airstrips; or a sharp improvement in the quantity and quality of opposing combat and support units (e.g., medical infrastructure). Indian analysts were quick to detect indications of conventional operations. In March 1999, for instance, analysts had picked up some signals of Pakistan military activity in the town of Gilgit.[40] The intelligence inputs available to the Indian army during the first half of 1999 indicated that one additional unidentified infantry battalion was in Gultari (opposite the Mushkoh sub-sector), that Pakistanis were dumping 100 tons of artillery ammunition in gun positions opposite Kargil, that 500 pairs of new snow boots had been provided to forward units, and that about 2,000 militants were present in the Gilgit region.[41] The Indian army did not respond to this information because it did not suggest that Pakistan was about to mount a major conventional operation. One additional infantry battalion did not pose a significant threat (besides, it also was impossible to confirm the presence of a new unit in the region using other sources). The presence of 100 tons of munitions constituted less than 2,000 rounds of field artillery ammunition, which Indian army sources correctly assessed as replenishment of winter stocks and ammunition expenditures in previous artillery exchanges. The three Pakistani army brigades stationed in the area also could have utilized 500 pairs of new snow boots.

The R&AW in its six-monthly reports submitted on October 6, 1998, had mentioned that in order to offset India's military advantage in the Lipa and Neelam valleys, Pakistan appeared "hell bent" on interdicting the Dras-Kargil Highway (NH-1A), and targeting the local population for vengeance.[42] The report said that Pakistan army was inducting more troops and guns from Mangla, Lahore, Gujranwala, and Okara to reinforce its units located on Pakistan side of Kashmir.[43] The report further added that during the period March–September 1998, Pakistan army had launched massive preparations to improve field defenses, and stock ammunition. The report had concluded that a "limited swift offensive threat" with possible support of alliance partners (an apparent reference to militants) could not be ruled out. The R&AW had shared this report with the IB, DGMI, and the JIC. However, when the HQ DGMI raised queries about the basis of R&AW's inference of a "limited swift offensive threat," according to the HQ DGMI, the R&AW officials failed to give a satisfactory reply. Also, the R&AW had omitted a similar assessment from their next six-monthly report sent in April 1999.[44]

In hindsight, this evidence might be seen as a clear indicator that something was brewing in Kargil, but the interpretation of this information at the time by India's intelligence analysts was reasonable. Nothing about these reports suggested that a major initiative was about to unfold. In fact, these reports generally reinforced prevailing Indian images of conflict in the region. Among Indian army officers and intelligence analysts, Kargil was seen as a quiet military front. The fact that the infiltrators wore civilian clothes and that their radio transmissions were in *Pashto* and *Balti* languages, which are often spoken by militants, apparently helped to reduce concern when a few stray communications were detected.[45] The Kashmir Valley generally was viewed as the center of low intensity conflict along the LoC, and the Siachen Glacier generally was believed to be the most likely location for high-intensity conventional combat. The difficulty of the terrain and the predominance of Shia population in the area suggested to Indian analysts that there were better places for Pakistan to launch an attack. Army officers and analysts responsible for Kargil planned to plug possible militant infiltration routes; however, they did not anticipate that Pakistani army units actually would use these routes to occupy the region.

Some Indian analysts such as Jasjit Singh believe that an objective analysis of the geopolitical situation and developments in the months leading up to the Pakistani effort to present India with a fait accompli should have alerted the Indian government and military to impending action in Jammu and Kashmir. They point to General Musharraf's emergence as the Chief of the Pakistan Army. According to these analysts, General Musharraf's ethnic origin as a Mohajir, his strong anti-India bias, his known, strong linkages with the militant organizations in the past, and his antipathy towards Shia population, should have raised concerns about new military developments in the region.[46] Immediately after becoming Pakistan army's COAS, Musharraf had visited Gilgit in November 1998 and March 1999.[47] Although Musharraf's background and preferences do not provide a clear signal of what was about to happen in Kargil, they should have alerted Indian officers and analysts to the possibility that a significant departure in Pakistani policy was possible.

In the months before Kargil, the Lahore process also raised high expectations that peace between India and Pakistan might be at hand. Yet, in the aftermath of the Lahore peace process, there was no cessation of Pakistan's artillery attacks across the LoC and Islamabad continued to offer military support to Islamic militants operating in Jammu and Kashmir.[48] Not much was made of the fact, however, that Pakistani military operations along the LoC failed to match the spirit of the Lahore process. If an alarm had been raised, Indian officers and analysts might have realized that the supply route to the Ladakh region along the Srinagar-Leh road was the most vulnerable sector of the Kargil region. Nowhere else in Jammu or Kashmir had the Indian army left such wide gaps in its defenses.

Conclusion

Once Indian officers and officials overcame the shock produced by the realization that they had been presented with a fait accompli by Pakistan, they slowly brought their superior military capability to bear against their opponents, and drove them out of their mountaintop positions. As the theory of surprise would predict, Pakistani forces achieved a great success when they did not face an active opponent, but the dialectic of war returned to the Kargil heights before the over-extended Pakistani units could cut the Srinagar-Leh road. The much-hoped-for help from the international community also failed to materialize for Pakistan, leaving their units in Kargil isolated and dependent on inadequate lines of supply.

In spite of inherent weaknesses in the Indian intelligence system on the eve of Kargil, the basis of the Pakistani surprise can be found in a pervasive idea generated by India's position as the stronger party in the enduring conflict with Pakistan. Indian officials and officers believed that it made little military sense for Pakistan to launch an operation in the dead of winter in the mountains along the LoC. After all, if Indian units were withdrawn from their mountain outposts in winter due to the incredibly harsh conditions, it would make little sense for

Pakistani units to attempt to occupy the vacated positions. Instead of many misinterpreted signals or faulty analyses, the story of Indian intelligence during the winter of 1998–1999 is really a story of an absence of signals. Indian intelligence only had a few extremely faint hints of what was transpiring on the Pakistani side of the LoC. Indeed, most of the information it had about Pakistani activity supported pre-existing beliefs that Kargil would remain a quiet sector of the LoC. Needless to say, because they did not suspect Pakistani activity, Indian officers and analysts did not concentrate collection efforts to discover Pakistani infiltration into Kargil. When activity was detected, India's military commanders at first were unsure about the identity and intentions of the intruders or the seriousness of the threat.[49] The first confirmation of the Pakistani army's complicity in the operation apparently occurred on May 26, 1999 when Indian intelligence intercepted a telephone conversation between General Musharraf and his deputy General Aziz.[50] In the annals of intelligence failure, Kargil is thus a rare instance of surprise in two respects: an action taken by the victim (i.e., withdrawal from the mountain outposts) suspended war's dialectic; and an absolute minimum number of signals (i.e., accurate indications of what was about to transpire) were within the Indian intelligence pipeline at the moment when the Pakistani fait accompli was discovered.[51] Kargil is probably best considered a failure of intelligence collection, produced by a failure to set effective intelligence requirements. Indian complacency was so pervasive that it affected the entire intelligence cycle, beginning with the identification of intelligence collection requirements, which should have reflected the decision to withdraw from mountaintop outposts.

When fully alerted, Indian intelligence analysts and officers responded quickly and effectively to indications that Pakistani units were on the move on their side of the LoC. This would suggest that Indian intelligence and command and control were capable of responding relatively quickly to indications of Pakistani operations once the possibility of movement across the LoC became salient. Reports of unusual Pakistani helicopter activity along LoC in the Turtok area were received in late April and between May 6 and 19, and Indian patrols identified small intrusions at five locations near the LoC. Two battalions from 102 Brigade were dispatched to the area and quickly captured these positions, and arrested a score of local inhabitants who were suspected of plotting to attack Indian troops and assist the intruders.[52] Psychology (i.e., the fundamental assumption used in the planning of the defense of Kargil in the winter of 1998–1999), not bureaucratic or technical weaknesses, is the primary cause of the Indian failure to detect the movement of Pakistani forces across the LoC.

Those who planned the Kargil operation also displayed much evidence of the cognitive bias that affects the weaker party in a conflict, the bias that makes the idea of using surprise to present their stronger rival with a fait accompli seem like an attractive option. Pakistanis became mesmerized by the possibility of generating a significant setback to India, so much so that they apparently failed to turn initial success into a local battlefield advantage by failing to hold the infiltrated heights, and using their positions to cut the Srinagar-Leh road. Pakistani ideas about how success in a region would translate into overall strategic and political gains were particularly vague and apparently based on wishful thinking.

The theory of surprise applied to the fait accompli at Kargil also offers a rather unsettling observation about Pakistani officials' behavior during the conflict. Instead of being deterred or reassured by the defensive dominance implied by a mutual nuclear deterrence relationship, they instead looked for ways to inflict a setback on a much stronger opponent. They saw surprise and the ability to suspend war's dialectic, as a way to obtain meaningful gains. As the theory of surprise would suggest, Kargil confirms the prediction that the weaker party is attracted to surprise, and this attraction does not seem to have been reduced by the specter of nuclear war.

Notes

1   Uri Bar-Joseph, *The Watchman Fell Asleep: The Surprise of Yom Kippur and its Sources*, (Albany, NY: State University of New York Press, 2005).
2   The Kargil Review Committee Report (KRCR), and a report compiled by India's Institute of Defense Studies and Analysis (IDSA) are prominent efforts in this category. Constituted on July 29, 1999. The KRC comprised of four members, K. Subrahmanyam (Chairman), Lieutenant General K. K. Hazari (ret.) B.G Verghese, and Satish Chandra, Secretary of India's National Security Council Secretariat (NSCS). The committee was charged with reviewing the events leading up to Pakistani intrusions in Kargil. The KRC submitted its 265-page report on 15 December 1999, entitled, *From Surprise to Reckoning: The Kargil Review Committee Report* (New Delhi: Sage, December 15, 1999). The IDSA report is Jasjit Singh, ed., *Kargil 1999: Pakistan's Fourth War for Kashmir* (New Delhi: Knowledge World, 1999).
3   Fred Ikle has brought this escalation dynamic inherent in the response to surprise to our attention.
4   T.V. Paul, *Asymmetric Conflicts: War Initiation by Weaker Powers* (Cambridge: Cambridge University Press, 1994).
5   The idea that the phenomenon of surprise transcends history and culture is reflected in the classic works on the subject see Richard Betts, *Surprise Attack: Lessons for Defense Planning* (Washington, DC: The Brookings Institution, 1983); and Alex Hybel, *The Logic of Surprise in International Conflict* (Lexington, MA: Lexington, 1986); and Robert Axelrod, "The Rational Timing of Surprise," *World Politics* Vol. 31, No. 2 (January 1979), pp. 228–246; and Michael Handel, "Intelligence and the Problem of Strategic Surprise," *The Journal of Strategic Studies* Vol. 7, No. 3 (September 1984), pp. 229–230.
6   Combat between Japanese and US forces in the Aleutian Islands in the Second World War had a similar quality. The harsh weather prevented effective reconnaissance, and conditions on the islands made them nearly uninhabitable. Both sides staged amphibious operations, only to find, after suffering numerous casualties, that they were unoccupied by the enemy.
7   James J. Wirtz and James Russell, "U.S. Policy on Preventive War and Preemption," *The Nonproliferation Review* (Spring 2003), pp. 113–123.
8   Roberta Wohlstetter, *Pearl Harbor: Warning and Decision* (Stanford, CA: Stanford University Press, 1962), p. 355.
9   Michael Handel, "The Yom Kippur War and the Inevitability of Surprise," *International Studies Quarterly* Vol. 21, No. 3 (September 1977), p. 468.

10 Wohlstetter, *Pearl Harbor*, p. 349.
11 Since the late 1990s, according to Sumit Ganguly, the Pakistani-aided insurgency in Kashmir was waning. The Indian security forces had most of the insurgents on the run. See Sumit Ganguly, *Conflict Unending: India-Pakistan Tensions since 1947*, p. 121.
12 For the role of artillery in this terrain, see Lt. Gen. V.R. Raghavan, *Siachen: Conflict Without End* (Delhi: Penguin Books, 2002), pp. 94–97.
13 Surinder Rana's interview with a senior Jammu and Kashmir state government official during his visit to Monterey, California in August 2002. According to this official, the Jammu and Kashmir State government agencies, based upon information gathered through their own sources, indicated to the Army that Pakistan's army regulars, and not militants were active in Kargil heights.
14 The statement by a former Indian Chief of Army of Staff (COAS) during an interview in New Delhi on February 26, 2002 that the origin of Pakistan's plan dates back to the late 1980s is an afterthought. Indian intelligence was not aware of any such plans prior to April 1999.
15 Feroz Hassan Khan, Peter R. Lavoy, and Christopher Clary, "Pakistan's Motivations and Calculations for the Kargil Conflict, in Peter R. Lavoy (ed.), *Asymmetric Warfare in South Asia: The Causes and Consequences of the Kargil Conflict* (Cambridge: Cambridge University Press, 2009), pp. 64–91.
16 There were eight Indian posts in the Kargil sector that in earlier years had been vacated in winter. Sensing the possibility of Pakistan attempting to capture them, Indian military commanders had decided to continue holding these posts during winter of 1998–99. Some observers thus believe that Pakistani officials had planned to send forces infiltrate through gaps between Indian defenses not necessarily with the intention of capturing vacated outposts. See V.P. Malik, *Kargil: Surprise to Victory* (Harper Collins, India, 2006), p. 90.
17 John H. Gill, "Military Operations in the Kargil Conflict," in Peter R. Lavoy (ed.), *Asymmetric Warfare in South Asia: The Causes and Consequences of the Kargil Conflict* (Cambridge: Cambridge University Press, 2009), pp. 93–129.
18 Shahbaz Hussain Khokhar, "Management of the Kargil Crisis: A Systemic Approach" (M.S. dissertation, Department of Defense and Strategic Studies, Quaid-i-Azam University, Islamabad, Pakistan, 2001).
19 When Polish leader Wladyslaw Gomulka learned in the summer of 1962 of the Soviet decision to present the United States with a fait accompli in Cuba, for example, he warned Khrushchev that the Americans would respond vigorously. "Khrushchev assured him," according to Ned Lebow and Janice Stein, "that all would turn out well. He told Gomulka the story of a poor Russian farmer who lacked the money to buy firewood for the winter. He removed his goat into his hut to provide warmth. The goat was incredibly rank but the man learned to live with its smell. 'Kennedy would learn to accept the smell of the missiles'." Richard Ned Lebow and Janice Gross Stein, *We All Lost the Cold War* (Princeton, NJ: Princeton University Press, 1994), p. 77.
20 Shaukat Qadir, "An Analysis of the Kargil Conflict 1999," *Journal of the Royal United Services Institute of Defense Studies* Vol. 147, No. 2 (April 2002), p. 24.
21 Zafar Iqbal Cheema interviewed by James Wirtz, 2 June 2003. Cheema's account is corroborated by the architect of this operation, General Pervez Musharraf, in his recently published memoirs. Pervez Musharraf, *In the Line of Fire* (New York: Simon and Schuster, 2006), p. 90.
22 In response to India's summer offensive to dislodge the infiltrated positions, the Pakistan Army failed to reinforce, counter-attack, or make any other diversionary maneuvers to

lessen the pressure upon the infiltrating troops, when they were attacked.
23 Evidence of Pakistani movement into the mountain positions was not a unique event in the annals of history, making it far easier to recognize it for what it was, compared to events that have no precedent, especially within living history. See Walter Laqueur, *The Terrible Secret* (Boston, MA: Little Brown, 1980).
24 According to an account written by the former Pakistani Minister of Information, Altaf Gauhar, an operational plan for occupation of Kargil heights in 1987 was dropped by the former Pakistani President Zia-ul-Haq, based upon a briefing by then-Foreign Minister Sahibzada Yakub Khan. According to Gauhar, in this briefing Yakub Khan was able to convince Zia that due to the difficulty of terrain, and treacherous weather, the plan for the occupation of the Kargil heights was militarily inappropriate. Extracts taken from Altaf Gauhar, "Four Wars One Assumption," *Nation*, September 5, 1999; as quoted in Jasjit Singh (ed.), *Kargil 1999: Pakistan's Fourth War for Kashmir* (New Delhi: Knowledge World, 1999), p. 133.
25 Nitin A. Gokhale and Ajith Pillai, "The War That Should Never have Been," *Outlook*, September 6, 1999, as quoted in P.R. Chari, "Introduction: Some Preliminary Observations," in Ashok Krishna and P.R. Chari (eds), *Kargil: Tables Turned* (New Delhi: Manohar, 2001), p. 18.
26 This implies that in 1999 there were apparent signs of decline in Kashmir insurgency (Pakistan called it Kashmiri struggle). Editorial in *Friday Times* (Pakistan), August 5, 1999, in *From Surprise to Reckoning*, p. 18.
27 The envisaged significant military activity included logistic support to maintain those heights, also, sending out protective and early warning elements around the occupied heights. Ibid., p. 17.
28 See B. Raman, *Intelligence Past, Present and Future* (New Delhi: Lancer Publishers, 2002), p. 1.
29 For the role and capabilities of the IB, see *From Surprise to Reckoning*, pp. 112–113.
30 *From Surprise to Reckoning*, p. 114.
31 In adopting winter posture, the concerned units vacated those posts that were considered hazardous and would result in exposing troops to the unacceptable risks from extreme weather conditions and avalanches. Certain posts were classified as winter cut-off posts, which were maintained throughout the year after adequate winter stocking. The units made decisions to vacate or maintain certain posts as winter cut-off posts, based upon tactical and logistical factors. In the winter of 1999, by thus adopting the winter posture, the Indian army had left large gaps in defenses astride the LoC in Kargil. See *From Surprise to Reckoning*, p. 83.
32 These patrols reconnoiter the unit's area of operational responsibility with a view to check any hostile movement in those areas, and liaise with the local civilian population of that area. During his active duty tenure with the Indian army in Kashmir the author, Colonel Surinder Rana (ret.) participated in such winter patrolling.
33 The then District Magistrate of Kargil, Shaleen Kabra reportedly told the Kargil Review Committee in September 1999 that army patrols hired civilian porters for these patrols. According to Kabra, no porters were hired for patrolling during the 1998–99 winter. Praveen Swami, "Kargil Questions," *Frontline*, September 1, 2000, p. 13.
34 Brigadier Surinder Singh stated this to the Kargil Review Committee during his testimony. See *From Surprise to Reckoning*, 158. In hindsight some reports suggest that Singh's decision not to send winter patrols was influenced by negative response from the Leh (3 Infantry Division) HQ, to his earlier suggestions of enhancing ground and aerial surveillance in 121 Brigade. Journalist Praveen Swami has quoted official

correspondence between the HQ 121, and HQ 3 Infantry Division, in which Singh's request for increased aerial surveillance of Kargil region had been rejected by his superior HQ. See Praveen Swami, "The Kargil Story," *Frontline*, November 10, 2000.
35 Shaukat Qadir, "An Analysis of the Kargil Conflict," p. 26.
36 *From Surprise to Reckoning*, p. 86.
37 Major General Ashok K. Krishna, "The Method Followed at Siachen Is Irrelevant in Kargil," www.rediff.com, August 18, 1999, accessed on August 8, 2003.
38 Ibid., p. 159.
39 *From Surprise to Reckoning*, p. 152.
40 Ibid., p. 152.
41 *From Surprise to Reckoning*, p. 153.
42 A majority population of the Dras-Kargil region is Shia. They had been non-cooperative in Pakistan's efforts of spreading militancy in the region, which has since 1997, made them targets of the Pakistan Army's punitive artillery bombardment. M.K. Akbar, *Kargil: Cross-Border Terrorism* (New Delhi: Mittal Publications, 1999), pp. 63–64.
43 Mangla, Lahore, Gujranwala, and Okara, are major army cantonments in Pakistan.
44 *From Surprise to Reckoning*, pp. 128–129.
45 *Kargil: Surprise to Victory*, p. 98.
46 Jasjit Singh, *Kargil: Pakistan's Fourth War for Kashmir*, p. 137.
47 Nawaz Sharif also visited Gilgit in January 1999.
48 *From Surprise to Reckoning*, p. 157. General VP Malik has also mentioned that when the Indian prime minister asked him about the pattern of cross-LOC infiltration in the aftermath of his Lahore visit, his reply was that there was no let up in the pattern of this infiltration. See *Kargil: From Surprise to Victory*, p. 98.
49 During a meeting of Cabinet Committee on Security (India's highest decision-making body) on May 21, 1999, the National Security Council Secretary (NSCS) said that 70 percent of intruders were militants and 30 percent were Pakistani regular soldiers. see *Kargil: From Surprise to Victory*, p. 111.
50 According to General V.P. Malik, when this conversation was intercepted, the Indian army was fairly certain about collusion of Pakistani military. Until this intercept, however, most intelligence reports had continued to point to the Jehadi militants. See *Kargil: From Surprise to Victory*, p. 99.
51 For an effort to explain Pearl Harbor as an instance of surprise caused by a lack of signals see Ariel Levite, *Intelligence and Strategic Surprise* (New York: Columbia University Press, 1987).
52 Y.M. Bammi, *Kargil: The Impregnable Conquered* (Noida, India: Gorkha Publishers, 2002), pp. 361–370.

3
SURPRISE AND THE NON-STATE ACTOR

Carl von Clausewitz, the famous military philosopher, never put much stock in denial and deception. Denial refers to practices intended to prevent accurate information from reaching the opponent, thereby creating the basis for deception, which involves deliberate activities intended to provide the opponent with misleading information so that the opponent perceives reality according to the deceiver's intentions. For Clausewitz, the attempt to deceive opponents was costly, diverting resources crucial for the main military attack, and was usually not worth the effort.[1]

Although much has changed since this Prussian philosopher offered his commentary on early nineteenth-century warfare, it remains a matter of debate whether the information revolution enhances or limits the prospects for contemporary denial and deception.[2] On the one hand, information about global events has become ubiquitous, making it difficult to hide significant developments from the outside world. The Internet, global television networks, and jet travel provide governments, corporations, grass-roots organizations and even individuals with ways to share information on a global basis. Given the myriad actors and communication channels involved, it is difficult to imagine how governments can reliably direct this information stream to mislead their opponents, while hiding the truth from the prying eyes of spy satellites, reporters, bloggers, or analysts who use powerful computers to monitor the flow of data across the Internet. On the other hand, a little bit of denial and deception may go a long way in an age of information overload. Unable to sift through the torrent of data confronting them, officials, intelligence analysts, and members of the general public may simply, in the end, pay attention only to information that supports their political, policy, or personal preferences, leaving them open to manipulation by astute opponents. The information revolution has done little to change the fundamental limits of human cognition: people will be slow to notice that their plans are not succeeding, that their concepts fail to account for reality, and that their preferences will not be fulfilled.³

There is virtually unanimous agreement that the information revolution has empowered individuals at the expense of governments and bureaucracies, giving everyday people communication, organizational, and analytical capabilities only possessed by national governments a few short decades ago. Nevertheless, there is less recognition of a new twist in the practice of denial and deception that has been facilitated by the information revolution. It is becoming increasingly difficult for states, despite their enormous resources, to hide military formations of virtually any size on the battlefield, while it is becoming increasingly easy for individuals or small groups with limited resources and nefarious intentions simply to "hide in plain sight" from law enforcement and intelligence agencies. In other words, it might be possible that the information revolution has empowered the individual vis-à-vis the state when it comes to denial and deception, giving terrorists and criminal organizations new abilities to blend in with civil society. Denial and deception has thus become the crucial enabler for contemporary terrorist cells, especially those operating within major urban areas.

To explore this important facet of denial and deception, the chapter will briefly describe what is meant by the terms "denial" and "deception" and why each term is important both in world politics and in military combat. It will then explain why terrorists or criminal organizations are constrained when it comes to how they conduct denial and deception. In other words, because terrorist organizations or spontaneous cells have limited resources they tend to practice denial rather than deception when it comes to preventing detection by the authorities. The chapter then briefly explores new ways the information revolution might, in the end, aid governments and other traditional state actors by making it increasingly difficult for terrorists to hide in plain sight.

Denial and deception

Denial and deception are activities that work together to misdirect or mislead opponents about the deceiver's presence, activities or intentions. They create the possibility that one's whole diplomatic or strategic outlook might be based on false assumptions or incomplete assessments of reality and that these erroneous assessments are the product of a sustained campaign carried out by one's opponents. If the developing situation is a bit too cut and dried, or if potentially threatening events seem to be unfolding in a particularly benign way, or if innocent explanations for unusual events seem to clutter reports from the field, or even highly classified intelligence estimates, then prudent policymakers and intelligence analysts should begin to suspect that they are falling victim to denial and deception. When it comes to denial and deception, policymakers and analysts alike should operate on the principle of *caveat emptor*.

Denial is based on secrecy and a keen awareness of the signatures—observable phenomena related to planning and preparing for action, and undertaking an operation itself—that can tip off an opponent about what is actually about to happen. When these signatures are denied to the opponent—as they largely were by Japan in the weeks leading up to Pearl Harbor—the "noise" of innocuous events or alternative erroneous explanations for an emerging situation can drown out "signals," accurate indicators of what is about to transpire.[4] In other words, opponents cannot determine what is about to transpire because they do not possess the information needed to develop an accurate and timely estimate of what is happening. Of course, efforts at denial vary in quality. United States intelligence analysts, for example, became suspicious when they discovered large-hatched ships involved in the Baltic lumber trade slowly moving from Soviet ports to Cuba in the late summer of 1962. The fact that these ships were riding high in the water and were being unloaded at night further raised the possibility that they were delivering something other than wood to Cuban ports.[5] The fact that the ships' cargo was not visible to US intelligence analysts did little to allay their suspicions about what the Soviets were up to in Cuba. Nevertheless, denial is a common practice in international relations and military operations. Governments and militaries rarely make public their fundamental objectives, or even their own estimates of their strengths and weaknesses, in a political or military contest. Denial is a "constant" when it comes to diplomacy and strategy: policymakers, strategists, and intelligence analysts can safely assume that their opponent is withholding information.[6]

Deception can take a myriad of forms and is limited only by the creativity and guile of the deception planner. Bogus stories published by legitimate media outlets, fake documents and plans, and false electronic signals or communications, have all been used to give an opponent a false sense of what is about to transpire. In contrast to denial, which generally requires only security or self-awareness when it comes to the "signatures" (i.e., observable electronic, seismic, social, or biometric evidence) generated by various activities, deception can be costly because it can require the expenditure of resources to create a convincing false front. For example, the Battle for Khe Sanh, which distracted US commanders from the looming threat posed by the Viet Cong to the cities of South Vietnam on the eve of the 1968 Tet offensive, involved several divisions from the People's Army of Vietnam. In this case, deception involved significant activity that was in fact so costly to the communist war effort that observers can still debate which action was in fact the main avenue of attack and which initiative was the effort at deception.[7]

Efforts at denial and deception rely on several factors for their success. Practitioners of denial and deception need accurate information not only about the way their opponents collect and analyze information, but also about their opponent's beliefs, plans, and expectations. In other words, denial and deception require good intelligence about the opponent. Without this information, it might be impossible to control the flow of information to the opponent or provide information that will be perceived as credible or compelling. Technical virtuosity also plays a part in denial and deception in the sense that the deceiver must employ artistry to attract the target's attention to misleading information without raising suspicion. Denial and deception works because it plays off an opponent's need for information, while heightening their sensitivity to the information that the deceiver intends to provide them, which often is a message that the opponent also happens to want to hear. According to Donald Daniel, "Denial plays against an adversary's eagerness while deception plays to it. That is, while the denier conceals information from the opponent, the deceiver happily provides him with false clues."[8] The opponent is desperate to learn about the deceiver's intentions, but the opponent has to discover the planted information "naturally" if the deception is to take a firm hold over their opposing intelligence community.

Although the practice of denial and deception in theory sounds highly demanding, in practice it can work splendidly, especially if the deceiver can channel the flow of information in a way that supports the target's preferred conception of reality. In the early 1970s, for example, Israeli officials based their defense policy on three assumptions that came to be described as "the Concept": Egypt would be at the center of any Arab coalition against Israel, Egypt would not launch a significant attack without a strong prospect of victory, and, unless Egypt destroyed the Israeli Air Force, an Arab victory would not be possible. Israeli officials also believed that their intelligence agencies would provide a "war warning," allowing them to mobilize their reserves or even launch a pre-emptive attack—actions that would produce an Arab defeat. The "Concept" held sway, despite some unusually compelling contradictory evidence and an Egyptian denial and deception campaign that was itself amateurish.[9] Even though Israel was equipped with an enormous amount of intelligence that should have raised flags—including actual Syrian and Egyptian war plans, reconnaissance photographs showing unprecedented force deployments along the Suez Canal and Golan Heights, a warning from a credible and trusted spy from the inner circle of Egyptian government, information that Soviet personnel and dependents were high-tailing it out of Cairo and Damascus, and signals intelligence suggesting that their opponents were about to strike—the Israelis never managed to act as if they were about to be hit by an all-out Arab assault. As a result, the outbreak of the 1973 Yom Kippur War was marked by one of the greatest intelligence-command failures in military history. Despite the availability of accurate, detailed, and compelling indications of what was about to transpire, Israeli analysts and officials could not overcome their existing concept of reality to act in time to head off disaster.[10]

Denial and deception is effective because it addresses the expectations of the target. Conventional wisdom, based on estimates made by Barton Whaley nearly fifty years ago, continues to support the notion that denial and deception is effective about ninety per cent of the time it is attempted.[11] Once the deceiver understands the target's biases, it is very difficult for the target to escape the trap. In fact, John Ferris, a leading historian of twentieth-century intelligence, has noted that only four qualities allow the target to escape effective denial and deception: "superior power and initiative; intelligence of outstanding quality or else so poor that it cannot pick up misleading signals, [and] an inability or unwillingness to act on any knowledge, true or false."[12] Ironically, two of the qualities identified by

Ferris can be characterized as sheer incompetence, while superior performance is often in short supply. Given the fact that most governments fall somewhere in the middle of this range of capabilities, it is not surprising that efforts at denial and deception are often effective.

Hiding in plain sight

Most of the literature, history, and practice of denial and deception involves state actors or military organizations that possess the resources required to (1) deny the opponent accurate information about their true intentions and (2) create a second misleading "image" that largely conforms to the expectations of the opponent. This is no small task. It requires a large team of analysts and operatives, as well as an effort to deny the opponent accurate information and signatures related to one's true intentions. It also requires an understanding of the preferences and expectations of the target, and an effective way to transmit information to the opponent in an attractive and compelling manner. Traditional denial and deception uses denial to set the stage for deception. In other words, denial is used to whet the target's appetite for information and then deception schemes are used to satisfy the need for information with stories that fit the needs of the deceiver. For many non-state actors—terror cells or even super-empowered individuals who would like to use violence to achieve their own political objectives—engaging in traditional denial and deception activities is likely to be beyond their capabilities. They simply lack the resources to generate and then offer an alternate reality to feed to the target. Yet, other forms of denial and deception are not beyond their reach—especially if they reverse the traditional balance between denial and deception.

Unlike states or large military formations, small terrorist cells or individuals face a less daunting challenge when it comes to denial. In contrast to an armored corps moving across the desert, for example, a terrorist cell does not generate a dust, heat, electromagnetic, or radar signature that can be detected from hundreds of miles away. The signature created by a terrorist group preparing to launch an attack is relatively weak and diffuse, making it difficult to detect against the noise generated by the normal everyday activities of the communities in its midst. Small cells, however, lack the human or material resources needed to undertake significant deception activities.[13] They cannot launch duplicate, redundant efforts to mislead the authorities. Furthermore, increasing the size of their organization or scope of their operations is unlikely to improve their prospects for success because it tends to increase the risk of detection. The more people involved in an operation, the greater the risk that someone will go to the police, speak to untrustworthy third parties, or risk detection or arrest following some minor run-in with local law enforcement.

Because of their weakness vis-à-vis the state, terrorist cells or individuals must incorporate denial as a fundamental principle of their operations.[14] Terrorists rely on denial for their very existence. Denial becomes a strategic asset for the terrorists because without it, they cannot hope to exist given the large asymmetry between their resources and the resources of local law enforcement and the state. Denial involves the tightest operational security, coupled with a rudimentary strategy of deception. For terrorists, "deception" involves maintaining a normal routine to the greatest extent possible as a cover for the nefarious plans and operations undertaken by the cell. This technique can be referred to as "hiding in plain sight." In fact, deception is based on an understanding of what the target of deception believes is normal, and the degree to which the target of deception can assimilate anomalies before responding. Deception is not based on feeding the target erroneous information, but on making one's actions comply with the expectations of the target.

Terrorists who hide in plain sight use their normalcy to appeal to the widely shared belief that what appears to be normal actually is normal in its entirety. In other words, because the image they present to the outside world fails to match a pre-existing notion of what (or who) constitutes a "threat," they are largely left alone, despite some anomalies in their behavior. Writing about the cell that bombed the World Trade Center in 1993, Bell notes, "no one in authority noticed the zealous sermons in the obscure storefront mosques or imagined that the wars of the Middle East might come to Manhattan. This lack of official concern persisted despite the visibility of militant Islam: the kidnappings and bombs of Beirut, the warnings in Algeria and Egypt and the threats of violence directed against the U.S. Homeland." Although analysts and a few local authorities knew about Sheikh Omar Abdel Rahman and the message he was delivering to his followers, no one took the blind cleric seriously. "His cover," according to Bell, "was that no American authority could imagine him as dangerous. He appeared to be an itinerant migrant who preached in seedy rented rooms."[15]

The persistent blindness of US elected officials, law enforcement personnel, and intelligence analysts about the true nature of the threat allowed Al-Qaeda cells to, once again, hide in plain sight in the months leading up to September 11, 2001.[16] Despite the fact that Osama bin Laden made little effort to hide his ambition of attacking US citizens and interests wherever he could find them, or that Al-Qaeda had established a track record of attacking US interests across the Middle East and Africa, or that various law enforcement officials and intelligence analysts were sounding alarms about specific events, the terror cells in the United States operated virtually unimpeded prior to the September 11 tragedy. Given this track record, it is hard to escape the conclusion that a little denial can go a long way, especially in the information age.

Toward counterdeception

Unlike most observers, Barton Whaley has expressed optimism about the possibility of counterdeception, the effort to detect and defeat the denial and deception strategies used by terrorist cells. He has devised a theory of counterdeception that is particularly well suited to detecting those who are hiding in plain sight. Counterdeception is relatively simple in theory, but more difficult to put into practice. But counterdeception sometimes does occur and could be more common in the future, especially if law enforcement officers, intelligence analysts, and elected officials recognize the principles behind the effort to detect individuals who are hiding in plain sight.

Counterdeception is based on the idea that every type of human endeavor has a large but knowable set of characteristics that must be present if it is true to form. Imitations of real activity, or "false fronts," will lack certain key characteristics, or will have extraneous characteristics added to a specific endeavor. The detection of these anomalies is the key element in discovering denial and deception because, according to Whaley, "every real thing is always, necessarily, completely congruent with all its characteristics."[17] Moreover, not all anomalies have to be detected before and analyst can uncover denial and deception. The detection of one anomaly is enough to raise the possibility that something is fundamentally amiss.[18] Whaley is not alone in offering what amounts to a scientific method for uncovering denial and deception. Richards Heuer has developed a similar technique—"analysis of competing hypotheses"—to validate the theoretical assumptions underlying intelligence estimates.[19] Heuer suggests that analysts can overcome cognitive biases and organizational preferences by comparing competing hypotheses and rejecting explanations that fail to account for key elements in a developing situation. Anomalies are evidence that something is amiss; they are the Achilles heel of deception planners.

Two factors, however, complicate this simple observation about what is needed to detect denial and deception. The first is the problem of measurement error. In other words, not every observation of reality is accurate, and errors can be read as either false positives or false negatives. No simple solution is available to overcome the problem of measurement error, in the sense that it is difficult to define and detect significant social anomalies in the first place. An analytical or political decision must be made to assess what sort of thresholds should be used to trigger further investigation once an anomaly is detected. The second problem involves the decision to respond to an anomaly, which again is a matter of political or analytical judgment. As Bell noted, some officials recognized that Sheikh Omar Abdel Rahman and his followers did not appear to be typical residents of Jersey City, but this awareness was not translated into effective action. The decision to respond to anomalies might be made on the basis on the principles of risk management: anomalies involving certain type of groups or certain types of targets might be selected for additional investigation by police officers or intelligence analysts. In that sense, the detection of anomalies might not be the end of an investigation, but a signal to refocus information collection and analytical efforts.

The information revolution makes it easier to hide in plain sight by facilitating the movement of ideas, people, and resources across international boundaries because the movements of outsiders, outside ideas, and outside resources are now an everyday occurrence. Nevertheless, the information revolution also might provide law enforcement officials and intelligence analysts with additional information needed to separate legitimate actors from those just masquerading as average people. Everyday life is increasingly digitized as people make full use of the services and resources made possible by the information revolution. This activity leaves a digital record in a myriad of unexpected ways and places. Templates and algorithms already exist that can detect anomalies in normal activities, such as the loss or theft of credit cards, unauthorized entry into secure facilities, or even increasingly routine airline baggage delays. There is no reason to subject anyone to this level of scrutiny on a daily basis, but it might be possible to explore the digital reality behind individuals or groups that somehow manage to attract the attention of intelligence and law enforcement officials. The requirement to fashion a convincing "electronic history" might be beyond the ability of small groups or terrorist cells. The absence of this history—living off the grid—in some settings might be cause for suspicion itself. In fact, the US intelligence community already has recognized the difficulty in manufacturing a credible electronic history to match the cover story supplied to its own clandestine operatives.[20]

Conclusion

Admittedly, if taken to its logical conclusion, the ideas presented here are downright Orwellian. But this is not a call to monitor people everywhere in real time to make sure that their "digital" lives roughly correspond to some template based on their geographic location, employment and family history, or their socioeconomic status. Instead, the article offers a tool that law enforcement can use to evaluate terrorist suspects quickly. It describes why terrorists need to hide in plain sight while undertaking their operations, and how their modus operandi differs from the more traditional practice of denial and deception. It also identifies a critical weakness in their tradecraft that might be beyond their ability to remedy quickly with available resources. In other words, once individuals come to the attention of law enforcement officials in the course of some investigation, their electronic bona fides could be matched against their stories. Anomalies would not be evidence of guilt, but prudence would suggest that they might require further investigation.

History has shown that terror cells have lived quietly in the United States, trying to give the appearance of normalcy until they can carry out their attacks. History also has shown that law enforcement and intelligence officials have not performed well in responding to anomalous behavior. Armed with rudimentary tradecraft, the September 11 hijackers were able to hide in plain sight while only attracting a modest amount of attention. They did reasonably well mimicking the behavior of average college students, who often lack visible means of support and have been known to spend more time lounging about or in bars than studying. But when cell members showed interest in learning how to take off and fly, but not land commercial airliners, they were not acting as "normal" student pilots. At that point, they had blown their cover. The September 11 hijackers never tipped their hand in terms of their plans, but they did fail to preserve their image as run-of-the-mill student pilots. The detection of anomalies might not be the final solution when it comes to discovering denial and deception or detecting terrorists, but it is a good place to start.

Notes

1 Because deception requires significant forces to be convincing, by definition it implies that these forces will not be available to support the main attack. Clausewitz judged that efforts beyond simple operational security—the attempt to minimize the opponent's ability to gather information about plans, troop movements, or the combat readiness of various units—were probably not worth the effort. Denial and deception might pay some dividends, but in all likelihood, these benefits would be modest compared to the resources required to create an effective diversion. Edward N. Luttwak, *Strategy: The Logic of War and Peace* (Cambridge, MA: Harvard University Press, 1987), pp. 9–10.
2 Michael Handel, *Masters of War* (London: Frank Cass, 1996), p. 131.
3 Kristin M. Lord, "National Intelligence in an Age of Transparency," in Loch Johnson (ed.), *Strategic Intelligence: Understanding the Hidden Side of Government* (Westport, CT: Praeger, 2007), pp. 181–200.
4 Roberta Wohlstetter, *Pearl Harbor: Warning and Decision* (Stanford, CA: Stanford University Press, 1962).
5 Raymond Garthoff, "U.S. Intelligence and the Cuban Missile Crisis," in James G. Blight and David A. Welch (eds), *Intelligence and the Cuban Missile Crisis* (London: Frank Cass, 1998), p. 23 [18–63].
6 James B. Bruce, "Denial and Deception in the 21st Century: Adaptation Implications for Western Intelligence," *Defense Intelligence Journal* Vol. 15, No. 2 (2006), pp. 13–27.
7 James J. Wirtz, "Deception and the Tet Offensive." *The Journal of Strategic Studies* Vol. 13, No. 2 (1990), pp. 82–98.
8 Donald C.F. Daniel, "Denial and Deception," in Jennifer E. Sims and Burton Gerber (eds), *Transforming U.S. Intelligence* (Washington, DC: Georgetown University Press, 2005), p. 139.
9 Israeli intelligence determined that the "exercise" that the Egyptians apparently intended to use as a cover for their mobilization was, in fact, not taking place.
10 Uri Bar-Joseph, *The Watchman Fell Asleep: The Surprise of the Yom Kippur War and Its Sources* (Albany, NY: State University of New York Press, 2005).
11 Barton Whaley, *Stratagem: Deception and Surprise in War* (Rand Corporation, 1969).
12 John Ferris, "'FORTITUDE' in Context: The Evolution of British Military Deception in Two World Wars, 1914–1945," in Richard K. Betts and Thomas G. Mahnken (eds), *Paradoxes of Strategic Intelligence: Essays in Honor of Michael I. Handel* (London: Frank Cass, 2003).
13 According to J. Bowyer Bell, "Organizations and movements, defined by … recognized and legitimate [governments] as illicit, must seek cover to operate … denial is so vital that it becomes a strategic necessity…" Bell, J. Bowyer. "Conditions Making for Success and Failure of Denial and Deception: Nonstate and Illicit Actors," in Roy Godson and James J. Wirtz (eds), *Strategic Denial and Deception: The Twenty-First Century Challenge* (New Brunswick, NJ: Transaction, 2002).
14 Ibid., p. 147.
15 Ibid.

16 Ahmed Rashid, "The Taliban: Exporting Extremism," *Foreign Affairs* Vol. 78, No. 6 (1999), pp. 22–35. See also *The 9/11 Commission Report: Final Report of the National Commission on Terrorist Attacks Upon the United States* by National Commission on Terrorist Attacks (New York: W.W. Norton & Company, 2004).
17 Barton Whaley and Jeffrey Busby, "Detecting Deception: Practice, Practitioners, and Theory," in Roy Godson and James J. Wirtz (eds), *Strategic Denial and Deception: The Twenty-First Century Challenge* (New Brunswick, NJ: Transaction Publishers, 2002), pp. 181–221.
18 Ibid.
19 Richard J. Heuer, *Psychology of Intelligence Analysis* (Washington, DC: Government Printing Office, 1999).
20 According to Jose Rodriguez, the outgoing head of the US National Clandestine Service, the widespread availability of public, real estate, and corporate databases has made creating convincing cover stories for clandestine agents "hard as nails," see Richard Willing "How U.S. Spies are Recruited, Trained is Morphing," *USA Today*, October 1, 2007, p. 10A.

4

DÉJÀ VU?

Comparing Pearl Harbor and 9/11

During my first trip to Hawaii, I made my way to a place considered sacred by most US citizens, the USS Arizona memorial at Pearl Harbor. Survivors often greet visitors to the memorial, answering questions and retelling their memories of the day the Japanese attacked the US Pacific Fleet. When it came to my turn, I asked what the weather was like that fateful morning. The answer was "like today." A few puffy clouds dotted the blue Hawaiian skies, a light breeze pushed ripples across the turquoise water of the harbor, stirring the warm tropical air to create one of the most idyllic anchorages on earth. September 11 also dawned clear and blue over New York City, the kind of late summer day that highlights perfectly the United States' front door, the spectacular edifice of promise and prosperity that is lower Manhattan. Given the setting, it is no wonder that the events of both Pearl Harbor and September 11 came as a complete shock to eyewitnesses. Neither could have happened on a more pleasant morning.

We now know, however, that initial eyewitness interpretations of both these surprise attacks, as bolts out of the blue, were incorrect. Indications of what was about to happen were available before the Japanese attack on Pearl Harbor. In fact, one of the accepted tenets of the literature on surprise attacks is that in all cases of so-called intelligence failure, accurate information concerning what is about to transpire can be found in the intelligence system after the fact. It is thus to be expected that revelations emerged about the signals that were in the intelligence pipeline before the terrorist attacks on September 11. And as in the aftermath of Pearl Harbor, the US government held a series of investigations to discover how organizational shortcomings or mistakes made by specific officials were responsible for the intelligence failure that paved the way for the destruction of the World Trade Center and the attack on the Pentagon.

It is not surprising that similarities exist between the attack on Pearl Harbor and the terrorist attacks of September 11 because both events are examples of a more general international phenomenon—the surprise attack. Despite the fact that they occurred over 50 years apart and involve different kinds of international actors with highly different motivations, a pattern exists in the events leading up to surprise and its consequences. Exploring these similarities can help cast the tragedy of September 11 in a broader context, an important initial step in reducing the likelihood of mass-casualty terrorism in the future.

Warning signs

Although Pearl Harbor and the September 11 attacks are sometimes depicted as totally unanticipated events both incidents were preceded by clear indications that the United States faced an imminent threat. Prior to Pearl Harbor, US–Japanese relations had reached a nadir. By the summer of 1941, the administration of US President Franklin Roosevelt had placed economic sanctions on the Japanese to force them to end their war against China. These sanctions were the proximate cause of the Japanese attack. Japanese officials believed that the US embargo against them would ruin their economy, while destruction of the US Fleet would provide them with some maneuvering room. They intended to quickly seize resource-rich lands in the Far East, fortify their newly conquered lands, and then reach some sort of negotiated settlement with the United States.

The Roosevelt administration recognized that it faced a crisis with Japan, although senior officials in Washington did not realize that Oahu was in danger until it was too late. In their minds, it made no sense for the Japanese to attack the United States because they simply lacked the economic resources or military capability to defeat the US military in a long war. In an ironic twist, the Roosevelt administration was ultimately proven correct in this estimate. The Japanese attack on Pearl Harbor eliminated the possibility of US acquiescence to the creation of a Japanese empire in the Pacific as well as the eventual peace arrangement Japan hoped to achieve.

The situation that faced the United States was even more clear cut, if not quite as grave, prior to September 11. Various studies and commissions (such as the government's Gilmore Commission) described the ongoing struggle against terrorism and predicted that a significant terrorist attack on the continental United States was a virtual certainty. The United States was actually in a war with Al-Qaeda, an international network of terrorist groups, throughout the 1990s. Al-Qaeda may have been loosely linked to the militias that battled US Ranger units in Somalia in 1993. Al-Qaeda also was involved in the bombing of the office of the program manager for the Saudi National Guard in Riyadh in November 1995 and in the attack on the Khobar Towers complex in Dahran in July 1996.

These attacks on US interests in 1995 and 1996 changed the way forward-deployed US forces operated within the Arabian Peninsula. New "force protection" regulations were promulgated to protect US military personnel, requiring commanders to observe stringent requirements to ensure their safety. In Saudi Arabia, US operational units were consolidated at Prince Sultan Air Base and advisory components were moved to Eskan Village, a housing complex south of Riyadh. Intelligence collection efforts also concentrated on the new threat, providing forces throughout the region with improved tactical and operational warning. At times, US forces were placed at "Threatcon Delta" in expectation of an immediate attack. The hardening of the "target" on the Arabian Peninsula forced Al-Qaeda to look for vulnerabilities elsewhere.

Any lingering doubts about the ongoing threat were dispelled by Al-Qaeda's bombing of the US embassies in Kenya and Tanzania in August 1988 and the attack against the USS Cole in October 2000. The United States even returned fire following the 1998 embassy attacks by launching cruise missile strikes against suspected terrorist training camps in Afghanistan and a pharmaceutical plant in Sudan that was believed to have links to Al-Qaeda. United States government agencies had a clear idea that Osama bin Laden was committed to attacking US interests globally. Bin Laden's 1998 *fatwa* represented a declaration of war on the United States and called upon supporters to kill US officials, soldiers and civilians everywhere around the world. This assessment of bin Laden's intentions was reflected in a variety of publicly available sources. The US Congressional Research Service published a compelling warning about bin Laden's campaign of terror entitled "Terrorism: Near Eastern Groups and State Sponsors" on September 10, 2001. A compelling description of bin Laden's alliance with the Taliban and his political agenda was even published in *Foreign Affairs* in 1999.

Pearl Harbor and the terrorist attacks on September 11 were not bolts-out-of-the-blue. But because they were generally perceived to have occurred without warning, they both have changed attitudes and produced policies that have reduced the likelihood and consequences of surprise attack. Pearl Harbor focused strategists' attention on the need to avoid the consequences of surprise attack, especially when it came to US nuclear deterrent threats. The fear of a surprise attack made the nuclear balance of terror appear delicate. As a result, enormous efforts were undertaken to guarantee that US strategic forces could survive a Soviet nuclear attack and still be able to assure destruction of the Soviet Union. The administration of George W. Bush also attempted to minimize the effects of a potential terrorist incident by improving homeland defenses and consequence management, spending US $35 billion on homeland defense programs. United States military forces also are pre-empting attacks by taking the battle to terrorists and by training foreign militaries to deal with the threat.

Structural vulnerabilities

Despite common misperceptions, it was the US Army, and not the US Navy, that was responsible for the defense of Pearl Harbor in December 1941. This division of responsibilities helped to create the conditions for surprise. When Washington issued a war warning to its forces in Hawaii, Army officers took steps to safeguard against sabotage, locking up ammunition and concentrating aircraft on the center of runways so they could be more easily guarded. In contrast, Navy officers thought that the war warning would prompt a vigorous effort on the part of the Army to use long-range aircraft to patrol the waters around Oahu. Army officers thought that Naval intelligence had been keeping tabs on the whereabouts of the Japanese fleet; they did not realize that Navy analysts had lost track of Japanese aircraft carriers in the weeks leading up to Pearl Harbor. Further, the Army and Navy staffs on Oahu never confirmed their expectation about what each other was doing to safeguard the islands from attack. Even perfect liaison between the services, however, might not have been enough to prevent disaster because no mechanism existed to collect and disseminate all-source intelligence to the operational commanders who could put it to good use. There is little evidence to suggest that the Japanese knew about these organizational weaknesses in Hawaii's defenses, but organizational shortcomings facilitated their effort to catch the US Fleet unprepared.

Al-Qaeda might have understood the organizational weakness that reduced the likelihood that its operatives would be detected before they struck. While there was a unified command structure in the Persian Gulf to address the local terrorist threat, organizational responsibilities in the US government largely diverged at the water's edge. The Department of Defense and the Central Intelligence Agency (CIA) focus on foreign threats and intelligence collection, while the Federal Bureau of Investigation focuses on internal security and investigating crime.

Local and state police forces operate in their own jurisdictions and US airport security at the time was largely the responsibility of private firms. Additionally, the definition of terrorism was not without organizational consequences. Was it a form of war or a type of natural disaster that would fall under the jurisdiction of the Federal Emergency Management Agency? Was it a homegrown threat involving high explosives (e.g., the destruction of the Alfred P. Murrah Federal Building in April 1995) or a new type of threat involving weapons of mass destruction (e.g., the Aum Shinrikyo attack on the Tokyo subway in March 1995)? And as this debate about the likelihood and form of mass-casualty terrorism unfolded in the years leading up to September 11, front-line government agencies in the war against domestic terrorism were allowed to atrophy. The US Customs and Immigration agents found themselves unprepared for their new role in combating domestic terrorism.

United States citizens tend to focus on technological solutions to problems, often forgetting that organization shapes the ability to respond to emerging challenges. Strong organization—the ability to orchestrate the efforts of a vast array of individuals and bureaucratic actors—is imperative if the United States is to effectively spend its resources in the war on terrorism. Despite inter-service rivalry and bureaucratic preferences, the organizational shortcomings that existed prior to Pearl Harbor were relatively easy to minimize compared to the bureaucratic and legal challenge created by the domestic response to terrorism. After Pearl Harbor, clearer lines of responsibility were drawn between the services. By contrast, legal questions and scores of jurisdictional issues complicate official efforts to create the governmental structures and relationships needed to generate a comprehensive answer to terrorism.

Technological surprise

The ability to utilize technology creatively played an important role in both the Japanese attack on Pearl Harbor and the terrorist attacks of September 11. When historians write about technical surprise, they focus on the unexpected introduction of hardware or weapons that cannot be quickly countered by an opponent. The attack on Pearl Harbor, for example was made possible when the Japanese developed an aerial torpedo that could function in the shallow waters of Pearl Harbor. But the Japanese success at Pearl Harbor was made possible by a broader integration of technology with a new concept of operations that brought the full capability of carrier aviation to bear in a decisive way. This demonstration of professional military prowess combined new technology, tactics, and strategy in a surprisingly devastating way. Carrier aviation itself was not a secret, but the Japanese exploited this new technology with so much daring and skill that it was impossible even for those who understood the threat posed by Japan to recognize that they faced such grave and immediate danger.

Al-Qaeda also achieved a technological surprise on September 11. Again, there was nothing particularly novel about the use of aircraft to conduct a suicide mission—ironically it was the Japanese who introduced the kamikaze during the October 1944 US invasion of the Philippines. But by using a host of modern technologies produced by the information revolution and globalization, Al-Qaeda operatives were able to plan, orchestrate, and execute a major "special operations" attack without the hardware, training, or infrastructure generally associated with conducting a precision strike at intercontinental ranges. Al-Qaeda used the Internet, satellite telephones, and cell phones to coordinate their international operations, especially to communicate with operatives in the United States. They also used the international banking system to fund cells in the United States without drawing undue attention. Al-Qaeda operatives rode the rails of the information revolution, harnessing international communication and financial networks to carry out their nefarious scheme.

In both instances of surprise, the opponent used technology in an innovative way to launch a devastating over-the-horizon attack. And prior to both attacks, the technology employed was actually well known to US officials and officers. Indeed, the case of the September 11 attacks, US citizens, as the major beneficiaries and supporters of globalization, were probably the world's leading experts when it came to harnessing new instruments of communication and commerce. However, they lacked a keen awareness of their enemies, leading them to underestimate opponents' willingness to find ways to circumvent defenses to gain the element of surprise.

The interest–threat mismatch

During the 1990s, the debate about the United States' role in world affairs revolved around concerns about the interest–threat mismatch. In the aftermath of the Cold

War, low-level, nagging threats—ethnic violence, terrorism, or just instability and unrest—permeated parts of the world. Some observers suggested that these threats had little effect on US national interests. People who suggested that the United States become involved in places like Rwanda or even Kosovo, for instance, were really thinking with their hearts and not their heads. The issue was not whether the United States should work to stop genocide. Instead, the concern was that intervention meant an open-ended US commitment to social engineering that realistically had little prospect of success. Intervention was an option available to the United States, but it was not without opportunity costs and significant risks. Intervening in faraway places like Afghanistan to stop Taliban human rights abuses or to deny Al-Qaeda a secure base of operations was never even considered. Bush ran his 2000 presidential campaign on reducing the United States' international "over-commitment" abroad. The Unites States' "casualty aversion" seemed to be a major factor in limiting US intervention to stop ethnic violence and other forms of carnage. Anti-democratic and anti-market forces, specifically a fundamentalist backlash against the way globalization spreads Western culture, was not deemed of sufficient strength to pose a significant security threat.

In the late 1930s, the US intelligence community also perceived a mismatch between US interests and the desirability of responding to the threats that were emerging across the globe. This perception is difficult to explain in hindsight, given the genocidal and aggressive policies of the Nazi regime and Japan's imperial ambitions. On the eve of Pearl Harbor, the Nazis had overrun virtually all of Europe and Japan had been engaged in a war in China for nearly a decade. Still, many in the United States seemed to believe that they could somehow escape the wave of fascism and violence that was sweeping the globe.

Both Al-Qaeda and Imperial Japan attacked the United States in an effort to limit US influence and to stop the spread of free markets, democracy, and liberal ideas into the Middle East and East Asia. Japan believed that US officials would not have the will to challenge their initiatives in Asia; Japanese leaders felt US "casualty aversion" would lead to a negotiated settlement in Asia. Bin Laden apparently expected a relatively ineffectual US military response (again driven by US concerns about casualties) that would in the end spark a revolution in moderate Arab regimes, if not a full blown clash of civilizations between Islam and the West. Bin Laden and the Japanese, however, underestimated how surprise attacks would alter the political balance within the United States and the way US citizens perceived foreign threats. Both also failed to recognize how quickly US military power could be brought to bear against them.

Aftershock

Many more points of comparison are possible between Pearl Harbor and September 11. At Pearl Harbor, the US military stopped about 8 percent of the attacking force from either reaching its target or returning home. On September 11, airline passengers actually stopped 25 percent of the attacking force from reaching its target, saving a US landmark from severe damage or total destruction. The US intelligence analysts issued a war warning before the Pearl Harbor attack, and the US military managed to engage the enemy. On September 11, intelligence reports of possible terrorist threats had not yet been translated into a compelling warning, and the US military failed to interfere with Al-Qaeda's suicide mission.

As time passes, the longer term effects of both events also can be compared. Japan's experience after Pearl Harbor was so unpleasant that the war inoculated Japan's leaders and public alike against aggression and armed conflict. By contrast, Al-Qaeda faces extermination. Pearl Harbor had a generational effect on young people in the United States, serving as a warning that the possibility of aggression and surprise can never be eliminated in international relations. Judging by the response from college students in Washington, DC to the news that bin Laden had met his demise in Abbottabad, the destruction of the World Trade Center and the Pentagon and the ensuing decade long "War on Terror" also left a mark on young people.

Pearl Harbor and September 11 are similar in at least one more important respect. Both surprise attacks renewed US interest in world affairs, creating a popular conviction that suffering and oppression in distant places can only be ignored at the expense of US security. Both attacks halted a creeping isolationism and both prompted changes in US government and a renewed commitment to the defense of democracy and economic liberty. The origins of the Department of Defense, the CIA, and a host of intelligence agencies and programs can be tied to that fateful morning over seventy years ago. The United States has changed again as the effects of September 11 rippled across government institutions and popular culture. Although it remains for history to judge, one can only hope that these changes have made the United States less vulnerable to mass-casualty terrorist attack.

PART II
Surprise and deterrence failure

5

THE BALANCE OF POWER PARADOX

Balancing behavior is important in world politics because it can deter conflict, at least according to its leading proponents and theorists. It is not just the presence of an international coalition ready to use diplomacy or violence that deters aggression, but the possible emergence of states willing to resist aggression that must be taken into consideration by leaders contemplating the use of force to achieve their objectives. As Jack Levy notes, "potential hegemons anticipate that expansionist behavior would lead to the formation of a military coalition against them, and refrain from aggression for that reason."[1] Indeed, one security motivation behind the formation of the United Nations, and the North Atlantic Treaty, for that matter, was to create standing coalitions to demonstrate to potential troublemakers that significant forces will respond to threats to international peace or to the security of member states. Collective security organizations are not supposed just to respond to war, they also are supposed to deter aggression.

By suggesting that balancing behavior can serve as a significant mechanism to deter war, however, balance of power theorists face an embarrassing anomaly: war often erupts between great powers and very weak states. Whatever theoretical school one follows—in other words, whether one believes that a parity in the balance between states preserves the peace or that a preponderance of power deters hostilities—the outbreak of war between states with gross disparities of military, economic or diplomatic resources defies the expectations of balance of power theorists.[2] It also defies the expectations of deterrence theorists, who predict that the awareness of a potential opponent's overwhelming military capability, combined with its stated willingness to use force, should deter a grossly inferior competitor from initiating hostilities. Deterrence theorists also would suggest that in circumstances where extreme disparities in capabilities exist, compellent strategies adopted by the stronger party should succeed in achieving their objectives short of war. Leaders equipped with even limited rational insight should comply with the demands of a greatly superior opponent. One would therefore think that the demands of a universal coalition of states would be irresistible.

Although few scholars have addressed the anomaly inherent in these "asymmetric conflicts," past efforts have focused on identifying the circumstances under which a weaker party might decide to initiate hostilities. By using the expected-utility model, for example, T.V. Paul has explained how weaker powers might initiate hostilities to obtain limited objectives, such as breaking a deadlock in negotiations or to highlight some perceived injustice in the status quo.[3] Theorists, however, usually focus on the reasons why unexpected outcomes occur, rather than on how the expectations of both sides can lead to war.[4] They fail to explain the calculations made by the stronger actor in the asymmetric conflict and why its balancing behavior or its deterrent or compellent policies fail. Asymmetric conflict would be better explained if it were viewed as a strategic interaction that produces a "balance of power paradox": the tendency of war to erupt during confrontations between weak and strong states—wars that strong states should strive to avoid and weak states cannot realistically expect to win. A complete explanation of the paradox would have to take into account the behavior of both sides in a conflict and how their interaction produces war.

In contrast to previous suggestions that weaker powers generally fight much stronger powers over limited objectives, the argument advanced here is that weak powers engages in conflicts with enormously superior opponents because their leaders believe that the great power will not be able to bring its full force to bear in the conflict. Leaders of weak countries tend to focus on the constraints imposed by the balance of power on the stronger opponent (e.g., the danger that another great power will be drawn into the conflict on the weak power's behalf). By contrast, leaders of the stronger side focus on the relative power imbalance between themselves and the weaker opponent. They fail to recognize that extremely weak opponents sometimes see reasons for optimism beyond a specific bilateral relationship. Because the strategic effect of the balance of power paradox is to make both sides extremely risk acceptant, conflict breaks out in crises that theory and logic would suggest should be resolved short of war.

A host of psychological explanations, not to mention an even more vexing array of idiosyncratic developments, could explain the outbreak of asymmetric conflicts or the workings of the balance of power paradox. Nevertheless, this chapter will suggest that these wildly divergent perspectives about the relative power positions held by both sides in an asymmetric conflict are inherent in balancing behavior. By focusing on only one facet of the balance, leaders tend to perceive the constraints facing their opponent, while their own strengths are highly salient to them. Leaders of strong powers thus take an "attritional" view of conflict, taking full measure of how their superior capabilities will clearly and inevitably crush weak challengers. By contrast, leaders of weak powers are likely to adopt an "asymmetric" view of conflict because they tend to believe that their strategies will prevent the stronger power from bringing its full weight to bear in a conflict. In Chapter 1, I identified the crucial role surprise plays in the calculations of weaker states planning to attack strong states. Here I identify the way that balance of power calculations themselves can create the balance of power paradox: the eruption of war between strong and weak states.

To address this issue, the chapter will first use Kenneth Waltz's *Theory of International Politics*, to explain how the balance of power paradox leads to indeterminate predictions of the behavior of weak and strong states in a bipolar system. It does so by examining the way balance of power considerations affected American and North Vietnamese perceptions of their relative positions during the Vietnam War. The chapter will then explore the recent failures of deterrent and compellent strategies in the 1991 Gulf War, to demonstrate how the conflict represents a transition point between the constraints created by the Cold War and a new situation that reflects more "soft balancing." The chapter is ambitious in the sense that it identifies not only the forces that shape the balance of power paradox, but also the forces that continue to foster it at a time when the United States enjoys a position of military, economic and diplomatic dominance in world politics.

The balance of power paradox in a bipolar world

In a bipolar system, the two dominant powers, which were referred to as superpowers, were preoccupied with one another's activities. "In the great-power politics of bipolar worlds," according to Waltz, "who is a danger to whom is never in doubt."[5] Because of the enormous conventional and nuclear arsenals possessed by both superpowers, only the United States and the Soviet Union could threaten each other's survival. Moreover, because of the enormous gulf between the capabilities and resources possessed by the superpowers and their nearest rivals, American and Soviet desires to strengthen themselves vis-à-vis their main competitor were best realized through internal efforts. Under these circumstances, allies objectively added little to the security of the superpowers, and even major changes in alliances had little effect on the existing military, economic, and political equilibrium between the United States and the USSR. To highlight this point, Waltz cited the minimal systemic effect produced by Beijing's withdrawal from the American "alliance" in 1949, and the de facto Sino–American alliance that emerged during the 1970s. In other words, if the world's most populous country could change sides during the Cold War without altering the balance of power significantly, then changes among lesser allies and rivals could not alter the equilibrium of a bipolar world.[6]

Given these structural realities, Waltz would suggest that both superpowers could be expected to shun military involvement in peripheral conflicts in the Third World. In 1967, for example, Waltz noted:

> Two states that enjoy wide margins of power over other states need worry little about changes that occur among the latter. ... Because no realignment of national power in Vietnam could in itself affect the balance of power between the United States and the Soviet Union—or even noticeably alter

the imbalance of power between the United States and China—the United States need not have intervened at all.[7]

At best, involvement in the periphery represents a "side show" that could do little to affect the balance of capabilities between the superpowers in a bipolar world. At worst, peripheral involvements could drain vital resources needed to maintain a superpower's position vis-à-vis its main rival.[8]

Conversely, bipolarity can provide superpowers with an incentive to become embroiled in peripheral conflicts. In a bipolar world, according to Waltz, great power leaders tend to view international relations as a zero-sum situation. Regardless of the causes of a particular setback, losses to one superpower are often interpreted to be a direct gain for its main rival. This zero-sum view increases both sides' preoccupation with changes affecting allies, lesser rivals, and non-aligned nations, despite the fact that these changes have little direct impact on the superpower competition. "Bipolarity encourages the United States and the Soviet Union to turn unwanted events into crises," according to Waltz, "while rendering them relatively inconsequential. ... Both gain more by the peaceful development of internal resources than by wooing and winning—or by fighting and subduing—other states in the world." Because of this zero-sum view of the world, according to Waltz, "the U.S. has responded expensively in distant places to wayward events that could hardly affect anyone's fate outside of the region."[9]

Thus, when the great powers in a bipolar world face "wayward" events in the periphery, Waltz's theory leads to two opposing propositions about their response. First, the two superpowers will avoid involvement in unrewarding peripheral conflicts to husband their resources for the paramount great power competition. This first proposition assumes that policymakers will be sensitive to the systemic constraints that they face and are reluctant to exploit the constraints—by definition, relative military inferiority—faced by weaker rivals. Second, faced with disagreeable, albeit relatively inconsequential, events in the periphery, the two superpowers will rush to intervene in less than vital regional disputes, to prevent even incremental gains by the rival superpower. This proposition supposes that policymakers are not sensitive to the systemic constraints that they face, and are instead anxious to exploit the weaknesses of lesser rivals.

How will weak states behave towards antagonistic superpowers? Waltz's analysis does not directly address this question, but a response can be deduced from his theory and the work of other balance of power theorists. Weak states, like the great powers that loom over them, face their own array of incentives and constraints, leading to indeterminate predictions of their behavior during confrontations with a superpower in a bipolar world.

Unlike the rough equilibrium that characterizes the relationship between the superpowers in a bipolar setting, the competition between the great powers and peripheral states was one-sided. The superpowers possessed overwhelming nuclear, conventional, economic, manpower, and natural resources when compared to weak states. Although there is often a discrepancy between the appearance of power and its reality in international relations, the gross disparity in capabilities between the superpowers and weak states is too overwhelming to misunderstand or ignore.[10] It would be unlikely, indeed quite foolhardy, according to many balance of power theorists, for weak states to risk a major confrontation with a great power. "Clearly," explained Inis Claude, "a potential aggressor is likely to be deterred more effectively by confrontation with preponderant, rather than merely equal power."[11] Given the superpower tendency to view changes in the periphery in zero-sum terms, Moscow and Washington could be expected to respond to even minor challenges made by weak states. From this perspective, the combination of the superpowers' enormous capability and willingness to respond to changes in the periphery should pose a strong deterrent to provocative behavior by the weak state. According to Klaus Knorr, because of the overwhelming power possessed by great powers, weak states do "not even consider certain courses of action because it is obvious that they are likely to incur the displeasure of a ... very superior state."[12]

If they focus on the systemic constraints faced by the great powers, however, policymakers in weak states will view their insignificant position in a bipolar world not as a liability, but as a major advantage. Bipolarity can offer weak states increased freedom of action, especially in risking potential conflict with a great power. Because the superpowers can be expected to concentrate primarily on the bipolar competition, weak states might calculate that the great powers would be unlikely to expend resources on trivial developments in the periphery. In the words of Arnold Wolfers, small states possess the "power of the weak."[13] Even though the great powers could easily crush them, weak states could gamble that they just are not worth the effort, and thus pursue their own policies regardless of superpower displeasure.

Why does the paradox lead to war?

The very existence of the balance of power paradox suggests that war is possible, but not inevitable. Thus, a parsimonious specification of balance of power theory cannot predict whether leaders will find their constraints or their opponent's constraints most compelling during a confrontation. For example, even though Waltz maintains that great powers will probably intervene in peripheral disputes to prevent cumulative, potentially significant losses, war is risky and could weaken a superpower, leaving it vulnerable to its main competitor.[14] Conversely, weak states also might engage in provocative activities to obtain limited objectives, but this generates the graver risk of superpower intervention. For the paradox to produce war, the leaders of both weak and strong states must believe that they can avoid the systemic constraints they face while their opponent cannot escape the constraints created by their relative power position.

The divergent ways that leaders of great powers and weak states perceive a brewing conflict can propel them to war. Leaders in strong states tend to take an attritional view of warfare, focusing on the overwhelming advantages they enjoy against weaker competitors and how this military superiority will inevitably produce a victory once battle is joined. Leaders in weaker states, however, take an asymmetric view of the coming conflict. They believe that it will be possible to avoid the full brunt of their opponent's superior capability, and thus achieve their objectives. For instance, surprise is often attractive to the weaker party in the conflict because it allows it to present a stronger opponent with a fait accompli without first having to do the impossible: defeat a much stronger opponent in attritional warfare. Similarly, John Mearsheimer suggests that policymakers are more likely to challenge conventional deterrence if they believe that they possess a strategy that will allow them to prevail quickly over their opponents with minimal cost. Mearsheimer's argument suggests that leaders of weak states will ignore the systemic constraints they face when they believe that they possess an asymmetric strategy, a strategy that would allow them to prevail quickly and cheaply in a conflict without facing the full military might of a vastly superior opponent.[15]

Key to this analysis is the fact that this divergence in perception tends to mask the systemic constraints faced by both strong and weak powers in a brewing conflict. By focusing on the attritional aspects of a brewing conflict, stronger powers overestimate the effectiveness of their deterrent, compellent and war-making potential, or at least they overestimate the effect this will have on their weaker adversaries. The leaders of weaker powers, by focusing on the opportunities created by asymmetric strategies, contemplate provocative moves because they believe that they can avoid the full weight of the great power's military capability.

Vietnam: Unlikely war, unlikely outcome

Given the gross disparity in resources, it is surprising that the regime in Hanoi could ever have hoped to challenge the United States militarily in South Vietnam and succeed. Given the low position of Vietnam on a long list of American strategic priorities, it also is surprising that the United States—despite claims, made from divergent political outlooks, concerning falling dominoes or the importance of Vietnam as a source of raw materials—ever devoted significant resources to stop North Vietnam's efforts to unify the country. Indeed, the so called Big-unit War, which erupted between the Viet Cong and their North Vietnamese allies and the Saigon regime and its American supporters, actually proved to be an unwelcome development from the perspective of both the victors and the vanquished. Even though North Vietnam eventually succeeded in uniting the country, the communist leadership in Hanoi initially expected to achieve their objectives without having to fight an enormously destructive war.[16] Conversely, the members of President Lyndon Johnson's administration did not initially expect to fight, and certainly not to lose, a long, costly war to preserve the Saigon regime, a war that would hurt America's global economic position and its military standing vis-à-vis the Soviet Union.

The view from Hanoi

Because the communists eventually won in Vietnam, scholars have a tendency to underestimate the problems confronting North Vietnam following American intervention in the ground war. Yet, the challenge posed by US intervention loomed large in the minds of communist leaders, political cadres, and soldiers. Indeed, a wave of "defeatism" swept the ranks following American intervention as the communists encountered the mobility, firepower, and motivation of highly trained and well-equipped American forces. According to Patrick McGarvey: "The move that caused the greatest anxiety among Vietnamese Communist leaders—if the sheer volume of writing is an accurate gauge—was the sudden influx of American ground forces in South Vietnam in mid-1965."[17]

Decisions made by North Vietnam to escalate its involvement in the south evolved over time. Following the renewal of guerrilla warfare in South Vietnam during the late 1950s, provoked by Ngo Dinh Diem's successful anti-communist campaign, members of the Viet Cong petitioned the Hanoi leadership to aid them in their fight for survival. In response, North Vietnam provided "regroupees," southern communists who had fled north following the 1954 Geneva accords, to support the Viet Cong. This relatively limited North Vietnamese aid had a significant impact on the battlefield. Prior to Diem's overthrow in November 1963, the South Vietnamese military position had deteriorated. In the aftermath of the Diem coup, however, the South Vietnamese position collapsed as Army Republic of Vietnam (ARVN) units and their commanders became caught up in the struggle to control the government in Saigon. The North Vietnamese, following a December 1963 meeting of the Central Committee of the Vietnamese Worker's (Communist) Party, decided to capitalize on this turmoil by escalating their involvement in the south. North Vietnamese Army (NVA) units were soon streaming down the Ho Chi Minh Trail.[18] By 1963, harassment of an American client had escalated to the point of a direct North Vietnamese threat to the continued existence of South Vietnam.

In acting provocatively, were the North Vietnamese so obsessed with the goal of unifying Vietnam that they were oblivious to the systemic constraints they faced? The answer to this question is no. North Vietnamese officials realized that the United States possessed overwhelming resources; they recognized that they faced systemic constraints. This awareness was a tacit product of their Marxist-Leninist ideology. Characterized as the "leading imperialist power," the United States enjoyed certain advantages, among them overwhelming military and economic resources. Marxism-Leninism, however, also identified the systemic constraints faced by the United States. Writing in September 1967, long after the Johnson administration had demonstrated its willingness to intervene massively in the war, General Vo Nguyen Giap noted that America's global commitments limited the resources it could devote to the conflict: "The U.S. imperialists must cope with the national liberation movement [in countries other than South Vietnam], with the socialist bloc, with the American people, and with other imperialist countries. The U.S. imperialists cannot mobilize all their forces for the war of aggression in Vietnam."[19] Giap was referring to the systemic constraints created by bipolarity as a factor that would limit the U.S. response in Vietnam. Even though their ideology identified the systemic constraints that they faced, as well as those of their opponents, in December 1963, communist leaders chose to emphasize the obstacles confronting the United States. In deciding to escalate the conflict in the south, they estimated that the United States probably would not respond massively to overt North Vietnamese intervention. At worst, the North Vietnamese predicted that the Americans might send 100,000 troops to support their Vietnamese clients, but they considered this eventuality to be unlikely.[20]

The North Vietnamese saw recent history as a reflection of the systemic constraints faced by the United States. In their view, Americans had a tendency either to abandon clients or compromise in the face of concerted challenges to "imperialism." North Vietnamese leaders pointed to the US decision not to save Chiang Kai-Shek's regime in China as an example of the American tendency to walk away from "no-win" situations. They regarded US acceptance of a compromise settlement of the Korean War in the same light, despite the fact that the Chinese communists, who relied on a different interpretation of the Korean analogy, continuously warned them of the danger of provoking a massive American response in Southeast Asia. Even though many North Vietnamese officials blamed their Soviet and Chinese allies for the "sell-out" that produced the 1954 Geneva accords, the agreements in their view again pointed to an American preference for compromise settlements. Finally, the North Vietnamese saw the 1961 agreement on the neutralization of Laos as further evidence of American reluctance to interfere in Asia. Given their reading of recent events, the communists apparently believed that if they could convince US officials that the situation in Saigon had deteriorated significantly, Americans either would accept a political settlement of the war or would simply withdraw from South Vietnam. In order to trigger the expected American response to a deteriorating situation, the North Vietnamese escalated their involvement in the south.[21]

In the minds of Hanoi strategists, People's War would largely negate the advantages enjoyed by the leading imperialist power, by allowing the North Vietnamese to control the level of violence in any confrontation with the United States. By shifting their *dau tranh* (struggle) to liberate the south towards the political realm, they could reduce casualties by increasing the duration of the war, thereby denying Americans a quick military victory. In other words, the North Vietnamese believed that they possessed a military strategy that would raise the stakes enough to force American officials to withdraw from Vietnam or risk wasting resources that needed to be preserved for the main contest with the Soviet Union.[22] Systemic constraints would prevent the United States from bringing its full power to bear in Southeast Asia.

The View from the Potomac

Prior to their decision to intervene in the ground war, members of the Johnson administration failed to realize that they ran the risk of becoming embroiled in a lengthy war that could reduce America's standing vis-à-vis the USSR. Warnings existed, however, about the gravity of the task they contemplated. France's unhappy experience in Indochina could not be ignored, even though many Americans denied its relevance as a guide to policy.[23] After all, as William Bundy noted in a November 1964 memorandum to the National Security Council (NSC) working group on Southeast Asia, "the French also tried to build the Panama Canal."[24] A war-game, code-named SIGMA I, conducted during late 1963, also suggested that after a ten-year commitment of 600,000 US combat troops, the VC would continue to expand their control of the South Vietnamese countryside. The participants in the exercise, with even more exact foresight, concluded that the American public would grow tired of such a costly, drawn-out conflict. Yet, the lessons offered by SIGMA I failed to have any discernible impact on the policies adopted by the Johnson administration.[25] Members of the Johnson administration were not particularly concerned about the systemic constraints they faced in contemplating intervention in Vietnam.

In contrast, members of the administration were alert to the possibility that not acting to stop the communists might produce negative consequences for the United States. They believed that they needed to maintain their reputation as a faithful ally. Since the administration's rhetoric highlighted the American commitment to South Vietnam, administration officials believed that US policy towards Southeast Asia would be interpreted as a test case of American resolve. As John McNaughton's July 13, 1965 memorandum to Secretary of Defense McNamara demonstrates, the administration's goals in Southeast Asia were intended:

> 70% – To preserve our national honor as a guarantor (and the reciprocal: to avoid a show-case success for Communist "wars of liberation"?)
>
> 20% – To keep SVN (and their adjacent) territory from hostile expansive [sic] hands.
>
> 10% – To "answer the call of a friend," to help him enjoy a better life.
>
> Also – To emerge from crisis without unacceptable taint from the methods used.[26]

If the US backed away from it commitment to South Vietnam, there was concern that it might damage "Free World" solidarity vis-à-vis the Soviet bloc. For many members of the Johnson administration, a quick humiliation in Vietnam, not a drawn-out war, was interpreted as the more conceivable threat to American standing in the global competition with the USSR. Ironically, systemic constraints were offered as a justification for intervention in Vietnam. A US failure to respond to the communists was seen to lead to prompt negative consequences, while the long-term threat of becoming embroiled in a quagmire appeared less salient to policymakers.

The objectives behind the American decision to respond to the NVA invasion of South Vietnam closely matched their perception of the way the international system constrained their Vietnamese opponents. The purpose of American policy towards Southeast Asia was not to win the war in Vietnam, but to demonstrate to the North Vietnamese that they could not obtain their objectives militarily. The Americans believed that if their actions could increase the salience of the systemic constraints faced by the North Vietnamese, in this case military inferiority, then the communists would abandon their quest to unite Vietnam through military action. Commenting on the conclusions reached by senior officials during an April 1965 meeting in Honolulu, McNamara noted that the American goal in Vietnam was "to break the will of the DRV/VC by depriving them of victory."[27] In the words of Maxwell Taylor, "a demonstration of Communist impotence … will lead to a political solution."[28] Years later, Taylor elaborated upon the expectations held by American officials at the time:

> In 1965 we knew very little about the Hanoi leaders other than Ho Chi Minh and General Giap and virtually nothing about their individual or collective intentions. We were inclined to assume, however, that they would behave about like the North Koreans and Red Chinese a decade before; that is, they would seek an accommodation with us when the cost of pursuing a losing course became excessive.[29]

American policymakers believed that officials in Hanoi had somehow experienced a strategic or intelligence failure, and had underestimated the potential forces that could be arrayed against them. By engaging in a gradual escalation of the conflict and by introducing combat forces into South Vietnam, the Americans expected that they would be able to compel Hanoi to abandon their effort to unify Vietnam through the use of force. If Ho Chi Minh and his followers had miscalculated, then a demonstration of force would bring them to their senses by highlighting the systemic constraints (i.e., their military inferiority) they faced. Two American mistakes thus smoothed the path to a disastrous conflict: (1) they failed to realize that North Vietnamese leaders believed they would not have to face the full brunt of American military power; and (2) they did not anticipate North Vietnamese willingness to suffer when the United States actually intervened in force. As Taylor noted in 1972, "the North Vietnamese proved to be incredibly tough in accepting losses which, by Western calculation, greatly exceeded the value of the stake involved."[30]

The balance of power paradox and the end of bipolarity: The 1991 Gulf War

If the North Vietnamese could look to the Soviet Union to constrain the United States, what force in the immediate aftermath of the Cold War prevented the United States from using its overwhelming military capability to punish or coerce weak states? Indeed, the balance of power paradox is even more perplexing in the aftermath of the Cold War because weak states can no longer hope that the remaining superpower will be constrained by a great power competitor. Nevertheless, US deterrent and compellent threats have failed repeatedly since the end of the Cold War (e.g., the 1999 war in Kosovo, or a near-decade-long terrorist campaign launched by Al-Qaeda), leading to brief conflicts between the United States (usually accompanied by many allies) and grossly inferior opponents. From a systemic perspective, the United States, as the sole surviving superpower, faces few constraints, which should leave weak states little hope of avoiding the full brunt of its military capability. Yet, weak states and groups continue to confront, defy and even attack the United States and its interests, while hoping to avoid defeat or even retaliation. In all cases, none of America's opponents doubted that the United States enjoyed significant military capability. Instead, they all believed that US officials, for one reason or another, would not be willing to use that power effectively.

The Iraqi invasion of Kuwait in August 1990 and the subsequent international effort to liberate the small nation occurred at the very moment the old bipolar order was crumbling; the conflict began during the Cold War but at its end only one superpower remained. It also represents both a failure of deterrence, in that the United States did not prevent the Iraqi invasion, and a failure of compellence in the sense Saddam Hussein did not withdraw from Kuwait but instead chose to battle a global coalition that was determined to eject Iraqi forces from the emirate. Although the Iraqi invasion of Kuwait is a poor case to assess deterrence theory because US officials failed to make a clear deterrent threat prior to the invasion, it does illustrate the fact that Saddam Hussein was not particularly concerned about the prospect of intervention.

The failure of deterrence

By all accounts, Iraq's invasion of Kuwait was prompted by a fundamental and well-understood motivation, money. With its economy wrecked by the Iran–Iraq war, with international creditors beginning to back away from loans, and with hundreds of thousands of veterans wanting to return to the good life that would follow their "victory" against Iran, Iraq was in dire straits. Saddam Hussein turned to extortion to shore up his economy and preserve his regime by putting pressure on Kuwait for territorial concessions, access to Kuwaiti oil reserves, and an outright gift of $10 billion. The war also highlighted rifts among members of the Organization of Petroleum Exporting Countries (OPEC), between those who championed long-term policies of price stabilization and those who sought quick profits by manipulating oil markets or at least increasing their production quotas. Ironically, the Gulf War was in fact all about oil, but it was driven by Saddam Hussein's unscrupulousness and OPEC's disarray.

Critics might charge that the United States never really suffered a deterrence failure prior to the Gulf War because officials in the George H.W. Bush administration failed to appreciate the nature of the threat posed by Iraq until just hours before the invasion. In the months leading up to the crisis, US officials were preoccupied with the collapse of Soviet power in Europe, German unification, and devising a way to support newly liberated states in Eastern Europe. Nor, in the weeks leading up to the crisis, was the gravity of the impending threat appreciated by the international community, thanks to a highly effective denial and deception campaign undertaken by Baghdad, which convinced all concerned that the crisis would be resolved after the Kuwaitis offered up some minimal concessions, or would terminate in some sort of small Iraqi land grab in Kuwait.[31] Although the United States did manage to issue some warnings to Baghdad before the invasion, the Bush administration, following requests made by friendly governments in the region, toned down its deterrent rhetoric to allow Arab mediation to settle the dispute.

Of crucial importance, however, is Saddam Hussein's estimate of the likely US response to the invasion of Kuwait. Saddam clearly believed that the United States could respond to Iraqi aggression, but he estimated that the Bush administration would choose not to expend blood and treasure to defend Kuwait. He even went so far as to make this assumption plain to the US Ambassador to Iraq, April Glaspie, that the Americans did not share Iraq's willingness to loose 10,000 people per day in battle, and that they risked terrorist attacks within the United States itself if they interfered in the dispute with Kuwait.[32] Saddam also might have hoped that the Soviet Union would act to restrain the United States, but as Lawrence Freedman and Efraim Karsh argue, the Iraqi dictator probably recognized that Soviet influence and power was fading rapidly. Other Arab states were beginning to reorient their foreign policies in response to the loss of their superpower patron; it is possible that Saddam saw a narrow "window of opportunity" in the summer of 1990 and decided to act before the Soviet Union disappeared from the scene.[33] In a speech delivered to the Arab Cooperation Council in Oman in July 1990, for example, Saddam noted that unless Arab states asserted themselves, Soviet decline would leave the United States as the dominant power in the Gulf.[34] Saddam also apparently believed that he could paralyze any potential Arab response to his seizure of Kuwait by linking his move to the "Israeli" issue. Without Arab acquiescence, he estimated that US policymakers would be unlikely to intervene in the Gulf. And for their part, Arab leaders initially were eager to find an "Arab solution" to the conflict—not out of some feeling of Islamic solidarity, but to forestall an increase in the military presence of the great powers in the region. In effect, Saddam was not deterred because he correctly estimated that he could seize Kuwait easily and then present the world with a fait accompli that would be difficult, albeit not impossible, to overturn. The Arabs would never form a common front with the West, the Americans did not have the guts to fight, and the Soviets might see the crisis as a way to reassert their fading influence in world affairs.

The failure of compellence

The failure of the international effort to compel Iraq to leave Kuwait without having to resort to war underscores the difficulty of creating and maintaining a solid international front against aggression. This problem was compounded by Saddam Hussein's ability to exploit every opportunity to sow dissension among his opponents, and the tendency of the Iraqi dictator to grasp at straws even as a global coalition massed overwhelming forces against him. The international coalition that slowly gathered strength during the second half of 1990 with the purpose of expelling Iraq from Kuwait nevertheless offers a textbook case of compellence.[35]

The international forces arrayed against Baghdad were indeed impressive. Iraq faced an economic embargo that was facilitated by its reliance on oil as its sole source of hard currency. Without oil exports, Iraq lacked the cash needed to entice officials or black marketeers to risk breaking the UN economic sanctions that were imposed just days after the invasion of Kuwait. Saddam attempted to torpedo the international coalition forming against him by playing the "Public Opinion," "Third World," "Arab," and Soviet cards. He seized hostages to split the coalition, offering to return nationals to visiting dignitaries who pleaded for their safety if only their governments would break ranks with the UN. He treated Western hostages better than those from the developing world, while simultaneously making overtures to governments of poor countries that he had common cause with them in their struggle against imperialism. (These efforts to manipulate public opinion, however, backfired as images of Saddam interacting with hostages, especially children, produced universal revulsion and anger.) He berated his Arab neighbors with the warning that any war among Muslims only strengthened Israel. Most Arab governments would agree with that sentiment, but they universally blamed Saddam Hussein for creating the conflict in the first place. And in a strange twist, Saddam taunted Soviet officials by noting that their failure to come to Iraq's aid demonstrated to all concerned that they were a state in demise:

> He who represents the Soviet Union must remember that worries and suspicions about the superpower status assumed by the Soviet Union have been crossing the minds of all politicians in the world for some time. ... Those concerned must choose this critical time and this critical case in order to restore to the Soviet Union its status through adopting a position that is in harmony with all that is just and fair.[36]

None of these gambits significantly disrupted the coalition forming against Saddam or the universal call for Iraq to withdraw from Kuwait. In fact, each of Iraq's moves actually hardened international public opinion in its opposition to the Iraqi occupation of Kuwait. In the end, Iraqi officials became highly dismissive of Soviet efforts to convince Saddam that they would not support him in his effort to hold onto Kuwait. Soviet Foreign Minister Eduard Shevardnaze noted that

Saddam Hussein's response to an August 23 letter from Soviet President Mikhail Gorbachev, advising him to comply with UN resolutions, was not even worth a comment.[37]

Compellence began in earnest following the Bush administration's October 31, 1990 decision (which was announced on November 8) to begin to deploy forces necessary not just to deter and defend against an Iraqi drive into Saudi Arabia, but also to expel Iraqi occupation troops from Kuwait by force.[38] United Nations Resolution 678 was passed on November 29, 1990, authorizing member states to "use all necessary means" to gain Iraqi compliance with all eleven previous resolutions regarding Kuwait. The deadline stated for Iraqi compliance was January 15, 1991.[39] Resolution 678 constituted an *international* ultimatum to Saddam Hussein to withdraw from Kuwait. Although a steady stream of official, semi-official and private initiatives to find a peaceful solution to the crisis were taken in the weeks and days leading up to the outbreak of hostilities, most of these emissaries reiterated the fundamental demand advanced by the United Nations: Iraq must withdraw from Kuwait before any of Iraq's demands would be addressed. The massive movement of coalition forces to the Persian Gulf accompanied this diplomatic activity. In the penultimate diplomatic meeting before the war on January 9, 1991, US Secretary of State James Baker attempted to deliver a letter to Saddam Hussein that clearly spelled out the size and nature of the military forces arrayed against him, made veiled threats about the "strongest possible response" that would follow any Iraqi use of chemical or biological weapons in the coming conflict, and the fact that Iraq would be left "weak and backward" following the terrible beating it would take in the coming war. Baker told Tariq Aziz, the Iraqi Foreign Minister, that if Saddam would not comply with the demands of virtually the entire international community, Iraq would suffer decisive defeat in a short war. Baker's warning to Aziz should not have been news to Iraqi officials. In the months leading up to the war, Soviet envoy Yevgeny Primakov repeatedly told Saddam Hussein that US military capabilities were vastly superior to anything in Iraq's arsenal.[40]

Although Aziz refused to deliver President Bush's letter to Saddam Hussein, he responded to Baker's brief by stating that it was the Americans and their allies who were in for a long and bloody conflict. He told him that the Arabs in the coalition would never fight alongside the United States, and that no Arab leader had ever been hurt by standing up to the West. In the days leading up to the war, Iraqi officials including Saddam Hussein harped on this theme, replete with references to America's inability to tolerate casualties, and references to the US experience in Vietnam. Iraqi officials were banking on the notion that the coalition could not withstand the negative political pressures generated by coalition losses in battle or the loss of civilian life from missile attacks on cities. Sometimes Iraqi officers actually claimed that the coalition lacked the necessary forces (3 million troops) to prevail over the Iraqi military, which was 1 million strong.[41] But more often they claimed that the coalition might be impressive on paper, but would in the end lack the stomach for war.

Conclusion

Although they debated different issues and in different strategic settings, the policy-makers on both sides of the Vietnam and Gulf War conflicts shared remarkably similar views of their prospects in the conflict. In one case, the great power leaders' predictions of the likely outcome came to pass: Iraq suffered a quick and decisive defeat during the Gulf War. In the other case, the limits of American power were reached in a long and bloody attritional war in Southeast Asia—a war that was won by the weaker party. In both cases, the balance of power produced war, even though Vietnam occurred at what might be considered the peak of bipolarity, while the Gulf War occurred at a time when the Soviet Union was no longer capable or willing to act like a superpower that faced a threat to one of its clients.

In both instances, officials in the great power adopted an attritional view of war, in the sense that they focused on the gross differences between the military capabilities of the parties in the conflict and the fact that the weaker party had little prospect for victory in the event of war. The compellent strategies adopted by American policymakers thus focused on changing the perceptions of their opponents, to communicate missing information somehow about the true weakness of their military forces vis-à-vis the great power. In Southeast Asia, members of the Johnson administration hoped that military demonstrations in the form of air strikes or the deployment of ground forces would force the North Vietnamese to recognize both their military inferiority and the US commitment to save the regime in Saigon. Prior to the Gulf War, officials in the first Bush administration thought that Saddam Hussein had never been given the unvarnished truth by a staff of sycophants who feared bringing the dictator an honest appraisal of Iraq's strategic prospects in the event of war. Baker's last-minute meeting with Aziz to deliver a letter from the President was intended to make sure that an honest appraisal of Iraq's prospects reached Hussein. The potential weaknesses in their position never dominated the view of the impending conflict held by leaders of the superpower.

While North Vietnamese and Iraqi officials recognized the overwhelming superiority of their potential superpower antagonist, leaders from both nations believed that the United States would not be able to bring the full weight of its military power to bear in a conflict. Leaders in Hanoi believed that America's world-wide commitments and the need to keep substantial forces in reserve to deal with a possible conflict with the Soviet Union, would limit the resources Washington could devote to blocking the unification of Vietnam under communist rule. Hanoi never really expected to defeat US forces on the battlefield, but sought to confront US officials with a long war that would end in a negotiated settlement favorable to the North Vietnamese. Similarly, Saddam Hussein also saw the Soviet Union and an unwillingness to spend blood and treasure as restraints on the US inclination to interfere with his plans for Kuwait. When the Soviets joined the global coalition to compel Iraq to abandon Kuwait, Saddam berated Moscow for its failure to play its traditional superpower role by restraining the United States.

And, like Hanoi, he assumed the weakest of asymmetric strategies: he willingly engaged the United States in an attritional campaign in an effort to get at what he perceived was the Western Achilles heel, an aversion to casualties.

What is clear in both conflicts is that American officials always framed the war in terms of a clash of military forces that the weaker party had virtually no prospect of winning, while the weaker party expected that for one reason or another the stronger party could not bring its full force to bear in a conflict. Both parties in both conflicts chose to fight instead of limit their demands—the stakes always involved who would control South Vietnam and Kuwait. But it is not surprising that a preponderance of power fails to generate a deterrent or compellent threat when it involves risk-acceptant opponents, especially one that views the conflict from an asymmetric perspective and one that views the conflict from an attritional perspective. Both see their opponent's weaknesses through a different lens, and both see paths to victory.

Notes

1 Jack S. Levy, "What Do Great Powers Balance Against and When?" in T.V, Paul, James J. Wirtz and Michel Fortmann (eds), *Balance of Power: Theory and Practice in the 21st Century* (Stanford, CA: Stanford University Press, 2004), p. 36.
2 George Liska, *International Equilibrium: A Theoretical Essay on the Politics and Organization of Security* (Cambridge, MA: Harvard University Press, 1957); and Inis L. Claude, *Power and International Relations* (New York: Random House, 1962), p. 56.
3 T.V. Paul, *Asymmetric Conflicts: War Initiation by Weaker Powers* (New York: Cambridge University Press, 1994).
4 Ivan Arreguin-Toft, "How the Weak Win Wars: A Theory of Asymmetric Conflict," *International Security* Vol. 26, No. 1 (Summer 2001), pp. 93–128; and Andrew Mack, "Why Big Nations Lose Small Wars: The Politics of Asymmetric Conflict," *World Politics* Vol. 27, No. 2 (January 1975), pp. 175–200.
5 Kenneth N. Waltz, *Theory of International Politics* (Reading, MA: Addison-Wesley, 1979), p. 170.
6 Kenneth N. Waltz, *Theory of International Politics*, p. 169.
7 Kenneth N. Waltz, "International Structure, National Force, and the Balance of Power," in James Rosenau (ed.), *International Politics and Foreign Policy* (New York: Free Press, 1969), p. 310.
8 Waltz's students were quick to build on this point. See Stephen Van Evera, "American Strategic Interests: Why Europe Matters, Why the Third World Doesn't," *Journal of Strategic Studies* Vol. 13, No. 2 (June 1990), pp. 1–51.
9 Waltz, *Theory of International Politics*, p. 172.
10 According to Arnold Wolfers: "There are several reasons for the frequent discrepancies between the appearance of power and its actual performance: one is the relativity of power, another is the gap between the estimate of power and its reality, and a third is the specificity of power, which means that it takes specific types of power to bring results under specific circumstances." Arnold Wolfers, *Discord and Collaboration* (Baltimore, MD: Johns Hopkins University Press, 1962), pp. 110–111. The point made here, however, is that the difference between the capabilities of the superpowers and weak states is so large that leaders of weak powers have ample reason to expect that the great powers will be able to confront a challenger with overwhelming resources.

11 Claude, *Power and International Relations* (New York: Random House, 1962), quoted in Robert Art and Robert Jervis (eds), *International Politics* (Boston, MA: Scott, Foresman & Co., 1985), p. 117. For a similar perspective, see A.F.K. Organski, *World Politics* (New York: Knopf, 1958), p. 293; and Robert Gilpin, *War and Change in World Politics* (Cambridge: Cambridge University Press, 1981), pp. 50–105; and K. Edward Spiezio, "British Hegemony and Major Power War, 1815–1939: An Empirical Test of Gilpin's Model of Hegemonic Governance," *International Studies Quarterly* (June 1990), pp. 169–170.

12 Klaus Knorr, *The Power of Nations: The Political Economy of International Relations* (New York: Basic Books, 1975), p. 10. The suggestion of an "implied" or "general" deterrent situation between the superpowers and weak states would be rejected on the basis of a strict definition, offered by Ned Lebow and Janice Gross Stein, of deterrence: "Deterrence requires that the 'defender' define the behavior that is unacceptable, publicize the commitment to punish or restrain the transgressors, demonstrate the resolve to do so, and possess the capabilities to implement the threat." In other words, the definition of deterrence offered here would only encompass the last two criterion suggested by Lebow and Stein. For a critique of this kind of "nebulous" deterrence theorizing see Richard Ned Lebow and Janice Gross Stein, "Deterrence: The Elusive Dependent Variable," *World Politics* Vol. XLII (April 1990), pp. 336–369.

13 According to Wolfers, "[W]henever two great powers are locked in serious conflict they can spare little if any of their coercive strength to deal with minor offenders and to impose their will on them over issues that have no direct bearing on the major struggle in which they are involved with their equals." See Wolfers, *Discord and Collaboration*, pp. 111–112.

14 Waltz, *Theory of International Politics*, p. 172.

15 John J. Mearsheimer, *Conventional Deterrence* (Ithaca, NY: Cornell University Press, 1983), pp. 23–24, 63–64.

16 William J. Duiker, *The Communist Road to Power in Vietnam* (Boulder, CO: Westview Press, 1981), p. 189.

17 Patrick McGarvey, *Visions of Victory* (Stanford, CA: Hoover Institution on War, Revolution and Peace, 1969), p. 5.

18 William J. Duiker, *Vietnam: Nation in Revolution* (Boulder, CO: Westview Press, 1983), p. 54; and Duiker, *Road to Power*, pp. 183–193; and Gabriel Kolko, *Anatomy of a War: The United States, and the Modern Historical Experience* (New York: Pantheon Books, 1985), pp. 99–101; and U.S. Grant Sharp and William Westmoreland, *Report on the War in Vietnam* (Washington, DC: U.S. Government Printing Office, 1968), pp. 81, 92.

19 Vo Nguyen Giap, "The Big Victory, the Great Task," Nhan Dan and Quan Doi Nhan Dan (September 14–16, 1967), contained in McGarvey, *Visions of Victory*, p. 237.

20 Duiker, *Road to Power*, pp. 221–223, 226; and Stanley Karnow, *Vietnam: A History* (New York: Viking Press, 1983), pp. 327, 329–330.

21 Duiker, *Road to Power*, p. 226.

22 Duiker, *Road to Power*, pp. 127–131; and Douglas Pike, *PAVN: People's Army of Vietnam* (Novato, CA: Presidio Press, 1986), pp. 213–253; and Douglas Pike, *Viet Cong* (Cambridge, MA: MIT Press, 1966), Appendix A "NLF Accounts of Dich Van Struggle Movements," pp. 385–397.

23 Douglas Blaufarb, *The Counterinsurgency Era: US Doctrine and Performance* (New York: Free Press, 1977), pp. 49–50.

24 "Memorandum for the Chairman, NSC Working Group on Southeast Asia (Mr. William P. Bundy, Department of State)," November 10, 1964, Document #228, contained in *The Pentagon Papers, The Senator Gravel Edition* Vol. III (Boston, MA: Beacon Press, 1971), p. 625.

25 Andrew Krepinevich, *The Army and Vietnam* (Baltimore, MD: Johns Hopkins University Press, 1986), pp. 133–134.
26 McNaughton's memorandum quoted in George McT. Kahin, *Intervention: How America Became Involved in Vietnam* (Garden City, NY: Anchor Books, 1987), p. 357.
27 McNamara quoted in Kahin, *Intervention*, p. 319.
28 Taylor quoted in Kahin, *Intervention*, p. 319.
29 Maxwell Taylor, *Swords and Ploughshares* (New York: Norton, 1972), p. 401.
30 Taylor, *Swords and Ploughshares*, p. 401.
31 Richard Russell, "CIA's Strategic Intelligence in Iraq," *Political Science Quarterly* Vol. 117, No. 2 (Summer 2002), pp. 191–207.
32 Iraqi transcript of the meeting between President Saddam Hussein and US Ambassador April Glaspie, *New York Times*, September 23, 1990, p. A 19.
33 Lawrence Freedman and Efraim Karsh, *The Gulf Conflict, 1990–1991* (Princeton, NJ: Princeton University Press, 1993), pp. 13–18, 52.
34 Janice Gross Stein, "Deterrence and Compellence in the Gulf, 1990–1991: A Failed or Impossible Task?" *International Security* Vol. 17, No. 2 (Autumn 1992), p. 158.
35 For the textbook, see Thomas Schelling, *The Strategy of Conflict* (New Haven, CT: Yale University Press, 1966).
36 Saddam Hussein quoted in Freedman and Karsh, *The Gulf Conflict*, p. 164.
37 Freedman and Karsh, *The Gulf Conflict*, p. 149.
38 Michael Gordon and Bernard Trainor, *The Generals' War* (Boston, MA: Little, Brown & Co., 1995), pp. 153–156.
39 Freedman and Karsh, *The Gulf Conflict*, pp. 233–234.
40 Stein, "Deterrence and Compellence," p. 174.
41 Freedman and Karsh, *The Gulf Conflict*, pp. 279–280.

6

DETERRING THE WEAK

Problems and prospects

Deterrence is a simple concept that is often difficult to put into practice. It involves creating the idea in the mind of the opponent that the gains enjoyed following some action will not outweigh the costs suffered in the wake of a threatened retaliatory blow or creating the impression in the mind of the opponent that a competitor can deny them their objectives through direct military action. A few conditions must be satisfied before threats—involving both conventional and nuclear weapons—actually deter an opponent from some unwanted endeavor. It is generally agreed that the effectiveness of deterrence is increased if threats are communicated clearly so that the opponent recognizes the "red lines" that will lead to the execution of a deterrent threat.[1] It makes no sense to surprise an opponent with unanticipated retaliation when a clear signal could have deterred unwanted activity in the first place. It also is generally agreed that deterrent threats require a combination of capability and credibility to be effective. In other words, one must have the capability to act on one's deterrent threats. Hollow gestures or threats that can somehow be circumvented or defeated carry little deterrent value. Deterrence also has to be credible in the sense that opponents must believe that those making deterrent threats will actually execute the threat if defined red lines are crossed. If opponents believe that the party issuing threats lacks the motivation, will, flexibility, or incentive to act on those threats, then deterrence might not appear credible in the mind of the beholder. Assuming that the deterrence target maintains even a tenuous grasp of strategic realities, the more clearly that deterrent threats are stated, the more unfettered the capability that a party possesses to execute the stated threat, and the stronger the incentive to act on the threat should deterrence fail, the greater are the prospects that deterrence will succeed.

Given this conception of deterrence, the ability of strong states to deter weaker competitors should be a foregone conclusion. Several observations support this assertion. The strong often believe that deterrence is a preferred strategy. Powerful states are attracted to deterrence because they would rather threaten to use their superior military capability to deter war than engage opponents on the battlefield. Deterrence is a cost-effective way to use superior military capability to prevent conflict before it starts. It prevents the outbreak of "unnecessary wars," conflicts that will be decided in favor of the stronger party but at some cost. Strong states embrace deterrence as a strategy against weaker competitors, and can be expected to take some care in crafting and communicating deterrent threats. Strong states have strategic incentives to embrace deterrence as a strategy and they possess the capability to make good on deterrent threats.

The difference in military capability between the strong and weak also becomes increasingly easy to perceive as the gap in capability grows. When disparities in capability are significant, both powers in a potential conflict generally share an accurate perception of those disparities. Under these conditions, one would expect that deterrent threats would be easily communicated by the stronger party and easily understood and recognized by the weaker party. Deterrent threats made by strong states against weaker competitors should be inherently credible, ceteris paribus, because the strong have the capability to make good on their threats. In other words, the structural conditions needed for deterrence to succeed—i.e., there is little doubt in the mind of the targeted state that the stronger power can make good on its deterrent threats—exist in conflicts between strong and weak states. In the words of Geoffrey Blainey, "Any factor which increases the likelihood that nations will agree on their relative power is a potential cause of peace."[2] Deterrence should work in these circumstances because an assessment of the nuclear and conventional military balance often leads the weak to recognize they are challenging a stronger state, and such challenges could lead to wars of attrition that the weak are destined to lose.

In a general way, the military balance between strong and weak states should also foster conditions for deterrence success. Because little in the military balance should create a sense of optimism in the minds of the leaders of the weaker state, they should refrain from challenging stronger states.[3] Provocative behavior not only could lead to the execution of deterrent threats on the part of the stronger state, it could foster the outbreak of a wider conflict that threatens the very existence of the weak state's regime. When disparities of power are significant, deterrence failure can create an existential threat to the weak state. Once again, under these circumstances, it makes little sense for weak states to challenge strong competitors because no matter what gains are expected from aggression, they are outweighed by the potential cost of challenging superior opponents.

Events, however, often fail to conform to the expectations of deterrence theory. Weak states challenge superior adversaries; deterrence failure is actually rather common in conflicts involving strong and weak states. In fact, deterrence often fails catastrophically, punctuated by some sort of action that presents the stronger power with a fait accompli or localized military defeat. Compellence, the effort to use threats to force a state to cease unwanted activity, also fares equally badly, sometimes in ways that are difficult to fathom. Saddam Hussein thumbed his nose at a global coalition when he ignored demands to withdraw from Kuwait. Slobodan Milosevic ignored calls to comply with international demands even though North Atlantic Treaty Organization aircraft carried out unimpeded counter-force and counter-value air strikes over Serbian territory. Although compellence is more difficult than deterrence and extended conventional deterrence can raise issues of credibility,[4] the fact that both of these leaders undertook actions that were bound to pit them against the interests of states and international coalitions that possessed overwhelming military and financial resources seems to make a mockery of the very tenants of deterrence. Deterrence of the weak by the strong is not as easy in practice as it is in theory.

This chapter explores the reasons why strong states often fail to deter vastly weaker competitors, and to identify factors that can increase the prospects that deterrence will succeed in these situations. The logic outlined here is applicable to deterrence involving conventional and nuclear weapons, or deterrence involving vital national interests or extended deterrence threats. It is applicable when potential conflicts involve states with significant disparities in nuclear and conventional military capabilities and becomes less theoretically and empirically relevant as states embroiled in a nascent dispute are more evenly matched in military capability. Deterrence fails between strong and weak powers not because the weaker party miscalculates the military balance or fails to perceive the existence of deterrent threats, but because of a perception that it is possible to circumvent deterrence. This perception, in turn, is often rooted in strategic, political and social factors that the leaders of weak states believe they can manipulate to their advantage. Deterrence fails because the weak believe that the strong will not be able to bring their superior military capability to bear in an effective way, not because they no longer believe that they are significantly weaker than their potential competitor. By contrast, the strong fail to recognize that weaker opponents have somehow discounted their superior military capabilities and have come to believe that they can neutralize or circumvent deterrent threats. In other words, the logic presented here describes a paradox that may lead to deterrence failure even when a challenger recognizes that they are the weaker party in a conflict and that the defender possesses vastly superior military capability and has made deterrent threats to maintain the status quo.

To illustrate these points, the chapter will describe the strategic, political and social factors that lead to sources of optimism on the part of the weak when it comes to circumventing deterrent threats issued by the strong. It then identifies several considerations that should govern the behavior of stronger powers as they contemplate efforts to deter weaker competitors. The strong can deter the weak, but the effort is facilitated by an awareness of how deterrence can fail.

The optimism of the weak

In surveying three hundred years of history related to the outbreak of war, Blainey noted that optimism about wars' outcomes generally characterized the attitude of both sides contemplating conflict.⁵ In other words, states become involved in wars that they believe they can win at a reasonable cost. The unforgiving venue of war tempers that initial optimism, leading to a reassessment of the relative utility of diplomacy when it comes to achieving national objectives. What is perplexing about the effort of the strong to deter the weak, however, is the fact that the weak should find little reason for optimism when it comes to crossing deterrent "red lines" or generally antagonizing or provoking stronger opponents. Deterrence should succeed and war should not occur because the weak should find it difficult to imagine how they can defeat stronger opponents.

Nevertheless, three sources of optimism often animate thinking when the weak challenge the strong. First, leaders in weaker states sometimes believe that they can capitalize on strategic surprise to circumvent deterrent threats, presenting stronger opponents with a fait accompli that cannot be easily overturned. Second, they sometimes believe that they can capitalize on an international political setting or on the domestic politics of stronger powers that will prevent the stronger power from actually executing a deterrent threat or, if executed, will prevent the stronger actor from bringing the full force of its military power to bear against the weaker opponent. Third, weak actors can come to believe that moral or political constraints—arising from international or domestic public opinion—that emerge in the course of some provocation, will restrain the strong, especially if threatened retaliation seems out of proportion or misdirected against innocent bystanders. In other words, the weak come to believe that the eruption of violence itself will force the stronger party to reassess the utility of the use of force in general, or the execution of specific deterrent threats. Equally perplexing is the fact that the leaders of strong states often fail to recognize these sources of weak-state optimism until it is too late, at the point when deterrence actually fails. The strong believe in deterrence as a strategy and in the efficacy of their deterrent threats, which helps explain why they are slow to recognize the circumstances when deterrence is likely to fail.

Strategic optimism: The problem of surprise attack

Michael Handel, a leading student of strategic surprise, noted that weaker states were often attracted to strategic surprise as an option when they contemplated challenging stronger opponents.⁶ Although Handel failed to trace out the logic inherent in this observation, this phenomenon is linked to the strategic path of deterrence failure. The link between weak state optimism, strategic surprise and deterrence failure is in fact explained by the theory of surprise.⁷ Strategic surprise suspends war's dialectic and removes an active opponent from the battlefield. Surprise transforms war into an act of administration, allowing the weaker opponent to achieve objectives that are literally impossible to attain when facing a fully prepared and engaged opponent.⁸ Strategic surprise is often a key component of what is known as "asymmetric warfare," because it creates a situation whereby the use of minimal resources can produce an overwhelming strategic and political effect. In a potential conflict, the weaker party is attracted to surprise because it allows them to achieve objectives that they cannot realistically achieve in a war against a vastly stronger competitor. Operations that rely on strategic surprise are extraordinarily risky because they will fail catastrophically if surprise is not achieved or if the effects of surprise "wear off" before objectives are reached. But when they succeed, they can produce spectacular results. Relying on strategic surprise, for instance, the Imperial Japanese Navy was able to destroy a large portion of the US Pacific Fleet at its anchorage at Pearl Harbor at the cost of a few midget submarines, under 40 aircraft and about 100 personnel.[9] Al-Qaeda was able to destroy the World Trade Center with the aid of box cutters and mace in about two hours at the cost of a few hundred thousand dollars and about twenty personnel.[10] Surprise allows actors to achieve objectives or accomplish operations that could not be undertaken in the face of a vastly superior active opponent.

The opportunities created by strategic surprise have a mesmerizing effect on the weaker party. Enormous amounts of effort and planning are invested in some gambit that is a true masterpiece of operational art, tactical brilliance or brashness, not to mention nerves of steel. Less effort is made, however, to devise a way for surprise or a fait accompli to be integrated into an overall strategy to overcome a stronger opponent. In attacking Pearl Harbor, for instance, Japanese officials believed that Americans would not think that it was worth the price in blood and treasure to reverse Japanese gains in the Pacific. They expected that they would reach some sort of compromise peace with Washington. Before occupying Kuwait, Saddam Hussein told the American Ambassador to Iraq that the West in general and the United States in particular did not have the stomach for a bloody fight to counter Iraqi ambitions in the region. After US opposition to the Iraqi occupation of Kuwait was obvious, Saddam still believed that American casualty aversion would lead the George H.W. Bush administration to reach a compromise settlement.[11] When multiple confidants warned Nikita Khrushchev, that the United States would react vigorously when it detected Soviet medium and intermediate-range ballistic missiles in Cuba, the Soviet leader reassured them that the Americans would simply learn to live with nuclear deployments close to their shores.[12] When Pakistani officials decided to occupy Indian-army positions that were temporarily abandoned due to the incredibly harsh winter conditions near the Siachen Glacier, they failed to think through what might happen when Indian military patrols discovered them.[13] Islamabad apparently believed that the crisis would somehow turn out to its benefit. They believed that Indian officials would agree to negotiations under international pressure to avert escalation.[14] In all of these situations, the weaker party recognized that it had attacked or provoked a stronger opponent. Nevertheless, they also all chose to believe that the stronger party would *choose* not to bring their superior forces to bear to reverse a fait accompli.

Stronger parties that rely on deterrent threats against weaker opponents are vulnerable to strategic surprise because they tend to focus on their superior capabilities when it comes to deterring weaker adversaries. Their military superiority and the strength of their deterrent threats shape their perception of the outside world. From their perspective, it makes little sense for inferior opponents to challenge them because they lack the military capability to achieve their objectives *in wartime*. As a result, they find it difficult to anticipate how weaker opponents might come to believe that they can challenge stronger competitors in a significant way. In the minds of leaders of strong states, deterrence is robust because the outcomes of plausible conflicts appear to be decidedly in their favor. In hindsight, the strong often appear to be complacent in the face of a potential threat; nevertheless, they perceive ex ante that their deterrent is virtually impossible to circumvent.

When confronted with signals of a brewing surprise attack, intelligence analysts and officials in strong states tend to dismiss these indications as too harebrained or far-fetched to be taken seriously. Prior to the 1973 Yom Kippur War, for instance, Israeli intelligence analysts and defense officials refused to believe that their deterrent was about to fail because in their minds, Egypt lacked the military capability to defeat Israel. For Israelis, it made "no sense" for a weaker opponent to launch a surprise attack, thereby starting a war that they were doomed to lose.[15] As a result, Israeli officers and officials failed to respond to several clear indications that deterrence was failing and that they were about to be attacked. Surprise often succeeds, and deterrence failures occur, because the strong fail to understand that the weak have imagined ways to achieve their objectives without having to confront directly the military capability of the strong.

When evidence emerges that deterrent postures might be challenged, strong states tend to take steps to highlight their military superiority. In the wake of Japanese aggression in the Pacific, the Franklin D. Roosevelt administration, over protests from US Navy officers, forward-deployed the US Pacific Fleet to Pearl Harbor in an effort to increase the salience of its military capability in the minds of Japanese officials. Although US Navy officers believed that the move increased the vulnerability of the Fleet, the Roosevelt administration apparently believed that moving the ships would deter further Japanese aggression by increasing the visibility of American military might. Ironically, the Japanese were undeterred by this show of strength and capitalized on the opportunity to destroy the US fleet.[16]

Strategic surprise and the failure of deterrence relationships between the strong and the weak are clearly linked in the history of international crises and the outbreak of war. The weak become captivated by the possibilities created by some surprise military initiative, which in their minds will allow them to present the stronger power with a fait accompli that will effectively nullify a deterrent threat. The weak believe that a fait accompli makes both conventional and nuclear deterrence irrelevant, because it presents the stronger opponent with strategic failure before it can bring its superior force to bear. In the minds of the weak, deterrence failure transforms the conflict into a test of who is willing to engage in an attritional struggle to reverse the status quo. The weak believe, and are in fact banking on the fact, that the strong will fail that test. The strong, by contrast, focus on their obvious military superiority and the inherent credibility of their deterrent posture. They remain strangely unmoved by indications that deterrence is failing because they find it incredible that the weaker party would intentionally initiate a conflict that they realistically cannot hope to win. The ultimate and dangerous irony involved in the relationship between strategic surprise and deterrence failure is that the initial estimates of both the strong and the weak are validated by ensuing events. The weak often manage to present the strong with a fait accompli, while the strong often emerge victorious following the failure of deterrence to keep the peace. In the history of international relations, the term "strategic surprise" generally corresponds to the failure of the strong to deter the weak.[17]

Political optimism: The balance of power paradox

"If the strong won't fight, and the weak can't win, why is there war?" is a question that captures the essence of the "Balance of Power Paradox."[18] The paradox emerges from an important indeterminate prediction of international outcomes contained in Kenneth Waltz's *Theory of International Politics*.[19] According to Waltz, in a bipolar setting, the superpowers should have sought to avoid becoming embroiled in peripheral conflicts because those would have constituted a dangerous and destructive sideshow that served as a distraction from the significant threat they faced, namely the *other* superpower. In 1967, for instance, Waltz explained his opposition to US military involvement in Southeast Asia:

> Two states that enjoy wide margins of power over other states need worry little about changes that occur among the latter. ... Because no realignment of national power in Vietnam could in itself affect the balance of power between the United States and the Soviet Union—or even noticeably alter the imbalance of power between the United States and China—the United States need not have intervened at all.[20]

From Waltz's perspective, the superpowers during the Cold War, and the great powers today, should strive to avoid conflicts on the "periphery." As a consequence, for the great power, the risks and costs of involvement in peripheral battles generally outweigh the benefits to be gained, especially when the benefits are a common good shared across the international community.

For the weak, the military balance militates against aggressive or disruptive policies because intervention by stronger competitors can lead to disaster. The weak can always engage in a series of minor provocations or "salami tactics" to inch themselves slowly closer to their objectives, but they risk inadvertently crossing important red lines, which would trigger a massive and overwhelming response by a far stronger antagonist. For the weak, an overwhelming imbalance of power creates a situation where the use of military force offers no realistic way to achieve objectives once far stronger opponents are engaged on the battlefield. International history, however, fails to support the intuitive deterrent effect that a gross imbalance of power should have on the weak when they face a stronger competitor. Conflicts that the strong should hope to avoid and that the weak cannot realistically hope to win populate the pages of diplomatic histories and are the stuff of current headlines. Iranian threats to close the Strait of Hormuz is a case in point. Two phenomena can account for this turn of events.

Although the leaders in weak states understand their inferior position, they believe that because of a variety of more pressing political and strategic reasons, the strong will not be able to bring their full power to bear to interfere with the weak's initiatives. The leaders of weak states actually accentuate the outcome of Waltz's cost-benefit calculations about the merits of Superpower intervention in the periphery. They often seem to believe that international and domestic political constraints will prevent Great Powers from intervening effectively in limited wars or responding forcefully to provocations.[21] As the North Vietnamese began to justify their decision to launch the Tet Offensive, for instance, General Vo Nguyen Giap offered an explanation of why the United States would not be able to bring its superior power to bear to stymie Hanoi's military effort to unify Vietnam:

> The U.S. imperialists must cope with the national liberation movements [in countries other than South Vietnam], with the socialist bloc, with the American people, and with other imperialist countries. The U.S. imperialism cannot mobilize all their forces for the war of aggression in Vietnam."[22]

Giap recognized that the United States possessed the military resources needed to end the conflict quickly, but he also believed that it faced competing interests and pressures that would restrain its freedom of action in Vietnam. Similarly, Saddam Hussein believed that "casualty aversion," a domestic political constraint, would prevent the United States from interfering with his occupation of Kuwait. As the United States and an international coalition increasingly appeared to use force to eject Iraqi forces from Kuwait, Saddam apparently believed that Soviet opposition to American intervention would deter US military action in the Middle East.[23] When Moscow, preoccupied with the collapse of its empire, failed to protect its client, Saddam berated the Soviet leadership for failing to act like a Superpower.[24] Both the North Vietnamese and the Ba'athist regime in Baghdad believed that the threat posed by other great powers, international political opposition or domestic political restraints, would be sufficient to hold superior US military power at bay.

The balance of power paradox thus sets up a different path to deterrence failure when compared to strategic surprise. Unlike strategic surprise, which creates a fait accompli that tends to render existing deterrent threats obsolete, the balance of power paradox helps leaders of weak states to believe that strong states will not be able to execute deterrent threats because of international or domestic constraints that will become highly salient as deterrence begins to fail. Surprise uses military action to render deterrent threats irrelevant by temporarily neutralizing the opportunity of the stronger party to react, while the balance of power paradox shapes the weaker party's perceptions of the stronger party's ability to execute the threat. The balance of power paradox undermines the political credibility of deterrent threats.

The balance of power paradox is also different in the sense that it tends to create situations in which stronger states confront a gradual failure of deterrence or compellence policies. As provocations continue to mount, stronger states often reinforce deterrent threats by restating them or by undertaking demonstrations of power to overcome what they perceive to be a misperception of reality by the leaders of weaker powers. The movement of the US Pacific Fleet to Hawaii in the months preceding Pearl Harbor is a case in point. It had little deterrent effect, however, because the Japanese believed that Washington would soon be preoccupied by the war in Europe and would not be able to bring all of its military might to bear in the effort to stop Japanese ambitions in the Far East. In the weeks leading up to the First Gulf War, the Bush administration repeatedly attempted to warn Saddam Hussein of the threat he faced if he failed to withdraw his forces from Kuwait. Soviet envoys also attempted to amplify and clarify increasingly specific threats emanating from Washington by informing their counterparts in Baghdad that America possessed overwhelming military power. Restating or reinforcing existing threats cannot overcome the negative effects produced by balance of power paradox, however, because the weaker power believes that political constraints will prevent the stronger power from fully executing its deterrent threats.

Ironically, when confronting deterrence failure produced by the balance of power paradox, the stronger party tends to believe that deterrence failure is occurring because the weaker party has somehow miscalculated the military balance. The strong tend to see deterrence failure as stemming from a misperception of capability, not a disagreement over the credibility of the threat. In order to rectify this situation, they engage in activities to demonstrate their military capability, short of an all-out response. In the early 1960s, for instance, US military actions against North Vietnam were intended to highlight the systematic constraints faced by Hanoi, namely military inferiority. Commenting on the results produced by a high-level meeting of Johnson administration officials in April 1965, for instance, Secretary of Defense Robert McNamara noted that the United States objective in Vietnam was to break the will of the North Vietnamese and their Viet Cong allies by "depriving them of victory." In other words, US policy was intended to alter Hanoi's apparent misperception of the military balance, thereby reinforcing deterrence and setting the state for a political solution to the conflict. Years later, Maxwell Taylor recalled that Washington knew little about Ho Chi Minh's and General Giap's objectives. Nevertheless, American officials were banking on the fact that Hanoi would seek an accommodation with the United States once it became clear that the costs of achieving these objectives exceeded the benefits they were seeking to obtain.[25] This strategy led to a deliberate policy to escalate American military pressure against the Hanoi regime gradually in an effort to bolster deterrence by highlighting the costs of conflict to the North Vietnamese leadership. These limited actions, however, tend to reinforce the perceptions of the weaker party who interprets restraint as evidence of the effects of strategic or political constraints. It also creates a situation in which deterrence fails incrementally.

Social optimism: The manipulation of the risk of death and destruction in local conflicts

Although it might make perfect strategic and political sense for the strong to issue a deterrent threat against the weak to prevent some unwanted action, would it actually be in the interest of the stronger party to carry out that threat in the face of deterrence failure? This question may in fact have to be answered in the negative. The costs of executing deterrent threats may outweigh the potential gains. Thus, deterrence can fail because the weak can come to believe that they can alter the incentives faced by the strong in the event of deterrence failure. They can come to believe that ex ante incentives to retaliate may lose their salience when politicians focus on the material and political costs of executing a deterrent threat, or begin to question the relevance of existing military options to reverse a deteriorating position on the ground at "acceptable" costs. Although the strong face an immediate trade-off between the costs of deterrence failure and the costs produced by the long-term erosion of the credibility of their deterrent threats, the weak can come to believe that they can alter this calculus in their favor.

Because the weak face potentially existential threats when confronting vastly superior opponents, they may have already recognized the possibility that they may suffer significant losses in the quest to achieve their objectives. In fact, they may seek to manipulate the risk that significant death and destruction will occur in territory under their control or territory in dispute as a result of their activities in an effort to actually deter the execution of deterrent threats by stronger opponents. In other words, the weak can manipulate the balance of interests that might exist between them and their stronger opponents by creating conditions in which retaliation by stronger powers will lead to widespread mayhem and destruction, especially among civilian populations. The weak may actually seek to create conditions that lead strong powers to see execution of deterrent threats as simply exacerbating an already perilous situation. The weak might gamble that their willingness to suffer death and destruction might exceed a stronger power's willingness to inflict death and destruction to achieve its political objectives. Conflict itself can highlight the asymmetry of interests that might exist between weak and strong powers, reducing the stronger party's perception of the efficacy behind its use of force or the relevance of executing deterrent threats in the face of a deteriorating situation.

An obvious path to achieve this objective is for the weaker state, or key political, economic or military elements of the weaker party, to somehow hide among innocent local civilians, neighboring third parties, or allies of the stronger state. By creating the impression that victims and victimizers are inseparable, or at least beyond the discrimination of available retaliatory instruments, the stronger party might find itself at a loss for options that will not exacerbate existing conditions, especially when provocations avoid targeting the homeland of the stronger state. If deterrent threats are executed, they could communicate to all concerned that existing political institutions or the status quo is unworkable, tilting the political balance in favor of the weaker party.

Concerns about the manipulation of material conditions to directly alter political perceptions regarding the relevance and effectiveness of traditional military options is a reoccurring concern among military analysts, particularly in recent decades. "Fourth generation warfare," is one of the latest terms used to describe the effort to influence outcomes in war through political, not military instruments.[26] According to Thomas Hammes, "Fourth generation war uses all available networks—political, economic, social and military—to convince the enemy's political decision makers that their strategic goals are either unachievable or too costly for the perceived benefit. It is rooted in the fundamental precept that superior political will, when properly employed, can defeat greater economic and military power."[27] Fourth generation warriors are not focused on defeating superior military opponents on some battlefield. Instead, they focus on using civil disorder or low-intensity warfare to manipulate social, political and cultural ties to alter local and global political perceptions in their favor. Innovative campaigns are designed to manipulate political perceptions of what is at stake in a given conflict and to create situations that make conventional military operations appear irrelevant or of limited utility. The goal is to create a situation in which the use of superior firepower and intelligence-surveillance-reconnaissance capabilities offer few good remedies to local turmoil. Under these circumstances, execution of advertised deterrent threats might be viewed by friend and foe alike as doing little more than exacerbating conflicts and increasing suffering among local civilians or third-party bystanders.

An even more pernicious manifestation of this path to deterrence failure has been described as the "deterrence trap." In other words, the weaker party might actually seek to provoke a stronger party to retaliate to create death and destruction in the hope of benefiting politically from the chaos that would follow. According to Emanuel Adler:

> In asymmetric conflict situations, which pit nation-states against terrorist networks and other non-state actors, such as insurgent groups and radical revisionist states that support them, deterrence may not only not prevent violence but may actually help foment it. ... The use of force against the weaker side enhances its social power and the credibility of its performance in front of domestic and foreign audiences, thus allowing it to win the war of the narratives, gain and maintain the support of the majority of the targeted population in question, delegitimize its enemies, and, ultimately weaken its victims until they are beaten.[28]

In a sense, weaker opponents might attempt to "hijack" the military forces of their opponents if they see the eruption of widespread violence and chaos as a means of achieving their goals. Terrorists who embrace purely negative goals or dark millenarian fantasies might also taunt stronger opponents in the hope that promised retaliation might further their objectives by destroying the existing social or political order.[29] Under these circumstances, the stronger party faces a dilemma.

Because executing deterrent threats can be politically very costly, immediate self-restraint by the stronger party might appear rational, though it comes at the price of generally undermining the future effectiveness of deterrence or deterrent threats directed at other parties.[30]

How do the strong respond to weaker parties that seek to manipulate the risk of death and destruction? Some simply retaliate. Adler points to the Israeli response to terrorist provocations. Another path would be to place forces on the ground to restore order, either directly or working through third parties. This might have been the path taken by the United States in dealing with the disorder that followed the defeat of Iraq in the Second Gulf War as various parties in the country attempted to use violence and disorder to achieve their objectives. Regardless of the response, deterrence fails because the weaker party no longer sees the eruption of violence as somehow being diametrically opposed to achieving its objectives. In extreme situations, deterrence fails because the opponent *recognizes* or even *welcomes* the capability and credibility behind the deterrent threat.

Responding to the new complexity

Although the foregoing survey offers a rather dismal appraisal of the prospects for successful deterrence when the strong face weaker opponents, it does lead to three observations that practitioners of deterrence should keep in mind when it comes to keeping weaker opponents at bay. Each of these observations is linked to a specific source of weak state optimism when it comes to their assessment of their ability to circumvent the deterrent threats made by stronger antagonists. Because the path to deterrence failure is different depending on the strategy adopted by leaders of weak states, the strong have to be aware that their strategies can also fail for different reasons.

In terms of strategic optimism generated by the opportunities created by surprise attack, the leaders of strong states have to be aware that their deterrent threats are tied to specific strategic contexts. Because strategic surprise can present the strong with a fait accompli, deterrent threats can be rendered irrelevant quickly. The capability and will of the strong remain unscathed, but the circumstances needed for deterrence to be effective no longer exist. Surprise changes the context in which deterrent threats were issued and it leaves the strong with few desirable options. The strong can live with the fait accompli, engage in a demanding compellence strategy to force the weaker party to give up their new gains, or simply take concerted military action to restore the status quo. The history of surprise attack suggests that the weak are banking on the hope that the strong will choose the first option.

The history of surprise attack also suggests that it is difficult for the strong to detect this impending deterrence failure.[31] In part, this might be because deterrence remains robust, and continues to appear robust, until if fails quickly and catastrophically. It behooves the weaker party not to alarm the stronger party by acting provocatively or seeking limited objectives because these can alert the opponent, which might curtail the opportunity to benefit from surprise. The strong also contribute to strategic surprise by taking steps to simply strengthen existing deterrent threats without reassessing the possibility that the weak intend to alter the strategic context without altering the fundamental military balance between the weak and the strong. To block the path to deterrence failure created by strategic optimism, the strong might be better served by not relying on static threats, capabilities and infrastructure. By posing a threat that remains static or narrow, the strong give the weak the time and opportunity to devise schemes to alter the strategic setting in ways that can circumvent what appear to be relatively robust capabilities. Instead, it might be better to confront weaker opponents with a changing problem. For instance, day alert postures could be altered in a random manner, making deterrent or war-fighting forces less vulnerable to pre-emptive attack. Operating plans and forces also should evidence ongoing change and evolution, making them less susceptible to long-term study in the effort to identify potential vulnerabilities. New weapons systems and strategies might also be introduced to continuously improve the material and strategic basis of deterrent threats. Increasing the redundancy across command and control systems combined with improving the resilience of operational forces can also make deterrent strategies appear less vulnerable to surprise attack.

In terms of political optimism produced by the balance of power paradox, the strong face a more gradual failure of deterrence. Here, gradual escalation of military action on the part of the strong tends to confirm the weaker party's optimism that domestic or international constraints will in the end prevent the strong from bringing the full weight of their military capability to bear. Under these circumstances, the strong must fight their tendency to believe that the weak are acting on the basis of some sort of misperception of the military balance. Instead, they need to assess why their weaker opponents might believe that political considerations will prevent them from executing fully deterrent threats. If this occurs, the strong would be better served by initiatives directed toward increasing their freedom of maneuver and not by actions that seek to more strongly communicate existing deterrent threats. The strong need to inventory their own political situation to determine if events are conspiring to create the impression that their ability to act on their threats is waning. Political optimism flows from the perception that politics will conspire to prevent the execution of deterrent threats. In that sense, the strong need to strengthen their political, not their military, position to defeat the more damaging manifestations of the balance of power paradox.

Social optimism is created by the perception that the balance of interests and the actual outbreak of violence actually favor the weaker party. It is based on the notion that the execution of deterrent threats will actually damage the stronger party's interests by contributing to an already dangerous and destructive situation or that the execution of deterrent threats will be out of proportion to the interests at stake for the stronger antagonist. Under these circumstances, developing a menu of options that directly threaten the interests or leadership of the weaker side without threatening civilians or parties not directly embroiled in the conflict can strengthen deterrence. In the words of Michel Fortmann and Stéfanie von Hlatky, the highly discriminate weapons created by the so-called Revolution in Military Affairs (RMA) "might become the basis of a new age of deterrence, because precision-guided warfare can be less destructive than nuclear war. RMA deterrent threats are credible because if deterrence fails, policymakers ... are likely to make good on their threats."[32] By developing precise military options that pose little risk of creating widespread death and destruction, the credibility of deterrent threats can be strengthened in the mind of the opponent. In this situation, the effectiveness of deterrence is less likely to be altered by the assessment that the stronger opponent cannot achieve its objectives without generating widespread death and destruction. Instead, deterrence is more likely to be strengthened by the perception that policymakers will actually act on their deterrent threats because they pose a politically and militarily effective response without the risk of widespread collateral damage.

Conclusion

From a systemic perspective, recent history supports the way that deterrence of the weak by the strong is depicted in this analysis. During the Cold War, for instance, deterrence became more stable as the Soviet Union and the United States approached a rough parity in their nuclear deterrent forces, leading to a situation of Mutual Assured Destruction. In other words, when optimism about a positive war outcome faded from both Soviet and American strategic calculations, both sides became reticent about challenging the status quo. Crises and provocative behavior waned as stability, defined as the absence of Great Power War, became the order of the day.[33] In fact, the Cuban Missile Crisis, the most dangerous confrontation of the Cold War, occurred when the weaker party attempted to present the stronger party with a fait accompli that was intended to alter the military balance quickly to circumvent existing deterrent threats. Nikita Khrushchev believed that the John F. Kennedy administration would simply accept the abrupt alteration of the nuclear balance,[34] a gamble that quickly came to be perceived by all concerned as a discernible path to nuclear war.[35] This sort of thinking is a common thread in the type of optimism created by strategic surprise. By altering the context of existing deterrent relationships, the weak hope to escape the execution of deterrent threats.

Other scholars have noted that the logic inherent in the effort of the strong to deter the weak is alive and well in today's strategic setting, although it is often ignored by scholars and policymakers alike. Thomas Christensen has noted that there is a peculiar twist in the ongoing debate about the "Rise of China." Whether or not scholars depict China's rise as relatively benign, resulting in a prosperous and increasingly democratic status quo state, or more sinister, leading to an increase in military rivalry and tension in Asia, both sides in the debate seem to accept the premise that Beijing would never confront the United States until it achieves conventional and nuclear parity with Washington. Instead, Christensen suggests that it is more likely that Chinese leaders, acting out of perceptions of their own weakness, might search for methods to distract, deter or bloody the United States in an effort to achieve some immediate objective. What is particularly disturbing, in Christensen's view, is that the thinking emerging in China is eerily similar to Japanese strategy on the eve of Pearl Harbor: a casualty-averse or financially strapped United States will seek a negotiated settlement following some military setback.[36] It is in fact easy to devise such a scenario. By launching a limited attack against US military bases on Guam, Pearl Harbor, Japan or San Diego, or a quick cyber or space campaign to temporarily curtail US information dominance, the People's Liberation Army might be able to separate Taiwan from US military support long enough to alter the political status quo on the island. Given the emergence of a fait accompli produced by strategic surprise, would US officials, despite the fact that they still enjoy a superior military position, be willing to execute deterrent threats given new strategic and political realities in Asia?

Globalization and the information revolution remain fixtures of international politics, linking developments in foreign lands with everyone's domestic politics. The opportunity to involve innocent civilians and third parties in localized conflicts is only increasing. Under these circumstances, conventional military responses to civil disturbances, acts of terrorism or social movements might in fact appear to observers as out of proportion to the interests at stake. Deterrent strategies thus have to become more finely crafted with an eye on shaping the domestic and international political and strategic situation while threatening minimal amounts of death and destruction in the event of deterrence failure. Unlike the Cold War, when the ability to inflict catastrophic societal damage under any circumstance created the basis of deterrence, the credibility of deterrence today seems to rest on the availability of militarily effective and politically acceptable uses of force. In the age of globalization, the credibility of deterrence increases as the amount of force used in deterrence threats to deny the weaker opponent its objectives decreases.

It is hard to escape the conclusion that the opportunities for the weak to sidestep deterrence by the strong are growing, especially when it comes to manipulating the incentives for the strong to actually execute their deterrent threats. The key to reversing this trend also does not lie solely in the realm of military capabilities. Instead, the leaders of strong states that rely on deterrence need to keep three notions in mind. They must be alert to the possibility that strategic surprise can eliminate the context for effective deterrence. They must be alert to the possibility that their response to limited provocations can actually undermine their overall deterrence posture. They also must be alert to the fact that their deterrence strategies need to minimize the potential for death and destruction while still denying their weaker opponents the opportunity to achieve their objectives.

Notes

1   Because deterrence theory is so sophisticated, it is possible to qualify virtually every definitive theoretical statement. For instance, identification of clear "red lines" might invite an opponent to engage in salami tactics—the practice of undertaking limited probes to achieve their objective over time without triggering a deterrent response.

Other deterrent strategies—French nuclear doctrine might be a case in point—embrace more ambiguity when it comes to defining vital interests in the hopes of inducing uncertainty and more caution in the target, thereby enhancing the general effectiveness and impact of deterrence. The choice of how to state deterrent threats in practice thus reflects an assessment of the type of risks one is willing to take in relying on deterrence as a defense strategy.

2 Geoffrey Blainey, *The Causes of War* (New York: The Free Press, 1973), p. 274.
3 According to Blainey, "Wars usually begin when two nations disagree on their relative strength, and wars usually cease when the fighting nationals agree on their relative strength," ibid. p. 172.
4 On the way that compellence is more demanding than deterrence see Thomas C. Schelling, *Arms and Influence* (New Haven, CT: Yale University Press, 1966), p. 100; and Robert Jervis, *The Meaning of the Nuclear Revolution: Statecraft and the Prospect of Armageddon* (Ithaca, NY: Cornell University Press, 1989), pp. 29–35.
5 Blainey, *The Causes of War*, p. 35.
6 Michael Handel, "Crisis and Surprise in Three Arab-Israeli Wars," in Klaus Knorr and Patrick Morgan (eds), *Strategic Military Surprise* (New Brunswick, NJ: Transaction Publishers, 1983), p. 113.
7 James J. Wirtz, "Theory of Surprise," in Richard K. Betts and Thomas G. Mahnken (eds), *Paradoxes of Strategic Intelligence: Essays in Honor of Michael I. Handel* (London: Frank Cass, 2003), pp. 101–116.
8 According to Edward Luttwak, "Without a reacting enemy, or rather to the extent and degree that surprise is achieved, the conduct of war becomes mere administration." See Edward Luttwak, *Strategy: The Logic of War and Peace* (Cambridge, MA: Harvard University Press, 1987), p. 8.
9 Roberta Wohlstetter, *Pearl Harbor: Warning and Decision* (Stanford, CA: Stanford University Press, 1962).
10 *The 9/11 Commission Report: Final Report of the National Commission on Terrorist Attacks Upon the United States* (New York: Norton, 2004).
11 Lawrence Freedman and Efraim Karsh, The Gulf Conflict: *Diplomacy and War in the New World Order* (Princeton, NJ: Princeton University Press, 1993), pp. 52, 236.
12 When Polish Communist leader Wladyslaw Gomulka learned during the summer of 1962 that Khrushchev planned to present the United States with a nuclear fait accompli in Cuba, he warned the Soviet leader that Washington would never simply ignore such a challenge. "Khrushchev assured him," according to Ned Lebow and Janice Stein, "that all would turn out well. He told Gomulka the story of a poor Russian farmer who lacked the money to buy firewood for the winter. He moved his goat into his hut to provide warmth. The goat was incredibly rank but the man learned to live with the smell." Kennedy would "learn to accept the 'smell of the missiles'." Richard Ned Lebow and Janice Gross Stein, *We all Lost the Cold War* (Princeton, NJ: Princeton University Press, 1994), p. 77.
13 James J. Wirtz and Surinder Rana, "Surprise at the Top of the World: India's Systemic and Intelligence Failure," in Peter R. Lavoy (ed.), *Asymmetric Warfare in South Asia: The Causes and Consequences of the Kargil Conflict* (Cambridge: Cambridge University Press, 2009), p. 217.
14 John H. Gill, "Military Operations in the Kargil Conflict, in Peter R. Lavoy (ed.), *Asymmetric Warfare in South Asia: The Causes and Consequences of the Kargil Conflict* (Cambridge: Cambridge University Press, 2009), pp. 92–129.
15 Uri Bar-Joseph, *The Watchman Fell Asleep: The Surprise of Yom Kippur and Its Sources* (Albany, NY: State University of New York Press, 2005).

16 Navy officers wanted the Pacific fleet to return to the West Coast to prepare for war and believed that the lack of facilities at Pearl Harbor made forward deployment a hollow deterrent that only served to give the American public a false sense of confidence in US defenses in the Pacific. When its commander, Admiral J.O. Richardson, failed to convince his superiors to reposition the fleet in California, he penned a message to President Franklin D. Roosevelt that led to his relief: "The senior officers of the Navy do not have the trust and confidence in the civilian leadership of this country that is essential for a successful prosecution of a war in the Pacific." See George W. Baer, *One Hundred Years of Sea Power: The U.S. Navy, 1890–1990* (Stanford, CA: Stanford University Press, 1994), p. 151.

17 Although it is difficult to make theory always conform to the procrustean bed of history, Nazi behavior at the outset of World War II in Europe generally fits the pattern of behavior outlined here. Hitler was deterred by the prospect of a long war of attrition against the French, British or the Soviets until he was convinced that the operational strategy of Blitzkrieg, which relied on initial and continuous surprise produced by the rapid movement of ground forces, could knock out opponents before they could bring their superior material resources to bear. This would suggest that he in fact did perceive Nazi Germany as the weaker party in the European conflicts that he was contemplating. He believed that surprise, combined with operational innovation and superior execution, could nullify an opponent's conventional deterrent. The Nazi strategy produced significant initial success but doomed Hitler and his fellow Nazis to defeat in a long war of attrition against opponents that in fact possessed superior resources. I would like to thank an anonymous reviewer for encouraging me to address this incident in light of the logic presented here. See John Mearsheimer, *Conventional Deterrence* (Ithaca, NY: Cornell University Press, 1985).

18 James J. Wirtz, "The Balance of Power Paradox," in T.V. Paul, James J. Wirtz, and Michel Fortmann (eds), *Balance of Power: Theory and Practice in the 21st Century* (Stanford, CA: Stanford University Press, 2004), pp. 127–149.

19 Kenneth N. Waltz, *Theory of International Politics* (Reading, MA: Addison-Wesley, 1979).

20 Kenneth N. Waltz, "International Structure, National Force and Balance of Power," in James Rosenau (ed.), *International Politics and Foreign Policy* (New York: The Free Press, 1969), p. 310.

21 Pakistan, for instance, might have been banking on the fact that diplomatic pressure, especially pressure exerted by the United States, might have served to moderate a potential Indian military response to the Mumbai attacks. I would like to thank an anonymous reviewer for referencing this example.

22 Vo Nguyen Giap, "The Big Victory, the Great Task," contained in Patrick McGarvey *Visions of Victory* (Stanford, CA: Hoover Institution on War, Revolution and Peace, 1969), p. 237.

23 Hope that the Soviet Union (Russia) would somehow constrain US freedom of action also seemed to influence Saddam Hussein's behavior leading up to the Second Gulf War and Slobodan Milosevic's actions in Kosovo in 1999.

24 Saddam Hussein quoted in Freedman and Karsh, *The Gulf Conflict 1990–1991*, p. 164.

25 Maxwell Taylor, *Swords and Ploughshares* (New York: Norton, 1972), p. 401.

26 For a description of how the issues identified by Hammes are in fact a long-standing development in international affairs, see James J. Wirtz, "Politics with Guns: A Response to T.X. Hammes's 'War evolves into the fourth generation'," in Terry Terriff, Aaron Karp and Regina Karp (eds), *Global Insurgency and the Future of Armed Conflict* (London: Routledge, 2008), pp. 47–51.

27 Thomas X. Hammes, "War Evolves into Fourth Generation," in Terry Terriff, Aaron Karp and Regina Karp (eds), *Global Insurgency and the Future of Armed Conflict* (London: Routledge, 2008), p. 42.
28 Emanuel Adler, "Complex Deterrence in the Asymmetric-Warfare Era," in T.V. Paul, Patrick Morgan, and James J. Wirtz (eds), *Complex Deterrence: Strategy in the Global Age* (Chicago, IL: University of Chicago Press, 2008), pp. 85–86.
29 S. Paul Kapur, "Deterring Nuclear Terrorists," in T.V. Paul, Patrick Morgan, and James J. Wirtz (eds), *Complex Deterrence: Strategy in the Global Age* (Chicago, IL: University of Chicago Press, 2008), pp. 109–130.
30 Adler, p. 86.
31 Although the problem of strategic surprise, intelligence failure and the failure of deterrence are linked in practice, scholars tend to study each subject separately. This is regrettable because the act of embracing deterrence as a response to a potential challenger could in fact weaken analysts and policymaker's ability to recognize indications that they face an imminent threat to their preferred strategy. For an analysis that traces the organizational and perceptual problems that prevents this sort of net assessment, see James J. Wirtz, "Review of *Special Issue of Journal of Intelligence and National Security*," H-Diplo ISSF Roundtable, Vol. III, No. 6, 2011.
32 Michel Fortmann and Stéfanie von Hlatky, "The Revolution in Military Affairs: Impact of Emerging Technologies on Deterrence," in T.V. Paul, Patrick Morgan, and James J. Wirtz (eds), *Complex Deterrence: Strategy in the Global Age* (Chicago, IL: University of Chicago Press, 2008), p. 317.
33 Robert Jervis, *The Meaning of the Nuclear Revolution: Statecraft and the Prospect of Armageddon* (Ithaca, NY: Cornell University Press, 1989).
34 Raymond L. Garthoff, *Reflections on the Cuban Missile Crisis*, rev. ed. (Washington, DC: The Brookings Institution, 1989), p. 15.
35 James Blight, *The Shattered Crystal Ball: Fear and Learning in the Cuban Missile Crisis* (Savage, MD: Rowman & Littlefield, 1990).
36 Thomas Christensen, "Posing Problems Without Catching Up: China's Rise and Challenges for U.S. Security Policy," *International Security* Vol. 23, No. 4 (Spring 2001), pp. 5–40.

PART III
Avoiding surprise: toward a new intelligence doctrine

PART III:

7
RED TEAMING SURPRISE

Can red teaming be used to preclude adversarial surprise?[1] This is the question that lies behind every war game. The effort to find unanticipated outcomes is the primary purpose for attempting to recreate the strategic interaction that constitutes war and other types of conflict. But because red teaming is based on the assumption that conflict is a strategic interaction (i.e., outcomes are determined by the interaction of at least two opponents), it encounters some fundamental limits when used as a tool to anticipate surprise. Surprise, as it approximates its ideal type, transforms war from a strategic contest into a matter of administration.[2] For some period of time and over some part of the globe, surprise can literally eliminate the blue team from the contest, allowing red to operate completely unopposed. Surprise allows one side in a conflict to reach the theoretical potential of a military action. The element of surprise enables asymmetric attacks and by itself can yield asymmetric results. Surprise made it possible to destroy the World Trade Center with the aid of only a box cutter in less than two hours.

Although it is not particularly encouraging or gratifying, the idea that surprise can eliminate the blue team from the war game, to say nothing of some actual battlefield, is well supported by history. Blue opposition was virtually nonexistent in the opening days of the Nazi offensive through the Ardennes in December 1944, in the first wave of the Japanese attack on Pearl Harbor, and on the three airplanes that found their targets on September 11, 2001. But by taking account of the actual effect of surprise on a specific conflict, it is possible to suggest more realistic ways of anticipating asymmetric attacks (made possible by the element of surprise) than simply applying games that are based on interaction between the players (which implies that some form of attrition will take place). By definition, there is no good way to anticipate asymmetric attacks or surprise, but it might be possible to devise better ways to game the effect surprise has on a conflict.

104 Avoiding surprise

To explore ways that red teaming might be used to help preclude adversarial surprise, the chapter will briefly state three key propositions drawn from the theory of surprise.[3] It then applies the insights offered by the theory to red teaming. It offers some observations about the inability of traditional games to model surprise. Finally, the chapter provides some general observations about effort to model surprise and some specific suggestions about how to capture the way surprise affects conflict.

The theory of surprise

Before one can game an interaction, it is necessary to have a theoretically informed description of the phenomenon to be modeled. Theory identifies the key elements of the phenomena of interest that need to be included to make an accurate and useful model. The theory advanced here is especially useful for red teaming because it is a two-level explanation of surprise that links the structure of a conflict to the psychology of the red and blue actors involved. In other words, it can describe how surprise changes the nature of a conflict and how the structure of the conflict influences the perceptual biases of the actors involved. These cognitive biases not only exist in real life, but also influence the way actors participate in gaming and simulation. It builds on the work of the Prussian philosopher of war, Car von Clausewitz by explaining how surprise can transform war's dialectic into a linear situation that can be controlled, at least temporarily, by one party in the conflict. The theory provides an explanation of why the red team is attracted to surprise, why blue finds it hard to anticipate and model realistically red's effort to attain surprise, and how surprise (and asymmetric attacks) transform the dialectical nature of the contest itself.

Three propositions drawn from the theory can be used to shape red team best practices to model surprise.

Proposition 1: Surprise temporarily suspends the dialectical nature of warfare (or any other strategic contest) by eliminating an active opponent from the battlefield

Surprise transforms war from a strategic interaction into a matter of accounting and logistics. Probability and chance still influence administrative matters and friction still can bedevil any evolution, whether it is conducted in peacetime or in war. But surprise eliminates war's dialectic: achieving a military objective is no longer impeded by opponents who can be expected to do everything in their power to make one's life miserable. This has a profound effect on military operations. For example, the amount of time it might take to arrive at and seize an objective can be derived from simple calculations about how fast a unit can drive down some highway. (Of course, more sophisticated analyses might be undertaken to determine the effects of equipment breakdowns, road conditions or crew fatigue to estimate probabilities of likely arrival times.) No account need be made for delays caused by roadblocks, blown bridges, pre-registered artillery or major enemy units astride one's path.

Although surprise often is described as a force multiplier, something that increases the effectiveness of one's forces in combat, as it approaches its ideal type it can transform war. Surprise, and the asymmetric attacks it facilitates, can thus yield spectacular results. Clausewitz disagreed with this judgment because he remained true to his dialectical depiction of war; for Clausewitz, the costs of creating surprise rarely outweighed the benefits it provided. But because surprise suspends war's dialectic and the attritional nature of warfare, Clausewitz's theory of war no longer applies when those attempting to achieve significant surprise succeed. The duel that is at the heart of war for Clausewitz simply cannot take place if one of the opponents fails to materialize on the battlefield.

Weaker parties in a conflict become mesmerized by the prospect of suspending war's dialectic because it allows them to contemplate operations that are beyond their reach in wartime. By avoiding the military forces of their opponent, weaker parties use surprise to avoid the attrition and opposition that is inevitable in war to inflict some sort of setback on their stronger opponents. Stronger parties prefer more predictable and less risky strategies based on attrition to achieve their objectives; they are extremely unlikely to risk a battle, to say nothing of an entire campaign, on achieving surprise.

Proposition 2: The weaker party in a conflict is far more likely than the stronger party to adopt strategies that require the element of surprise to succeed

Proposition 2 applies to actors that rely on surprise for success, not as a more mundane force multiplier. This is an important qualification because strategists everywhere recognize the benefits of surprise. Across cultures and history, military doctrines have encouraged soldiers to incorporate surprise, along with other force multipliers such as the use of cover or maneuver. In ritualistic fashion, for instance, US officials and officers often report that some attack has achieved surprise, even though the United States rarely attempts to surprise opponents in a significant way. As the stronger party in the conflict, it generally seeks to intimidate or deter its opponents without fighting by telegraphing its intentions to fight and the general size and severity of the blow that is about to land. In the rare instances where the United States attempted to use surprise to deliver a war-winning shock to its opponent (e.g., the use of nuclear weapons in World War II), contingency plans for an attritional campaign (the invasion of Japan) were ready to be implemented if surprise failed to break the opponent's will to resist.

The weaker party in a conflict, by contrast, generally cannot engage in coercive strategies to intimidate its opponent into complying with its wishes. In fact, even the potential threat the weaker party poses is often not recognized by the stronger opponent. Japan had been engaged in a war in Asia for nearly a decade prior to Pearl Harbor. It had abandoned the international arms control regime governing naval deployments and had joined the original "axis of evil" with Germany and Italy. Yet, US officers and officials never really took the Japanese threat seriously, although they believed that it likely that the Japanese might attack someone else. Similarly, Al-Qaeda had been linked to the 1993 bombing of the World Trade Center, battles with US Army Rangers in Somalia, the bombing of the Khobar Towers, attacks on US embassies in Africa and the attack on the USS *Cole*. The United States had even fired back at Al-Qaeda, but it is clear in hindsight that US officials and intelligence analysts failed to appreciate the severity of the threat posed by bin Laden.

The leaders of the weaker side in a conflict are more likely to risk all in attacks that depend on surprise to succeed because they lack credible alternatives to defeat their stronger opponents. They cannot win force-on-force engagements so they become preoccupied with using surprise to deliver a devastating blow to an unsuspecting enemy. The weaker party begins to focus on what might be possible in war if military operations could unfold without opposition. By contrast, the stronger party in the conflict remains focused on the attritional nature of warfare and thus fails to perceive the opportunities created by surprise. Moreover, even if the stronger party detects evidence of the weaker party's initiative, it will dismiss the threat as extraordinarily reckless or simply too fantastic to be taken seriously.

Proposition 3: Strategies based on surprise appear to all concerned as extremely risky or even foolhardy ex-ante and often turn out to be reckless and ill-advised

A paradox inherent in surprise is that both sides generally share the same perception of the risk inherent in relying on surprise in some sort of war-winning strategy. But because blue assesses any potential threat surprise attack as doomed to eventual failure, it tends to dismiss evidence of an impending threat. Michael Handel captured this phenomenon in what I have called the risk paradox that is at the core of the theory of surprise: "The greater the risk, the less likely it seems, and the less risky it becomes. In fact, the greater the risk, the smaller it becomes."[4] At this point the structure of the conflict or game becomes linked to the perceptual biases of the parties involved. The weaker party plays down the extreme risks inherent in the effort to gain and benefit from surprise because of the prospect of achieving gains that otherwise are beyond its grasp. The stronger party, armed with an attritional perspective, focuses on the real impediments (i.e., a superior opponent) that red faces in achieving any gain at all. Both parties' perceptions of risk also are validated. The weaker party generally succeeds in surprising its more capable opponent; while the more capable opponent usually goes on to defeat the weaker party.

In sum, the stronger party views a potential conflict through the lens of war's dialectic: conflict will involve a clash of wills and combat on some battlefield. This attritional view of war shapes the stronger side's evaluation of information about potential initiatives by the weaker side. By contrast, the weaker side focuses on what might be possible if the opposition turns out to be a "no show."

Putting theory into practice

In his fine overview of the way red teaming can shape the transformation process, John Sandoz[5] describes four types of games that can be used to "question conventional wisdom, challenge favorite ideas, confront technical issues, expose flaws in our understanding, and discover how adaptive adversaries might counter our concepts and capabilities." "What if-ers," according to Sandoz, "look for unexpected scenarios or unintended consequences of particular concepts or approaches to problems." "Technical peer reviews" search for flaws in technology or engineering, while "system red teams" explore the way adversaries might use technology to develop low-cost countermeasures. "Surrogate adversaries" involve groups with diverse technical, operational and cultural backgrounds to challenge US strategies, concepts and capabilities in creative ways. None of these approaches to red teaming, however, capture the essence of surprise. Technical and system red teams identify flaws in systems that could be easily exploited by the enemy, which imply some force-on-force interaction. Surrogate adversaries engage in attritional battles, an outcome that is not on the mind of those who seek surprise. "What if-ers" seem to hold out some promise of capturing surprise, but Sandoz states "this style of red teaming is often informal and involves free-flowing dialogue between proponents for an idea and those who play devil's advocate." It is unclear if blue or red is the proponent of the initiative in this case. And when it comes to surprise, a devil's advocate (or, for that matter, the proponent of some concept or program) would dismiss a proposed surprise initiative as unrealistic.

The theory of surprise would suggest that the way ahead begins by devising a method to account for the different psychologies of blue and red, psychologies that are reflected both in reality and in the game. Most importantly, those creating and refereeing war games must recognize the different mindsets involved in playing blue and red, to make sure both sides are allowed to play the game in a way that approximates reality. It also suggests that the hardest period of the conflict to game is the moment when surprise is the strongest: at that time red really can be considered to have a bye in a round of game play. When the game involves US forces, red should play the part of the weaker party in the conflict and blue (America and its allies) should be played in an attritional way. To play the United States so that it bases a campaign's success on attaining the element of surprise or on some extraordinarily ambitious asymmetric strategy is simply unrealistic. As the stronger party in all foreseeable contests, the United States will prefer attritional strategies that engage the opponent's military.

Roles can be reversed, however, if the game begins in the aftermath of surprise or if the scenario is deliberately crafted to place the United States at a significant disadvantage. Following surprise, political or strategic considerations that might have restrained a blue response to red also should be relaxed. Indeed, in the aftermath of surprise, operations that were once considered politically and militarily impossible are often viewed as imperative. For example, US intervention in the European theater in World War II, elimination of the Taliban regime, and even abandonment of the ABM Treaty were all considered at one point to be unlikely if not virtually impossible. Similarly, the 2002 Nuclear Posture Review suggests that US nuclear testing might be necessary to create nuclear forces optimized to meet emerging threats, although such a move is politically impossible. Yet, one could imagine a set of circumstances (e.g., nuclear, radiological, chemical or biological warfare) that would alter politics in favor of a resumption of US nuclear testing. Surprise at first vastly weakens and then enhances blue's already superior capability against red.

Surprise takes blue out of the game

When the red team plays the role of the weaker party, they can be expected not to attack blue's military forces directly, but instead to attack blue's critical nodes, infrastructure or counter-value targets. Red in fact might never really engage blue's military forces. By definition, games that are intended as "experiments" (i.e., to test the results of an attritional interaction between red and blue) can never really capture a red effort to surprise blue. In fact, by holding a plethora of variables constant, an outstanding experiment would be nothing less than a horrible war game. Those planning an exercise must decide in advance if they intend to conduct a scripted experiment or a war game played by real adversaries acting in a truly adversarial manner. To mix the two activities in a single event only creates acrimony.[6]

Red's surprise initiative should be gamed in a non-attritional way, allowing red to achieve a significant percentage of its objectives with only minimum casualties or interference from blue. On the morning of December 7, 1941, the defenders of Pearl Harbor succeeded in shooting down about 8 percent of the attacking force, while on September 11, average US civilians did better, inflicting about a 25 percent casualty rate on the attackers and preventing them from reaching one of their targets.[7] It would have been reasonable to expect, for example, that Al-Qaeda could have destroyed all of the US Navy's aircraft carriers that were in port on the morning of September 11, 2001.[8] If surprise is to be gamed accurately, blue has to be taken out of the game for a specific period of time, allowing red to achieve the immediate military objectives of a specific attack.

In the aftermath of surprise, blue will find itself on the defensive or at least in a position in which it must respond to red's initiatives. Even a highly successful surprise attack, however, is unlikely to win the overall campaign or war for red.[9] After suffering the initial setback created by surprise, blue can be expected to marshal its superior forces in an attritional battle against red. Surprise can make war go away, but it cannot prevent war from returning.

Blue cannot take on red's attributes

Despite brave talk about asymmetric attacks and utilizing surprise, it is unrealistic to expect that blue will deviate from its preferred attritional approach to a campaign. Red should thus know blue's general capabilities and strategy. In theory and practice, blue will want to obtain the maximum amount of deterrent and coercive effect from its superior force, and might have even demonstrated these capabilities repeatedly in past military actions. Red might be surprised by some tactical development or new technological capability deployed by blue, but the level of surprise inflicted by blue will not eliminate red from the game. This final observation applies more in theory than in practice: game organizers or designers are unlikely to design and play scenarios in which surprise eliminates red from the contest.

Can blue ever retain the initiative against red? The answer is yes, but only if blue takes the initiative from the start of the game. The theory of surprise suggests that preemption—getting in the first blow following tactical warning of red's impending attack—is unlikely to succeed because blue will not recognize or respond to tactical indicators. The only path open to blue is preventive war. Preventive war is driven by the perception that war has become inevitable and that it is better to attack red deliberately now, while costs are low, instead of waiting until later, when the costs of war are likely to be higher. By taking the war to red first, blue can disrupt red's plans to inflict surprise. As the Bush administration's preventive war against Iraq suggest, however, it is extraordinarily difficult for democracies to build the political consensus necessary to engage in preventive war. Game designers can give their blue team both the iron will and keen insight needed to engage in preventive war, but they must recognize that in reality both qualities are in short supply. Of course, in the aftermath of surprise, some critics of preventive war will become incredulous at the fact that no preventive action was taken to stop the surprise from occurring, but it is difficult to foster this cognitive shift in both game participants and policymakers ex ante.

Similarly, red teams should not take on blue's attributes. The idea that red will initiate an attritional campaign against blue is far-fetched because this type of campaign will predictably end in failure. In other words, red does not seek surprise or asymmetric strategies because it underestimates blue's strengths, but because it recognizes them and seeks a way around them. Thus, red might undertake extremely risky strategies, but never risky attritional strategies. In fact, red can be expected to be extremely conservative until it devises some way to achieve its objectives without having to fight directly against blue's superior strength.[10]

Gaming the absurd

One of the highest hurdles to overcome in red teaming surprise is to game the absurd by allowing red to undertake operations that appear to make little sense ex ante. Not only blue players, but also game organizers are likely to be influenced by an attritional mindset that will constrain red's surprise moves and asymmetric attacks. In other words, red's initiatives that are directed against non-military targets or targets not directly listed in blue's order of battle will be disallowed as being beyond the scope of the game. Similarly, blue will object that red cannot destroy important military or counter-value targets by listing a variety of factors that will doom any enterprise to failure. For example, one could easily imagine attempting to game the Japanese attack on Pearl Harbor and being handed the long list of blue objections to the practicality of such an attack: naval intelligence would detect the movement of the Japanese fleet towards Hawaii; reconnaissance aircraft would detect the Japanese fleet as it neared Oahu; radar would alert defenses of an incoming attack; Japanese torpedoes would prove to be ineffective in the shallow water of Pearl Harbor; or the Fleet would be out at sea engaged in some exercise at the time of the attack. With the exception of the lone technical point involving the performance of torpedoes, each of these objections is attritional in nature because they all presuppose the presence of an active blue opponent.

Reservations about the strategic logic of a move also are likely to be raised when red suggests using surprise to take on a stronger adversary. Although surprise can yield positive political effects—the shock of the 1968 Tet offensive and the Egyptian attack in the 1973 October war paved the way for political victory for the side initiating surprise—it usually ends in disaster. The effect of surprise usually fades before overall victory is achieved in a given campaign; the stronger side then brings its superior capability to bear with predictable results. Surprise initiatives also are rarely linked or are weakly linked to an overall theory of victory. Red often fails to contemplate what will happen when blue and the prospect of attrition return to the battlefield. The Japanese, for example, expected that the United States would reach a negotiated settlement with them after Pearl Harbor, not realizing that the surprise they inflicted on American forces would make it politically impossible for the Roosevelt administration to negotiate with them. In game play and in reality, blue often recognizes the possibility that red might undertake a surprise or asymmetric attack, but it usually dismisses this possibility as illogical. Just because red's initiative appears to lack long-term strategic logic does not mean that it should not be played.

Conclusion

In the aftermath of the September 11 tragedy, the problems of surprise, asymmetric attack and red teaming have taken on a sense of urgency and importance. Some people apparently believe that if we could have just done a better job at imagining what was possible and then gaming these unlikely scenarios, it might have been possible to avert disaster. The theory of surprise suggests, however, that we are not particularly inept when it comes to imagining bizarre and extremely threatening behavior on the part of our adversaries. After all, it is not hard to imagine that enemies wish to do us harm. Al-Qaeda had established a long track record of attacking US interests, and US forces had actually fired back in Somalia and against its camps in Afghanistan in 1998. What actually is missing from the study of intelligence, asymmetric attack and red teaming are ways to help blue recognize the obvious, albeit often illogical, indications of what is about to transpire.

The theory of surprise suggests that the fundamental problem encountered in red teaming surprise is gaming the interaction that leads to surprise itself. Because surprise eliminates an active opponent from the battlefield, surprise transforms the game from an interaction between opposing forces to a one-sided matter of administration and logistics. This observation is not particularly gratifying to individuals who are charged with constructing war games because it really calls for a temporary suspension of play while red is allowed to make unilateral changes to the fundamental strategic situation. Surprise and the notion of "game" (a conflict in which the outcome is determined by the interaction of at least two actors) are far from synonymous, making it difficult to "game" the effects of surprise.

The theory also suggests that it will be difficult for blue and game organizers (at least when these positions are populated by Americans) to appreciate the non-attritional outlook and style that should be adopted in game play and will be adopted in reality by red. By definition, blue and game organizers want interaction with and attrition of enemy forces; by definition, red wants to avoid blue's forces while accomplishing its goals. Red wants to avoid attritional engagements that it cannot realistically expect to win. In order to red team surprise, it will first be necessary to capture the way surprise temporarily transforms strategic interaction. It will also be necessary for blue to accept the ability of red to affect situations unilaterally, at least for the opening moves of the game.[11]

Notes

1   The October 2001 Concept of Operations published by the United States Joint Forces Command, Joint Futures Lab (JFL) states: "The challenge to the JFL is to accurately identify, analyze, and portray the future global environment and then determine those concepts or technical vulnerabilities based on potential future threats. The JFL accomplishes this task via experimentation, which enhances our competitive advantage and precludes adversarial surprise," United States Joint Forces Command, Joint Futures Lab, "World Class Adversary Concept of Operations," October 25, 2001, p. 1–1.
2   Edward Luttwak, *Strategy: The Logic of War and Peace* (Cambridge, MA: Harvard University Press, 1987), p. 8.
3   James J. Wirtz, "Theory of Surprise," in Richard K. Betts and Thomas G. Mahnken (eds), *Paradoxes of Strategic Intelligence: Essays in Honor of Michael I. Handel* (London: Frank Cass, 2003), pp. 97–111.
4   Michael Handel, "The Yom Kippur War and the Inevitability of Surprise," *International Studies Quarterly* Vol. 21, No. 3 (September, 1977), p. 468.
5   John F. Sandoz, "Red Teaming: Shaping the Transformation Process," IDA Document D-2590, Institute for Defense Analysis, June 2001.
6   Sean Naylor, "Fixed War Game: General says Millennium Challenge 02 was 'Scripted'," *Army Times*, August 26, 2002, p. 8.
7   Most, if not all, of the casualties were inflicted during the second wave of the Japanese attack on Pearl Harbor. And when Al-Qaeda lost the element of surprise over the skies of the United States, they lacked the capability to maintain control of the aircraft they had hijacked when faced with mobilized and motivated passengers and crew.
8   Of course, an attritional perspective would suggest that a lone 757 on a suicide mission is unlikely to penetrate the protective screen provided by a carrier's battle group. By contrast, it is possible that a lone 757 might have been capable of destroying or severely

damaging all three carriers that were docked next to each other in Norfolk in early September 2001.
9 Wirtz, "The Theory of Surprise."
10 John Mearsheimer, *Conventional Deterrence* (Ithaca, NY: Cornell University Press, 1985).
11 In real life and in game play, blue already is quick to dismiss ex-ante indications of red's asymmetric intentions. That part of red teaming is in no need of modification.

8
INDICATIONS AND WARNING IN AN AGE OF UNCERTAINTY

Indications and warning intelligence is an important and time-tested methodology employed by intelligence analysts to warn military officers and policymakers about changes in an opponent's operational "posture," which indicate that the likelihood of dangerous or aggressive activity is increasing. In recent times, it has fallen out of fashion because policymakers and the public alike have come to expect that the intelligence community will be able to provide "specific event predictions" of an opponent's future actions. In other words, people tend to believe that intelligence analysts should be able to state who is about to undertake some unwanted activity, as well as where, how, when and why the action will unfold. There is also an expectation that these specific event predictions will be offered early enough so that policymakers and operators can take effective action to prevent the occurrence of some nefarious act or attack. Specific event prediction is indeed the "holy grail" of intelligence analysis and sometimes analysts do manage to warn of specific events before they unfold. Naval intelligence analysts predicted the Japanese attack on Midway. The intelligence community detected Soviet efforts to place medium range missiles in Cuba before these actions became a fait accompli.[1] But for theoretical, bureaucratic, and cognitive reasons, specific event prediction is extraordinarily difficult to achieve in practice. Success tends to be the exception, not the norm.

Indications and warning intelligence offers a powerful and important alternative to a focus on specific event prediction that might in fact be better suited to contemporary threats posed by non-state actors or rogue regimes. To be effective, however, analysts and policymakers must both understand the philosophy and methodology that animates indications and warning intelligence. They not only have to comprehend its strengths and limitations, but they also must understand the part they have to play to best utilize indications and warning intelligence to deter or defend against an opponent's pending initiatives.

To explore the role indications and warning intelligence can play in an age of uncertainty when novel threats seem to populate the strategic horizon, this chapter will first define what is meant by the term "indications and warning" intelligence. It will then describe how indications and warning intelligence has been utilized in the recent past and explain why this history tends to shape perceptions of the appropriateness of this methodology in a contemporary setting. The chapter then describes today's intelligence setting and offers a justification for why indications and warning intelligence can address many contemporary threats. It concludes by suggesting that indications and warning provides a national strategy to counter today's security challenges.

Indications and warning intelligence defined

Indications and warning intelligence is an effort to identify and monitor changes in an opponent's operational posture. It is an effort to assess whether or not opponent's military units or other types of operational capabilities are in a "day alert" or "generated alert" status. Day alert represents a normal, or peacetime, status in which assets are maintained in a routine posture and are not highly capable of conducting offensive operations or even any significant operation at all. By definition, most units most of the time are in a day alert status—their activities are centered on undertaking routine maintenance, training, or other activities required to preserve the potential for real operations. Each organization also possess a unique day alert posture because bureaucratic procedures, equipment maintenance demands, funding cycles and personnel practices combine to create routines and patterns of activity that are not easily broken. At any given moment in time, for instance, about two-thirds of the ships in the US Navy are in port undergoing routine maintenance or major overhauls that are planned years in advance, which would suggest that the day alert status of the US Navy roughly corresponds to a situation in which thirty percent of available assets at any given time are deployed at sea and are capable of undertaking military operations.

A generated alert status represents a break with this normal peacetime pattern of activity. It constitutes a halt in routine and instead focuses on making the largest possible force available to undertake operations. Maintenance and other housekeeping measures are curtailed and deferred as units take up attack positions or are otherwise postured to undertake actual operations. The process of force generation generally follows a bell curve—as a majority of a force is brought up to operational readiness, its capability tends to peak for a limited period of time and then begins to diminish as deferred maintenance and other housekeeping requirements tend to reduce operational capabilities. The decision to generate forces thus implies real costs that will have to be paid in the form of reduced operational capabilities in a future day alert posture as units are forced to complete deferred maintenance and other routine matters that were ignored during generated alert. The fact that the act of generating forces is not without long-term operational costs and risks is extraordinarily important because it ties the operational decision to generate forces with fundamental strategic and political calculations of the government or non-state actor that places its units on a state of maximum readiness.

The movement of forces from a day alert to a generated alert status often creates a string of observable actions that can be detected by the collection efforts of intelligence agencies. For military formations, leaves are cancelled and reservists are mobilized, units depart bivouac and move to staging areas, command and control networks are activated, and even rumors about impending military action begin to circulate among civilian populations and government agencies. In terms of non-state actors such as criminal organizations or terrorist cells, deviations can be observed in what constitutes normal activity as efforts begin to focus on launching initiatives, not simply maintaining clandestine cells. Chatter on Internet-enabled terrorist networks might increase as coded messages are relayed to fellow travelers to prepare to face enhanced law enforcement activities and a break with "peacetime" command and control procedures. Talk might begin to circulate within criminal or terrorist circles about the increased likelihood that a major operation is about to unfold, which can be picked up by informers. Paradoxically, the very absence of signals of normal activity also can suggest a sharp increase in operational security that could indicate that military forces or terrorist and criminal organizations are attempting to hide last-minute preparations to stage a significant operation. The absence of chatter on Internet networks or indications that routine activities have inexplicably been curtailed can serve as important signals that the opponent might be changing its readiness posture. The presence of unique signals or the absence of routine signals—the presence or absence of data—can both serve as important indicators that an opponent is moving from a day alert to a generated alert status.

Indications and warning intelligence is thus focused on detecting changes in the operational posture of the opponent to provide warning that the likelihood of dangerous or otherwise unwanted activity is increasing. It is a continuous effort to reassess the likelihood of enemy action over the short to medium term (days or several weeks). It is not necessarily intended to estimate exactly what is about to unfold, but is instead intended to warn policymakers, officers and law enforcement officials that the threat they face is increasing. In this sense, it is not a single event prediction, but a risk assessment that can be used to alert military forces to move to a heightened state of defensive alert or to inform law enforcement officials that the time has arrived to implement heightened security procedures. This type of information is crucial because military organizations or law enforcement also cannot operate on maximum defensive alert indefinitely. Thus, indications and warning intelligence must be tied to appropriate action on the part of the recipient in order to increase defenses or security activities to meet an attack or, better yet, to have a deterrent effect on the party contemplating some nefarious activity. If the success of an attack depends on a complacent opponent, indications and warning intelligence that is followed by a change in defensive posture can deter or derail an attack or some other undesirable action.

Indications and warning: The traditional view

During the Cold War, the US intelligence community devoted vast resources to monitor the status of Soviet conventional and nuclear forces in an effort to provide warning of nuclear attack against the United States and its allies or a Warsaw Pact offensive against the North Atlantic Treaty Organization. It was not uncommon for individual analysts to be given responsibility for the day-to-day monitoring of individual Soviet military formations or key parts of its strategic nuclear force. Checklists were drawn up to help analysts monitor routine "life-cycle events" (e.g., maintenance and training activities) so that anomalies in normal patterns of activity could be identified for additional analysis. By subjecting previous findings to continuous scrutiny, minor alterations in behavior could also be analyzed in the search for evidence of a gradual change in readiness that might constitute a pattern of denial and deception intended to lull the observer into a false sense of security intended to bolster a clandestine movement toward generated alert. If changes were detected, warnings could be delivered through dedicated communication channels directly to officials and officers who possessed a series of pre-planned responses to meet specific warnings or changes in the opponent's day alert posture.

This traditional use of indications and warning intelligence was facilitated by several factors that emerged during the sustained confrontation between the Soviet Union and the United States during the Cold War. The likely and most threatening dangers posed by the USSR were understood and generally accepted across the intelligence community. The Warsaw Pact posed a threat of a massive conventional-nuclear attack across the inter-German border along recognized invasion corridors that permitted the movement of large armored formations (e.g., the Fulda Gap). The Soviet Union also posed a threat of nuclear attack by sea-based and land-based ballistic missiles and long-range bombers following a period of force generation that was intended to strike a devastating blow against US strategic nuclear forces, limiting the damage they could inflict against the USSR in a retaliatory strike. Deviations to these general threats were also identified and understood. In Europe, analysts recognized that the Soviets might launch a "standing start" attack under the guise of a large exercise without placing the entire Warsaw Pact on generated alert, seeking to capitalize on the element of surprise in a mad dash to the English Channel. In the strategic nuclear realm, the Soviets also retained the capability of launching a "bolt-from-the blue" attack by utilizing capabilities available on day alert in an effort to destroy a significant portion of the US nuclear force caught on its bases in a day alert posture. But even these "day alert" deviations in Soviet strategy were subjected to indications and warning analysis. Analysts not only monitored signs that the Soviets were generating their forces to launch an all-out attack, they also searched for evidence that the Soviets were preparing to launch standing start or bolt-from-the-blue attacks from a day alert posture. Indications and warning methodologies were institutionalized by developing standard procedures within the intelligence community and pre-planned responses to warnings issued across dedicated communication channels. There was a conscious effort made to get within the opponent's "decision and operation cycle," so that a response to warning could actually outpace the opponent's preparations for attack.

The fact that large forces faced each other across the Cold War divide actually facilitated indications and warning intelligence because even small changes in their alert status tended to generate signals that were not easily concealed or ignored. Sustained interaction and collection and analysis activities over decades also led to a deep understanding of what actually constituted a normal "day alert" posture. Conventional and strategic arms control negotiations facilitated understanding of the opponent's doctrines and standard operating procedures by increasing transparency. The fact that both sides also relied on similar military technology produced an abundance of technical and operational expertise that enhanced the analytical process—US Army officers with experience in armored operations, for instance, provided a ready supply of technical and operational knowledge when it came to understanding Soviet armored operations and doctrine. Because they relied on large bureaucracies to produce their military capabilities, organizational behavior provided an additional commonality in practices and procedures that were easily recognizable across the ideological divide of the Cold War. It was no coincidence that "bureaucratic politics" was a major area of practical and theoretical interest within the US academic and policymaking communities during the 1960s and 1970s because it did much to explain operational, procurement and doctrinal forces that shaped the activities and initiatives of military organizations.[2] Organizational behavior was the dominant explanation used to account for "irrational consistency" on the part of Soviet military organizations in the face of a changing political, strategic and technological environment.[3] The shared history of strategic interaction that emerged during the Cold War also facilitated indications and warning intelligence because it created reference points that could be used as a benchmark for Soviet responses to various kinds of incidents, creating a basis for diplomatic and military-to-military contacts that increased transparency into Moscow's motives and alert decisions. The fact that the analytic assumptions behind the assessment of Soviet procurement decisions, day alert postures, and doctrine were subjected to sustained academic, intelligence and policy debate only guaranteed that the basis of indications and warning methodologies were subjected to continuous revision and refinement.

Indications and warning: The contemporary setting

Since the end of the Cold War, indications and warning intelligence is no longer a leading element of the tradecraft employed by the US intelligence community, although it is still highlighted as an important analytical technique by leading intelligence scholars and practitioners.[4] This state of affairs is probably related to the fact that indications and warning intelligence is apparently linked to its Cold War applications, and seems unsuited in the minds of many to address current threats posed by non-state actors or rogue regimes whose behavior appears highly unpredictable and difficult to track using existing collection techniques.

Two objections are often mentioned in negative assessments of the ability of indications and warning methodologies to address contemporary threats. First, it is sometimes stated that contemporary threats, especially those posed by non-state actors, fail to generate signals of sufficient strength, novelty or significance to be subjected to analysis using traditional indications and warning techniques. Admittedly, the signals generated by a clandestine terrorist cell that is about to launch an attack are different than the signals created by several armored corps as they move out of their bases towards forward attack positions. Nevertheless, terrorist organization or criminal syndicates also generate discernible signals as they too shift from day alert to generated alert in the days and weeks preceding an actual operation. It is also clear that the intelligence community can discern these signals. As the 9/11 Commission report stated, the "system" was "blinking red" in the summer of 2001, highlighting the fact that intelligence officials and policymakers had detected a significant change in Al-Qaeda's operations that suggested that an action, directed against the airline industry, was increasingly likely.[5] Even before the September 11, 2001 terror attacks against the Pentagon and the World Trade Center, the intelligence community was capable of monitoring changes in the status of terrorist organizations and other non-state actors.

Second, there is a belief that the threats posed by non-state actors are so novel and unpredictable, that it is impossible to identify likely avenues, methods and targets of attack. In other words, unlike the Cold War, where invasion corridors were known and the nature of the danger seemed obvious, the threats posed by non-state actors now appear too diabolical and innovative to be anticipated in advance. But the idea that intelligence analysts and policymakers lack the requisite imagination to anticipate probable threats is also a bit of a red herring. The motives and modus operandi of clandestine networks are usually well known and are sometimes even announced by non-state actors who wish to bolster political support for their objectives. It also is true that non-state actors' behavior is not constrained by the standard operating procedures or regulations of state actors that rely on bureaucracy to generate military power. Nevertheless, the exigencies of operating clandestinely and the sheer difficulty of undertaking significant action with limited resources channels their behavior and initiatives along relatively predictable paths.[6] Al-Qaeda's preference for the use of explosives or its interest in targeting transportation networks remained a feature of the organization both before and after the September 11, 2001 attacks.

By contrast, several less well-recognized issues have emerged that tend to complicate the contemporary use of indications and warning techniques. The perceptions of analysts and policymakers alike are often shaped by a rationality bias when it comes to assessing the likelihood of some potential threats. Often the actions of non-state actors or rogue regimes appear "harebrained" or bizarre ex ante, because they seem to lack either strategic or political purpose or appear extremely unlikely to yield significant effects, especially against mobilized national defenses or the law enforcement establishment.[7] It is thus difficult for analysts to make a convincing case to themselves or to policymakers that significant and costly responses must be made to what appears to be far-fetched or ill-conceived plans that seem to offer little prospect for success. This perception, in turn, exacerbates a fundamental dilemma inherent in the political decision to respond to warning. Specifically, contemporary threats often appear vague, probabilistic and highly unrealistic, while the costs of response are known, high, and certain.[8] This forces policymakers to bear real political and financial costs to head off possible threats that appear from their perspective ex ante as ludicrous or strategically unsound for the party launching the initiative. This dilemma is compounded by the fact that policymakers often prefer "all or nothing" responses to warnings—they want options that are guaranteed to head off the threat detected by analysts. It is virtually impossible, however, for analysts to supply this guarantee because indications and warning methodologies do not yield a specific event prediction, which prevents them from determining if a potential response will deter or defeat an attack before it occurs. As a result of the tradeoffs involved, policymakers sometimes adopt a "wait and see" attitude when it comes to responding to warnings of an apparent change in the alert status of the operational units of non-state actors. A wait and see attitude, however, undermines the effort to get inside the opponent's decision and operational cycle—a defensive response has to be undertaken before an opponent is fully prepared to launch some initiative if indications and warning techniques are to yield their greatest benefit.

Another issue that complicates the contemporary use of indications and warning methodologies is the fact that non-state actors and (sophisticated) rogue regimes are likely to direct their attacks or initiatives against the military or security weaknesses of their opponents. This would suggest that contemporary indications and warning methodologies must incorporate a net assessment on the part of analysts and policymakers when it comes to responding to changes in the alert levels of opponents' units. In other words, analysts and policymakers must have some awareness about the ability of non-traditional targets and civilian infrastructure to respond effectively to warning, and not simply assume that changes in opponents' alert levels will meet with an appropriate response. For instance, as some of the Al-Qaeda terrorists boarded aircraft on the morning of September 11, 2001, they did draw attention on the part of airline personnel, but the security procedures triggered were inappropriate to the threat they faced.[9] It appears that when warnings are issued to policymakers, they should be accompanied by some form of assessment of why the increased threat is particularly alarming in the sense that it may be directed at targets that are ill-prepared to deter or defeat an attack.

Several observations can be offered about the threat posed by emerging non-traditional threats (i.e., terrorist cells, criminal networks, rogue regimes) in relation to the benefits offered by indications and warning analysis. Compared to the signals generated by the large military bureaucracies that were subjected to scrutiny during the Cold War, the signals generated by non-state actors are limited in number and relatively faint. At the same time, the resources available to non-state actors are also limited compared to state actors, and their operations are constrained by the availability of minimal resources and the exigencies of clandestine operations. Moreover, their operations must be undertaken on the finest of margins because the effort to devote additional material resources or personnel simply increases the probability of detection by opposing intelligence agencies. It is also clear that ideology, culture and expertise—to say nothing of their political agenda—make it relatively easy to discern their modus operandi and operational objectives. The fact that they must attack an opponent's weaknesses and not their strengths in order to generate a significant political impact also can be used as a guide to understand likely threat vectors. When subjected to sustained collection and analysis, it is theoretically possible to monitor the day-to-day activities of non-state actors to understand what in fact constitutes their "day alert" status and to detect subtle changes in the signals they generate to warn that they are in fact moving to a "generated alert" posture. In other words, it is somewhat harder to detect the threat posed by non-state actors when compared to state actors. But given the more limited nature of the threat constituted by non-state actors, it is possible to suggest that more limited responses might be sufficient to deter or defeat the threats they pose.

Towards a modern indications and warning capability

Indications and warning methodologies are based on key concepts and assumptions that must understood and accepted by analysts and policymakers. Foremost among these assumptions is that indications and warning intelligence does not necessarily yield specific event predictions, only indications that the threat posed by some opponent is increasing. If commanders or policymakers insist on receiving specific details about what is about to transpire, or responses guaranteed to head off an attack, or compelling explanations for why an opponent is about to undertake an extremely counterproductive initiative, then warnings are likely to yield few positive results. If analysts wait until the situation unfolds to the point where answers can be offered to these questions, it will likely be too late to respond effectively. Analysts and policymakers must overcome the dilemma inherent in indications and warnings methodologies—they must devise a way to overcome policymakers' preference for an "all or nothing" response when it comes to selecting a response to warning.

Indications and warning also is based on the detection of anomalies, which requires sustained analysis so that patterns of activity that reflect "normalcy" can be identified. In the absence of a clear conception of expected behavior and well-defined checklists of warning indicators, however, indications and warning methodology can still provide a valuable service because it can serve as a way to direct scarce collection and analytical resources towards individuals, groups, facilities, organizations or military units that appear to be engaging in unusual activity or that are failing to exhibit the signals expected by normal patterns of activity. Investigators who arrive at some facility might in fact find perfectly innocent and compelling explanations for the emergence of some anomaly, but anomalies require additional analysis because they offer a good way to penetrate denial and deception techniques employed by state and non-state actors. Detecting anomalies among individuals or groups might appear impossible to achieve, but the Al-Qaeda operatives involved in the September 11, 2001 terror attacks left signals that were in fact detected by their flight instructors, which were subsequently discussed within the Federal Bureau of Investigation. The fact that the law enforcement or intelligence communities did not investigate why groups of students were interested in learning how to fly, but not necessarily land, aircraft suggests that both analysts and policymakers alike failed to recognize what actually constitutes raw intelligence and warning data.[10]

Once anomalies are detected, policymakers must understand the range of appropriate responses that are available to respond to heightened threats. At a minimum, they need to understand that a change in defense and security postures can derail an opponent's plans. A change in defense posture can deter an opponent from taking undesirable action because it can deny the opponent the element of surprise needed to achieve a fait accompli, which changes the strategic setting in a way that makes existing deterrent threats less relevant. A change in security postures also can delay some nefarious scheme concocted by a non-state actor because it negates the assumptions behind some finely crafted plan that is intended to exploit weaknesses in day alert security procedures intended to safeguard critical infrastructure or vulnerable aspects of civil society. Delay also provides law enforcement with the additional time needed to investigate leads and to explore anomalies detected in the behavior or status of non-state actors, providing an opportunity to disrupt activities by identifying and detaining individuals that are key to impending operations. Because non-state actors are forced to undertake operations on the finest of margins, a change in defensive and security operations should force them to reassess planned operations in order to guarantee that they will still be effective against new defense postures or security procedures. In this sense, time is on the side of the defense because a "mission kill" provides the opportunity for law enforcement or intelligence agencies to target key parts of the opponent's infrastructure, which can ultimately eliminate the threat.

Because small changes in defensive and law enforcement postures can deter a potential attack or produce a mission kill when it comes to initiatives launched by non-state actors, intelligence and warning intelligence can overcome policymakers' preferences for an "all or nothing" response to warning. Intelligence analysts no longer have to present policymakers with specific event predictions that identify exactly what is about to unfold or offer a compelling explanation for why an opponent is about to undertake some actions that appear ex ante as strategically ill-advised or self-destructive. Instead of requiring policymakers to adopt costly and extreme responses to potential threats, analysts only have to request relatively modest changes in defense and security postures to deny the opponent the element of surprise or to derail an opponent's plans that are crafted to meet specific strategic settings. By reducing the known costs of a response to potential threats, intelligence analysts can increase the probability that policymakers will undertake changes in defense and security postures needed to deter or derail threats. For example, a modest change in airline security procedures before the September 11, 2001 terror attacks might have forced Al-Qaeda operatives to re-evaluate their plans to ensure that they would not run afoul of airline security. The Japanese fleet moving towards Pearl Harbor in December 1941 also had instructions to abandon their operations if they lost the element of surprise. Ultimately, indications and warning techniques offer the possibility of deterring attack by increasing defensive readiness, a metric that might constitute a new "holy grail" for intelligence professionals.

Conclusion

Indications and warning methodologies are significant tools that offer important ways to organize strategic responses to today's threats. They offer important insights into collection techniques, suggesting the importance of long-term research to develop a broad awareness of emerging threats. They also offer a way to direct more focused collection efforts to investigate anomalies in known patterns of behavior of both state and non-state actors. For analysts, indications and warning methodologies also offer a way to defeat an opponent's efforts at denial and deception by highlighting the collection and analysis techniques needed to investigate and explore anomalies that emerge. Intelligence and warning methodologies also offer a way to overcome response dilemmas and the general reluctance of policymakers to incur substantial and known costs in response to possible threats that appear ex ante as unrealistic or ill advised. In effect, indications and warning methodologies offer a strategic way to organize national intelligence and response efforts across the entire intelligence, defense and security enterprise.

Although indications and warning methodologies offer a constructive response to today's security challenges, they have clearly have fallen out of fashion among intelligence professionals. In part, indications and warning is often viewed as better suited to a different setting—the prominence of the technique during the Cold War might make it appear unresponsive to present circumstances. As a result, intelligence managers and policymakers have failed to consider how indications and warning techniques can be applied to meet today's challenges. Another stumbling block is the fact that indications and warning methodologies have to be implemented across the entire intelligence cycle—collection, analysis, and response—in order to be effective. Because there are few mechanisms to organize and inform both intelligence professionals and government officials about their role in the indications and warning process, it is unlikely that indications and warning will see a resurgence as a key instrument of intelligence and strategic policy. The failure to consider and apply indications and warning methodologies in the effort to exploit the opportunities for collection and analysis created by the information revolution is especially unfortunate. Nevertheless, indications and warning intelligence remains an important and effective tool in the national effort to avoid surprise and to deter opponents who seek to exploit defense and security weaknesses to achieve their objectives.

Notes

1 In the words, of Sherman Kent, photographic evidence of efforts to deploy Soviet medium-range ballistic missiles in Cuba was a "moment of splendid," Kent quoted in Loch Johnson, *National Security Intelligence* (Cambridge: Polity, 2012), p. 50.
2 Some scholars even suggested that the use of similar military technology and the reliance on large bureaucracies was leading to a process of "convergence" between the United States and the Soviet Union. In other words, the need to exploit similar technologies via large bureaucracies was leading to the adoption of similar standard operating procedures, technical solutions and military doctrines when it came to the military competition between the Superpowers. See Zbigniew Brzezinski and Samuel P. Huntington, *Political Power: USA/USSR* (Westport, CT: Greenwood Press, 1982).
3 The best known of these studies was Graham Allison, *Essence of Decision* (Boston, MA: Little Brown, 1971).
4 Richards J. Heuer and Randolph H. Pherson, *Structured Analytic Techniques for Intelligence Analysis* (Washington, DC: CQ Press, 2011).
5 *The 9/11 Commission Report: Final Report of the National Commission on Terrorist Attacks Upon the United States* (New York: Norton, 2004), p. 254.
6 For a description of how the exigencies of a covert or clandestine existence shape the operations of non-state actors, see J. Bowyer Bell, "Conditions Making for Success and Failure of Denial and Deception: Nonstate and Illicit Actors," in Roy Godson and James J. Wirtz (eds), *Strategic Denial and Deception: The Twenty-First Century Challenge* (New Brunswick, NJ: Transaction 2002), pp. 129–162.
7 James J. Wirtz, "Theory of Surprise," in Richard K. Betts and Thomas G. Mahnken (eds), *Paradoxes of Strategic Intelligence: Essays in Honor of Michael I. Handel* (London: Frank Cass, 2003), pp. 101–116.
8 According to Jack Davis, policymakers are acutely sensitive to the "wrenching shift in defensive resources that would be required if … warnings were taken seriously," see Jack Davis, "Strategic Warning: Intelligence Support in a World of Uncertainty and Surprise," in Loch K. Johnson (ed.), *Handbook of Intelligence Studies* (New York: Routledge, 2007), p. 186.
9 *The 9/11 Commission Report*, p. 1.
10 Ibid, pp. 272–276.

9
FROM COMBINED ARMS TO COMBINED INTELLIGENCE

Philosophy, doctrine and operations

Combined arms operations, what Steven Biddle has called the modern system of force employment, emerged during the last century. Those who master combined arms operations generally achieve victory in war, while those who ignore it or concentrate on a single dimension of combat operations generally go down in defeat.[1] The mastery of combined arms operations, however, is no simple matter. Organizational culture and bureaucratic preferences can impede the integration of forces and operations. The quest for quality and professionalism remains a constant struggle; it is often easier to preserve the appearance rather than substance of competence in peacetime when the only true test of a military is battle itself. Serious militaries also must constantly work to integrate new technologies, weapons, and operations into the most effective combinations to maximize combat synergies. And even the most exquisitely conceived and brilliantly executed combined arms operations can fail if they are not tied to strategic realities and plausible political objectives.[2]

What can intelligence professionals learn from combined arms operations? Combined arms operations are influenced by an underlying philosophy that also can be used to shape the contribution of intelligence to statecraft and national security, especially the effort to defeat denial and deception. Intelligence professionals do battle with opponents who wish to hide their true intentions and capabilities from outside scrutiny. The basic logic of combined arms operations can be applied to the equivalent of the combat arms in the intelligence domain: the functional disciplines of imagery intelligence, which is now more commonly referred to as geospatial intelligence (GEOINT),[3] signals intelligence (SIGINT), measures and signals intelligence (MASINT), human intelligence (HUMINT), and open source intelligence (OSINT). It could also be applied to other aspects of the intelligence enterprise, including counter-intelligence, partnerships with foreign intelligence services, and collaboration across state, local and tribal authorities, and the private sector.

Each intelligence discipline offers unique strengths, but exhibits serious limitations (including susceptibility to countermeasures), especially when applied in isolation. It is their combined employment that amplifies their impact for intelligence professionals seeking to confer a decisive advantage to national officials and homeland security and law enforcement customers. Without an integrating philosophy, the disciplines and their sponsoring intelligence agencies tend to pursue independent efforts in relative isolation, which produces limited combined effects or synergies. It was the effort to overcome this organizational dynamic of bureaucratic "stove piping" that has animated many reform efforts, including the Intelligence Reform and Terrorism Prevention Act of 2004.[4]

Collaboration between and among the intelligence disciplines is certainly not new to the intelligence community. Skilled intelligence professionals have, by necessity or accident, worked across discipline boundaries to address specific problems posed by closed societies or inscrutable trends. There have been many examples of their coordination to meet the tactical challenges in specific operations, particularly since World War II. Since September 11, 2001, the interaction has increased to meet the very operational needs of those on the front-line of combating terrorist groups, the details of which quite rightfully remain classified. But these efforts have occurred largely case-by-case, with little development of a theory—or a family of theories—for how the disciplines work together more generally so that success can be replicated, let alone scaled. Just as research into the interactive dynamics of the military combat arms yielded combined arms theory that Biddle crystallized with empirically based assertions to explain variations in military power, constructing theory about the interactive effects of the intelligence disciplines can provide insight about what makes intelligence a more or less effective tool of national power.

Combined arms operations rely on doctrine to put this underlying philosophy into practice. Intelligence professionals generally do not think of doctrine when it comes to organizing for intelligence, but a doctrine that shapes the way information is collected, fused and analyzed could facilitate efforts to obtain optimal performance from information age technologies. In an operational sense, combined intelligence operations, much like combined arms operations, also can produce synergies when it comes to collection and analysis, including for counter-intelligence purposes. The strengths of one intelligence discipline can overcome, or at least minimize, limitations in other disciplines.

To support these assertions, this chapter first describes the philosophy behind combined arms operations and how this philosophy is related to integration of intelligence disciplines. It describes the attributes, strengths and limitations of the major intelligence disciplines. The chapter then turns to a brief discussion of the role of doctrine, and how it can help operationalize a combined arms approach to intelligence. The chapter concludes by briefly highlighting some operational implications of adopting a combined intelligence approach, enabling subsequent consideration of how to apply it to posture, manage and employ national intelligence capabilities.

Combined arms philosophy

The philosophy behind combined arms operations is simple, although extremely difficult to put into practice. The philosophy suggests that whenever possible, a commander should employ multiple categories of forces and weapons in an integrated manner that maximizes their individual effectiveness, offsets their limitations and produces greater combined effect. In sum, combined usage creates synergy. It also implies that combat objectives can often be achieved with fewer resources and less effort, thereby overcoming opposing units, which may enjoy superior numbers but lack the skill needed to undertake combined arms operations. Like an orchestra, the whole of a combined arms operation is greater than the sum of its parts. An orchestra can achieve a qualitatively different musical effect when compared to a mass of musicians playing various instruments because the orchestra combines its efforts in a purposive and meaningful way. Similarly, a combined arms operation can produce a battlefield effect far greater than one would expect by simply tallying some quantitative balance of forces. Combined arms operations can allow numerically inferior opponents to defeat far larger armies. By accurately identifying the *Schwerpunkt* (point of main effort) or disrupting an enemy's normal operational pattern, combined arms attacks can cause an entire army to collapse quickly, without horrific attritional engagements that might kill thousands more combatants.

The philosophy of combined arms operations also turns enemy strengths into weaknesses in potentially myriad ways. For example, if opponents deploy to engage or counter a specific type of weapon or to carry out a particular type of operation, they generally make themselves vulnerable to attack by other types of weapons. In the 1991 Gulf War, for instance, Iraqi armor was buried to hide it from air attack, but then it found itself an easy target when it was engaged at long distance by US armored formations. In the Afghan war, Taliban fighters found it difficult to concentrate to resist the advance of Coalition ground forces; the movement of Taliban ground units was almost immediately subject to air attack. In the 1973 Arab–Israeli war, Israeli armor formations, which lacked adequate infantry support, suffered heavy casualties at the hands of Egyptian infantry armed with new wire-guided anti-tank rockets. Some observers were quick to announce that the tank had met its match in war, but a combined arms approach in this context soon nullified the advantages enjoyed by infantry armed with man portable anti-tank weapons. In fact, the only ways to defeat a combined arms assault are with a superior combined arms defense or asymmetric strategies and tactics, which are intended to circumvent or deny the opponent the benefits of the victory achieved on some battlefield.

Nevertheless, several issues complicate the execution of combined arms operations. First, from an operational perspective, it is difficult to determine in advance how best to integrate a wide variety of weapons, units and tactics into an effective operation, especially as technological advances alter the capabilities of some systems at the expense of others. The particulars of an operation—geography, leadership objectives, and the capabilities and intent of specific enemies—create significant challenges when it comes to devising the optimal combined arms operation. Second, ongoing changes in technology, doctrine and the social and economic aspects of warfare complicate efforts at keeping an effective approach to combined arms operations current. For example, the information revolution has produced ongoing advances in so-called smart weapons, command and control systems, and reconnaissance and surveillance capabilities that require integration into doctrine and planning on a continuous basis. Third, militaries, much like the intelligence community, are made up of competing organizations with their own agendas, institutional processes and hierarchies.[5] Dominant sectors of the bureaucracy seek to preserve their autonomy and their parochial interests at the expense of organizational interdependence and support to relatively ambiguous collective goals.[6] Such institutional inertia curries support from current bureaucratic beneficiaries, but doctrines and tactics that exist only to satisfy organizational preferences can lead to disaster on some future battlefield. Fourth, militaries, at least the US military, tend to value technology above other facets of combined arms operations. There is a proclivity to search for a "silver bullet" that can guarantee victory regardless of military proficiency. Or, as a British officer once said, "When all else fails we have the Maxim gun and they don't." Ironically, Biddle's suggestion that it was the professionalism of the US military that produced rapid victory in the First Gulf War actually was met with criticism. Some observers wanted to believe that victory had little to do with the skilled execution of combined arms operations, but was instead based on US technological superiority.[7] One wonders if the intelligence community also looks to technology as a panacea, making up for the ever-present possibility that human frailty, organizational pathologies, or politicization will lead to intelligence failure.[8]

Another issue that can emerge is that planners and policymakers can become mesmerized by the operational level of war and fail to pay adequate attention to how combined arms operations serve overall strategic objectives and political realities. The history of war is replete with brilliant military maneuvers that end in strategic disaster. As long as navies ply the oceans, for example, sailors will talk about the well conceived and executed Japanese attack on Pearl Harbor; what is forgotten is that the attack itself doomed Japan to a long war of attrition it could not win. The successful surprise attack eliminated the political basis of Japanese war plans (i.e., US willingness to reach a compromise settlement in the face of Japanese aggression). Several US military operations during the Vietnam War—the defense and relief of Khe Sanh and the urban warfare in Hue during the Tet offensive—demonstrated US military prowess in conducting combined-arms set-piece battles, air-mobile operations, and urban warfare, but these successful operations could not overcome the negative impact of unrealistic political objectives. From the intelligence perspective, this idea is equivalent to saying that good tradecraft cannot compensate for misdirected strategy or for embracing objectives that fail to correspond to political realities. As Richard Best recently noted, "Intelligence analysis can inform policymaking, but it does not substitute for it."[9]

Several key facets of the philosophy behind combined arms operations are thus of interest to intelligence managers and analysts. By combining forces and weapons into a coherent and purposive whole, a synergy can be achieved that produces combat capabilities that cannot be achieved by systems operating independently. The enemy becomes vulnerable to defeat because a successful defense against one type of system or tactic leaves it vulnerable to attack by other elements of the combined arms team. Similarly, combined arms operations can prevent the opponent from exploiting one's vulnerabilities because combat synergies can cover the weaknesses that are inherent in any weapons system or operation. Most importantly, combined arms operations embrace interdependencies and are based on a systematic analysis that matches operational objectives with the strengths and weakness of opposing forces, placing this analysis against the backdrop of adversary capabilities and intent. Officers and planners have to believe they are empowered to achieve combat synergies at the expense of organizational and cultural preferences. Military organizations that actually achieve real innovation have to find a way to protect the careers of their "young Turks" as they follow non-standard career paths integrating new technologies, tactics and doctrine into existing organizations.[10]

Intelligence disciplines: Strengths and limitations

Every intelligence discipline has strengths and limitations. As a result, reliance on a single type of collection and analysis would at best only create a partial picture of an unfolding situation. At worst, reliance on one phenomenology could be subject to spoofing or manipulation by the target, or simply fail to contain the data needed to uncover activities of interest. During the Cold War, for example, Soviet intelligence officers valued state secrets obtained through espionage as the single most important type of evidence they could obtain about their opponents' activities. Information gained from open sources was given short shrift, while analysis was looked upon as virtually meaningless opinion.[11] But what happens when needed information is not contained in an opponent's secret communications? Under these circumstances, access to even the most secret communication channels will not yield positive results. The Soviets actually encountered this situation in the months leading up to the Cuban missile crisis. When the KGB was tasked to discover how President John F. Kennedy's administration would react to the placement of missiles in Cuba, their agents fanned out across Washington, DC, hoping to pick up snippets of conversation. They were unsuccessful in their effort because Soviet activity in Cuba at the time had not yet been discovered by US intelligence. American officials could not talk about a situation that they knew nothing about.[12] By contrast, a scholarly study of the impact of domestic politics on the Kennedy administration's foreign policy stance might have highlighted the fact that administration might have felt compelled to take a strong stand on the issue of Soviet activity in Cuba, especially after the setback at the Bay of Pigs.

The state of intelligence disciplines, as well as the relative strengths and weaknesses of their associated capabilities, varies over time. Changes in technology, the amount of resources devoted to a specific discipline, adversary countermeasures and the nature of the target set all alter estimates of the effectiveness of each intelligence discipline. In other words, analysis of the disciplines' roles and contributions hinges on the strategic and operational context. Each discipline, however, has been the focus of real intelligence coups and real intelligence disasters. Rarely does one offer a silver bullet that guarantees success. The Israelis, for instance, had gained access to the inner reaches of the Egyptian government on the eve of the Yom Kippur war, but the accurate information gleaned from this source still failed to stave off surprise.[13] Understanding the inherent attributes, strengths and weaknesses of each intelligence discipline provides a foundation for undertaking a more contextual analysis concerning how to integrate them according to a combined arms philosophy. While many aspects remain classified, a review of openly available information provides a sound starting point for the purposes of developing theory.

GEOINT

Although experiments with balloons and cameras occurred during the American civil war, imagery intelligence emerged during World War I with the combination of aircraft and photographic equipment. By World War II, aerial reconnaissance was used by all combatants for identifying troop formations and industrial targets and for the conduct of battle damage assessment. In 1960, the United States went one step further when it sent a Corona satellite into earth orbit, thereby providing reconnaissance capabilities across vast portions of the Soviet Union. Today, satellites can provide high-resolution surveillance capabilities. Digital images are transferred to ground stations in near real time, although a constellation of satellites is needed to provide continuous coverage of specific regions. Other satellites provide real time radar and infrared imagery to ground stations.[14] Since the 1970s, for example, the US Defense Support Program infrared satellite provided early warning of missile launch.[15]

Imagery analysis is easy for policymakers to understand and utilize. After all, a picture is worth a thousand words. Sometimes images are extraordinarily compelling and provide concrete evidence of critical activities or major departures in national policy—here the important role played by aerial reconnaissance during the Cuban Missile Crisis comes to mind.[16] Imagery also can yield insight in a change in status in the operational readiness of an opponent's forces. The fact that satellites and reconnaissance aircraft can capture imagery at a distance is a significant positive attribute because personnel and equipment do not have to be placed in harm's way to achieve mission objectives.

GEOINT, however, has several important limitations. The effects of weather or camouflage and evasion techniques can degrade the effectiveness of satellite sensors and the utility of the resulting images. If satellite coverage is not continuous, for instance, targets can limit their activities to times when overhead sensors are not in position to capture imagery. Additionally, not all pictures speak for themselves; some require significant analytical effort to interpret the specific objects or activities captured by the sensors. Activities occurring underground may also lie beyond the reach of overhead imagery, although analysts can come to understand what is occurring underground or behind closed doors by monitoring "life cycle" activities occurring near suspect installations.

SIGINT

Signals intelligence is a highly guarded form of collection and analysis that involves intercepting and monitoring electronic signals generated by various types of activity. One type of SIGINT is communications intelligence, whereby a target's communications are intercepted and read by analysts. Many means of electronic communication can be monitored by listening devices operating in space, in the air, on the ground and even underneath the ocean. SIGINT collection also can involve clandestine penetration of denied territory and even specific facilities. During the Cold War, for instance, US submarines reportedly tapped Soviet underwater cables to monitor classified communications.[17] Even if intercepted communications resist decryption, traffic analysis can reveal important information about command structures, ongoing operations or a change in the status of forces. In other words, communication patterns can often reveal much about an opponent's activities.

Another type of SIGINT is electronic intelligence, which collects and analyzes various kinds of electronic emissions. Radars, for example, are of interest to analysts because it is important to know their locations, coverage zones and operating patterns when it comes to planning air operations and countermeasures. Analysts are also interested in collecting telemetry about an opponent's military systems. Aircraft and missiles, especially when they are being tested, transmit information about their performance to ground stations. This type of telemetry is key to verifying arms control agreements and in terms of shedding light on fundamental weapons characteristics.[18]

The ability to eavesdrop on the conversations of others without them knowing is a priceless asset when it comes to intelligence production. It can offer insights into plans and intentions, and provide enormous advantages to the side that can clandestinely monitor an opponent's communications. The Allies' ability to break German and Japanese codes—producing intelligence known by the code words ULTRA and MAGIC—saved thousands of lives by appreciably shortening World War II.[19] Signals can be detected from remote locations, which often eliminates the necessity of placing personnel in harm's way to collect intelligence.

Signals intelligence, however, presents several limitations. First, the amount and types of information that can be intercepted is virtually limitless, making it increasingly difficult to separate the wheat from the chaff when it comes to detecting important messages. The sheer mass of material that can be collected presents a problem for analysts. In 2005, for instance, the Federal Bureau of Investigation held

8,000 hours of counter-terrorism wiretaps that were still waiting to be translated.[20] Second, without context, it is difficult to understand the exact meaning of intercepted communications. In the three months preceding the September 11, 2001 terrorist attacks, US intelligence analysts intercepted thirty conversations containing veiled references that a major attack, disaster or incident was imminent.[21] Third, someone has to understand what is being said in intercepted communications—the US government for a time simply lacked analysts who could understand the languages spoken in Afghanistan.[22] Fourth, relatively simple countermeasures such as use of couriers, secure landlines, elaborate code languages, or simply "staying off the grid," can curtail the effectiveness of modern collection techniques. These measures increase operating costs and can slow the tempo of operations, but for some opponents pursuing certain objectives, speed is not a prerequisite for success.

MASINT

Measurement and Signals Intelligence is similar to signals intelligence (electronic intelligence, for instance, is often characterized as MASINT), and is generally the least understood INT. Infrared and optical sensors that generate data without imagery are also considered to be MASINT. Radar images can also be used to identify targets once their unique characteristics are catalogued. Seismic, acoustic and magnetic sensors can be used to sample the environment, and materials sampling can be used to test effluent streams, debris, and exhaust plumes. Sensors also are configured to detect radiological, chemical and biological hazards. More exotic types of sensors also are coming online. According to Jeffrey Richelson, "Hyper-spectral imagery employs at least sixty narrow contiguous spectral bands ... the data produced by examining those bands allows analysts to detect an object's shape, density, temperature, movement, and chemical composition."[23] Hyper-spectral imagery might be put to use to identify the dyes used in an opponent's uniforms. Smart weapons could then be created that would hone onto those signatures. MASINT thus appears to be similar to touch, taste and smell, while GEOINT resembles sight and SIGINT is similar to hearing.[24]

MASINT is useful when the location, timing and nature of an unfolding event are known; cueing is crucial in measurement and signatures intelligence. In other words, the right sensors need to be in the correct location to observe an unfolding event. Once in place, however, MASINT sensors can offer definitive information about an unfolding situation by helping to defeat denial and deception efforts geared toward traditional GEOINT and SIGINT capabilities.

MASINT suffers from several of the drawbacks inherent in other technical collection systems. For example, MASINT data can require a good deal of processing and analysis to discern meaningful information. As a result, policymakers do not readily understand raw MASINT data. In contrast to other technical collection capabilities, some MASINT sensors need to be brought into close proximity to the target. Sampling effluent streams or particles in exhaust gases often means that the sensors themselves have to be brought to the location of interest. If targets are aware of MASINT capabilities, they also can take steps to hide signals of interest.

HUMINT

Human intelligence, which is gained through interpersonal contact conducted in secret, is known in the vernacular as espionage. In this classic formulation, espionage qua HUMINT usually involves cooperation of an official in an adversary's government, who, for various reasons, is willing to betray the trust placed in them to compromise classified information. Espionage is a clandestine activity, in the sense that the side undertaking the espionage needs to maintain the secrecy of its operations.[25]

But more generally, HUMINT can take a variety of forms. Officials in their everyday interactions with foreign counterparts can gain insight into the intentions of other governments. Sometimes these representatives take a low-key approach when contacting foreign officials to avoid publicity and to keep their activities in other countries as quiet as possible. Officials stationed overseas—ambassadors, military attachés, representatives of various agencies—also report their observations. The intelligence community also undertakes a variety of debriefings of émigrés, business executives and subject matter experts to track development in foreign countries.

HUMINT can provide fundamental insights into an opponent's objectives, political setting, command and control procedures, and military doctrine. Sometimes agents hit the jackpot. Oleg Penkovsky, from his position inside Soviet military intelligence, for instance, literally turned over the operating manuals for the medium-range and intermediate-range ballistic missiles that the Soviet were deploying to Cuba in the Fall of 1962, while informing the Kennedy administration that General Secretary Nikita Khrushchev faced significant domestic opposition to his Cuban gambit.[26] Most of the time, however, intelligence provides "cueing": it provides indications that an opponent is undertaking some sort of initiative before that initiative is fully underway and begins to generate observable activities. Espionage allows intelligence managers to focus collection efforts on the suspected activity.[27]

Of all the intelligence disciplines, human intelligence is the most coveted by intelligence consumers because of its prominence in the culture of intelligence, but it is also probably the most idiosyncratic and unpredictable. For HUMINT to succeed, it can take years to develop reliable and productive contacts within an opposing regime. Contacts also can have mixed motives when it comes to compromising information and agents always have to be aware of the possibility that dangles or false leads are being offered. Double agents, which can take the form of reliable sources detected by their own side, also are another downside to HUMINT. Opposing governments can use double agents to feed misleading information into collection channels. In many parts of the world, Americans are no longer seen as the "good guys," which makes it very difficult to operate in foreign societies and makes it less likely that individuals will turn over classified information out of ideological or political sympathy. The fact that many intelligence officers lack familiarity with emerging languages and cultures of importance makes it increasingly difficult to carry out HUMINT.[28]

OSINT

Definitions of open source intelligence, the most recently formally recognized INT, are subject to debate. OSINT constitutes insight gleaned from publicly available information that anyone can access by overt, non-clandestine or non-secret means to satisfy an intelligence requirement.[29] Using this expansive definition, information that is proprietary but acquired by legal means, e.g., certain law enforcement or industry data, falls under the rubric of open source intelligence. More commonly, when scholars refer to OSINT, they generally are referring to various forms of publicly available media: television and newspapers (especially in foreign languages); Web-based user-generated content like wikis and blogs; public data, such as government reports, patent applications, and speeches; academic sources like doctoral dissertations and conference proceedings; commercial data, such as private satellite imagery; and "gray literature," such as research reports and working papers that were generally intended for limited distribution.[30] Its acquisition may or may not be free, but, in general terms, OSINT is far cheaper and carries much less operational risk than the other INTs, though it does require a fairly large number of people and time. But just because OSINT leverages publicly available information does not mean that findings derived from this information are necessarily unclassified. In fact, some of the most penetrating insights based on open source information can be deeply classified because they can form the basis of foreign and defense policies.

OSINT has historically been a stepchild within the intelligence community. Intelligence professionals have a cultural preference for information gleaned from secret sources. The intelligence community also seems to believe that their consumers prefer insights gained from sources that are not commonly available. It also is difficult to glean adversaries' specific strategic motivations or long-term intentions from open source data, especially if the opponent practices a modicum of operational security. In addition, the unlimited volume of and variation in open source information poses questions about processing and exploitation capacity. In other words, how could anyone possibly identify all the appropriate sources for analysis, place the inputs gathered into a meaningful typology or framework, and decipher what was relevant, accurate and useful?

Nevertheless, OSINT has several unique attributes beyond its relative low cost compared to other intelligence disciplines. The large and public marketplace of open source information can often correct false or misleading information by providing multiple sources to fill in esoteric details on almost every conceivable topic. OSINT provides context within which the other INTs can bring insight to bear and forms the basic framework and reference point for analysts to do their work. It also gives indispensable strategic warning through its broad coverage of leading economic, cultural and political indicators. Most OSINT can be shared widely—from foreign partners to non-traditional partners like first responders—to provide a common starting point for further collaboration.

OSINT's significance and the ease with which it could be leveraged have increased over the past twenty years for a number of reasons. First, the demise of Soviet communism, the singular focus of the intelligence community for fifty years, and proliferation of other threats has spawned the need for a foundation of global coverage that is eminently suitable to OSINT. The other intelligence disciplines could not possibly provide the necessary coverage to meet the broad range of topics of policymaker interest, and often their specialized perspectives were not appropriate to the basic questions being asked by intelligence customers. Second, OSINT may be the best weapon to meet many twenty-first century threats that are less a function of high-tech weaponry guarded tightly by a regime's security forces, and instead operate as social and political movements or self-organized interest groups that plan, communicate and recruit their participants in the relative openness of cyberspace. Third, the availability of a preponderance of open source information through the internet has enabled greater access to a wider range of materials. Going to city hall to look up tax records or real estate deeds, for instance, is an anachronism. Third, the problem of processing and exploitation continues to wane as new software and hardware becomes available that can identify, sort and sift through structured and unstructured data with increasing speed, at lower cost.

Benefits of combined intelligence

There are several important parallels that can be drawn between the combined arms philosophy and the world of intelligence. A combined intelligence philosophy would provide the intelligence community further advantages over intelligence services maintained by state actors and the networked operations of non-state actors. The US intelligence community already possesses unequaled human, technological and financial resources. What is lacking is a philosophy to integrate these capabilities into a combined effort. It is impossible to predict the nature or quantify the extent of the superiority generated by this type of synergy, but combined arms militaries often handily defeat far larger enemies. Marrying a superior philosophy of operations to the already significant resources devoted to intelligence should give the United States a fundamental and persistent winning advantage in the conduct of its foreign and defense policies.

Second, employing a combined arms philosophy yields operational advantages. On the defensive side, it defangs adversary attempts to penetrate, deceive or deny information to an intelligence apparatus through counter-intelligence means. Such enemy tactics are the bane of good intelligence and ultimately sound policy. Effectively integrating the vice and virtues of the intelligence disciplines can shore up the weak points in the intelligence process, while buttressing the strong ones.

For example, prudent management of the SIGINT discipline can offset the risks of adversary intelligence services spoofing human operators.

On the offensive side, enabling more accurate and incisive intelligence about adversaries, while creating new opportunities to gain additional intelligence insight about adversaries. By fusing HUMINT, SIGINT, OSINT, GEOINT, and MASINT, an intelligence organization would possess a far more powerful basis for analysis and indications and warning than would be created by relying on any one phenomenology or information source. Fusion across Law Enforcement Sensitive (LES) information, and information gathered by the Department of Homeland Security, would cast even a wider net. Gathering information from domestic or foreign sources would create important synergies at a time when globalization generates transnational threats.[31] This sort of fusion should be capable of penetrating even the most concerted efforts at denial and deception because it may be difficult for an opponent to create such a convincing false front that it would be capable of hiding simultaneously from the scrutiny of all of these collectors. In all probability, the effort to hide from one type of sensor would increase the likelihood of detection by other sensors because a successful effort to deny or deceive one type of sensor is likely to leave evidence of deception that is detectable by sensors based on different phenomenologies. Visual deception based on the construction of a fake manufacturing facility, for instance, would have to be accompanied by MASINT deception too or else risk creating an easily detectable anomaly. A combined intelligence approach increases the geographic or spectral area observed, which is a fundamental tactic in defeating denial and deception.[32]

A combined intelligence approach also should improve the sophistication and accuracy of finished intelligence by allowing more data and analysis from various geographies and spectra to be incorporated in the analytical process on a regular basis. The purpose here would not be to simply inundate analysts with more data and supporting analysis, but to allow analysts to draw upon appropriate data streams to construct and validate richer explanations and predictions. The fusion of data and analysis would help make the world more transparent. By improving situational awareness and the ability to offer quick and accurate attribution when it comes to understanding an unfolding event, a combined intelligence approach can mitigate damage, prevent cascade effects and generally lead to more effective consequence management.

Fourth, a combined arms approach to intelligence confers institutional benefits, providing a singular lens to assess a complex enterprise and promotes more economical uses of scarce intelligence resources. It would provide both a framework and a metric to judge virtually every process related to the intelligence community. Judging the appropriateness of organizational and procedural reform usually follows two paths. One way is by judging the quality of organizational output, in this case finished intelligence. But if output is not satisfactory, it is difficult to adopt appropriate changes in the absence of an overall design that specifies a desired end state. This leads to the second method for judging performance, especially in the absence of intelligence "victories" that are often apparent only in hindsight. This method involves comparing organization, processes and output against an idealized vision of the desired end state. In this sense, the combined intelligence philosophy resembles an ideology. It describes why some intelligence analyses end in success while others end in failure, and what needs to be done to improve intelligence performance in support of national objectives.

Intelligence concepts and doctrine

To translate this new philosophy into practice ultimately requires concepts and doctrine. Concepts provide specific principles for how and when to employ different intelligence disciplines based on a general set of conditions. They provide guideposts to understand which discipline has greater or lesser utility given the security landscape, leadership objectives and enemy capabilities, and rules for how to meter, sequence and otherwise combine their employment. A capstone concept might describe general parameters for how the disciplines should combine, while more detailed concepts would delineate derivative insights, e.g., how SIGINT enables HUMINT operations, or how to apply combined intelligence approach for a mission area like counterproliferation.

Doctrine is the next step in the process of translating the combined arms philosophy into operations, providing guidance to organizations and processes that contribute to overall mission achievement. In other words, doctrine is a "game plan" for turning philosophy into organizational and procedural realities. It reflects an ongoing, deliberate planning process. Doctrine allocates tasks and responsibilities across the entire enterprise, searching for efficiencies while guaranteeing redundancy is purposive. It also describes processes, especially how information moves across organizations and who is responsible for making specific decisions. It prevents unproductive examinations of the first principles behind previous bureaucratic and policy decisions, while allowing analysts and managers greater initiative in their designated areas of responsibility. It lays out the basic framework of responsibilities and tasks, showing the "lanes" that organizations should follow in working toward completion of a common task. While the military developed doctrine in many areas to institutionalize combined arms, e.g., the Army's field manual on AirLand Battle, the intelligence community has little of such formal guidance that the different elements plan to consistently or authoritatively.

Doctrine tells all concerned how mission success will be achieved in a general sense so that they can use their own subject matter expertise to adopt or devise practices that match organizational priorities. It identifies the themes that should be followed and principles that should be implemented across the entire organization. It goes so far as to tell planners and managers which errors to make and the desirable objectives that will be set aside to achieve the goals set by doctrine. For example, combined intelligence doctrine would encourage managers to sacrifice the benefits of complete organizational independence to better integrate organizational outputs into the collective effort. It identifies the general principles that all personnel should attempt to put into practice.

Doctrine also is important to the staff and support units of an organization by helping to set priorities. Today, scholars and practitioners increasingly bemoan the fact that administrative and accounting demands are slowly but surely taking over the workplace, making it impossible for analysts and managers to concentrate on the substance of their jobs.[33] Doctrine would discourage the staff from turning analysts and managers into the de facto "staff to the staff," allowing them to focus on producing finished intelligence and serving the needs of policymakers. Housekeeping functions would be standardized as much as possible to allow a commonality of best practices across the intelligence community, reducing the bureaucratic impediments to community-wide collaboration. The professional development and education and training regime can reinforce such "joint doctrine" by creating joint expertise and a joint culture. Illustrative initiatives include the current joint duty effort (where promotions to senior ranks are contingent on service in another element); a coherent graduate and executive educational program for all intelligence officers (vice by intelligence element); and research on community-wide ideas and ideology.

Operational implications

Effective doctrine should provide a philosophy to animate operations, breathing life into organizational structure and procedures. At the enterprise level, a combined arms approach would galvanize integration of the intelligence community, providing a unifying framework to consider strategic choices about force structure and posture, and to weigh tradeoffs. It would also inexorably lead to greater emphasis on mission-focused entities that cut across the intelligence disciplines to tackle problems as a more coherent unit, rather than as a number of activities pursued by individual agencies only loosely connected to an overarching purpose.[34] Existing bureaucracies might also be designated as lead agencies for specific types of collection or analysis. In other words, certain organizations might not be designated as the lead agencies on terrorism or counterproliferation as instantiated in post-9/11 national centers, but also drugs, health issues or financial markets. Combined intelligence would not mean that every agency should maintain full-spectrum capabilities, or that every analyst has to be well versed in every aspect of the intelligence production process. A commanding general, for instance, might not know all of the steps involved in putting an artillery round down range: to be effective, all he needs to know are the general limits and strengths of the artillery units under his command. This sort of "operational" familiarity could be a guiding principle behind combined intelligence production. Analysts and managers should be steeped in the capabilities of other agencies and "INTs," while being well versed in the intricacies of their own agency and related subject matter expertise.

Combined intelligence doctrine for instance, might lead analysts to expect that high-quality finished intelligence will be derived from multiple sources and different analytical products. Cueing of the combined process might be based on a single type of data or analysis, which would then prompt the use of multiple sources and methods. Alternatively, more systematic use of combined analysis could improve target collection. Anomalies could receive greater scrutiny from collection systems tailored to address specific problems and threats.

At the mission level, a combined arms approach to intelligence would provide a repeatable methodology for assessing how the intelligence disciplines should interact to best effect. Analyses of the range, type and amount of each intelligence discipline that might be needed to address a specific issue would rest on a much more analytical base.

And at the tactical level, where innovation in combined intelligence practices has already begun, practices would further adapt as well. Collection strategies against known targets would have a firmer foundation for determining which intelligence disciplines to bring to bear given the adversary's capabilities. Analysts working on finished intelligence reports would be more able to identify and leverage the kinds of disciplines most relevant to the questions they were addressing. When holes in collection or analysis occurred, a combined arms methodology would more likely indicate what discipline could contribute to address the gap in collection or analysis.

Development of concepts and doctrine at the enterprise, mission area, and tactical levels can also provide analysts and managers with analogies or idealized scenarios that can serve as templates to guide current operations. The various military services, for instance, often rely on certain battles to illustrate the essence of their organization and to offer an example to be emulated by their rank and file. For members of the US Army, the performance of Union forces during the battle of Little Round Top during the Civil War or the heroic stand at Bastogne during World War II, highlight what are considered to be ideal qualities, attitudes, and performance. For the Navy, the Battle of Midway remains as the quintessential naval battle, not only because it was a blue-water fleet engagement, but also because it demonstrated determination and resourcefulness. The Marines have their World War II island-hopping campaign in the Pacific, captured in the imagery of the flag raising on Mount Surabachi. For the Air Force, the First Gulf War is becoming iconic in the sense that air power alone paralyzed an opposing military, preventing Saddam Hussein from mounting a defense when land-power was eventually employed.[35]

It is possible to speculate endlessly about the potential operational implications of combined intelligence doctrine. Nevertheless, for all phases of intelligence production and other types of intelligence activities, the notion that synergies can be achieved by working with several agencies and capabilities would guide managers and analysts.

Conclusion

While the histories that are cherished by each of the military services reflect combined arms operations, they highlight the performance of a single service, i.e., their own. Regardless of the fact that many operations are today clearly joint in nature, the services still tend to celebrate their own unique contribution to the joint and combined arms environments. This suggests that the effort to create "combined" effects relies on a conscious effort among disparate entities to synchronize their operations and goals. It also suggests that combining operations should be considered a process, not a specific end state.

For the intelligence community, a "combined" philosophy holds out a number of intriguing possibilities. It offers a way to integrate the efforts of disparate agencies, while allowing them to further perfect their unique capabilities. Combined intelligence doctrine also would provide the United States with a capability that is enjoyed by no other state and is far beyond the capability of non-state actors. The synergies created by implementing a combined intelligence philosophy would produce capabilities that actually remain unimagined. It is time that the intelligence professionals begin to address the organizational limits of current intelligence structures and practices.

Notes

1 Stephen Biddle, *Military Power: Explaining Victory and Defeat in Modern Battle* (Princeton, NJ: Princeton University Press, 2004).
2 Combined arms operations sometimes are referred to as the "operational level of war." Critics are quick to point out, however, that by focusing on the operational level of war, officers and planners can avoid the strategic issues that govern warfare by concentrating on the mechanics of military operations. As they devise exquisite military evolutions, planners sometimes lose sight of how their operations can produce strategic consequences that can hurt the effort to attain political objectives. Robert M. Citino, *Blitzkrieg to Desert Storm: The Evolution of Operational Warfare* (Lawrence, KS: University Press of Kansas, 2004).
3 In the last few years, imagery intelligence (IMINT) has been subsumed under a larger discipline called "geospatial intelligence" (GEOINT), as reflected in presidential executive order 12333, as amended July 30, 2008, available at www.fas.org/irp/offdocs/eo/eo-12333-2008.pdf. The term IMINT, however, sometimes is used as short-hand for this category of intelligence.
4 See for example, the US Senate report that accompanied that chamber's view of the 2004 law, available at http://frwebgate.access.gpo.gov/cgi-bin/getdoc.cgi?dbname=108_cong_reports&docid=f:sr359.108.pdf, in particular pp. 4–12.
5 Carl Builder, *The Masks of War: American Military Styles in Strategy and Analysis* (Baltimore, MD: Johns Hopkins University Press, 1989).
6 Edward L. Katzenbach, Jr. "The Horse Cavalry in the Twentieth Century: A Study in Policy Response," in Richard G. Head and Ervin J. Rokke (eds), *American Defense Policy*, 3rd ed. (Baltimore, MD: Johns Hopkins University Press, 1973), pp. 406–422.
7 Stephen Biddle, "The Gulf War Debate Redux: Why Skill and Technology are the Right Answer," *International Security* Vol. 22, No. 2 (Fall 1997), pp. 163–174.
8 Richard Betts, for example, long ago noted that it was the inability to fine tune standard operating procedures to meet future circumstances that made intelligence failure inevitable. By contrast, Betts failed to even mention the possibility that technology might overcome the fundamental limitations encountered in generating predictive intelligence see Richard K. Betts, "Analysis War and Decision: Why Intelligence Failures are Inevitable," *World Politics* Vol. 31, No. 1 (1978), pp. 61–89.

9 Richard A. Best, Jr., "U.S. Intelligence and Policymaking: The Iraq Experience," *CRS Report for Congress* (Order Code RS21696, Updated December 2, 2005), p. CRS-6.
10 Stephen Peter Rosen, *Winning the Next War: Innovation and the Modern Military* (Ithaca, NY: Cornell University Press, 1991).
11 Alexander Orlov, "The Theory and Practice of Soviet Intelligence," *Studies in Intelligence* Vol. 7, No. 2 (Spring 1963), pp. 45–65.
12 Aleksandr Fursenko and Timothy Naftali, "Soviet Intelligence and the Cuban Missile Crisis," in James G. Blight and David A. Welch (eds), *Intelligence and the Cuban Missile Crisis* (London: Frank Cass, 1998), pp. 64–87.
13 Yuri Uri Bar-Joseph, *The Watchman Fell Asleep: The Surprise of Yom Kippur and Its Sources* (Albany, NY: State University of New York Press, 2005).
14 Jeffrey T. Richelson, "The Technical Collection of Intelligence," in Loch Johnson (ed.), *Handbook of Intelligence Studies* (London: Routledge, 2007), pp. 105–108.
15 Glenn W. Goodman, Jr., "Space-Based Surveillance: Reconnaissance Satellites are a National Security Sine Qua Non," in Robert Z. George and Robert D. Kline (eds), *Intelligence and the National Security Strategist* (Lanham, MD: Rowman & Littlefield, 2006), p. 150.
16 James J. Wirtz, "Organizing for Crisis Intelligence: Lessons from the Cuban Missile Crisis," in James G. Blight and David A. Welch (eds), *Intelligence and the Cuban Missile Crisis* (London: Frank Cass, 1998), pp. 120–149.
17 Sherry Sontag and Christopher Drew, *Blind Man's Bluff* (New York: Public Affairs, 1998).
18 Richelson, "The Technical Collection of Intelligence," pp. 109–110.
19 Alan Harris Bath, *Tracking the Axis Enemy: The Triumph of Anglo-American Naval Intelligence* (Lawrence, KS: University of Kansas Press, 1998).
20 Patrick Radden Keefe, "The Challenge of Global Intelligence Listening," in Loch K. Johnson (ed.), *Strategic Intelligence: The Intelligence Cycle*, Vol. 2 (Westport, CT: Praeger, 2007), p. 34.
21 Ibid., p. 35.
22 Senate Report No. 107-351 and House Report No. 107–792. Report of the US Senate Select Committee and US Permanent Select Committee on Intelligence, *Joint Inquiry Into Intelligence Community Activities Before and After the Terrorist Attacks of September 11, 2001*, 107th Congress, 2nd Session, December 2002, p. 336.
23 Richelson, "The Technical Collection of Intelligence," p. 113.
24 John D. Macartney, "John, How Should We Explain MASINT?" in Robert Z. George and Robert D. Kline (eds), *Intelligence and the National Security Strategist* (Lanham, MD: Rowman & Littlefield, 2006), pp. 219–221.
25 Norman B. Imler, "Espionage in an Age of Change: Optimizing Strategic Intelligence Services for the Future," in Robert Z. George and Robert D. Kline (eds), *Intelligence and the National Security Strategist* (Lanham, MD: Rowman & Littlefield, 2006), p. 150.
26 Frederick P. Hitz, "Human Source Intelligence," in Loch Johnson (ed.), *Handbook of Intelligence Studies* (London: Routledge, 2007), p. 123; and Wirtz, "Organizing for Crisis Intelligence, pp. 128–132.
27 Imler, "Espionage in an Age of Change," p. 221.
28 Hitz, "Human Source Intelligence," pp. 127–128.
29 Intelligence Community Directive Number 301, signed July 11, 2006, available at www.fas.org/irp/dni/icd/icd-301.pdf and P.L. 109–163, Sec 931.
30 Amy Sands, "Integrating Open Sources into Transnational Threat Assessments," in Jennifer E. Sims and Burton Gerber (eds), *Transforming U.S. Intelligence* (Washington, DC: Georgetown University Press, 2005), pp. 64–65.

31 Recognition of the breakdown in the distinction between domestic and international threats has been a staple of intelligence estimates for well over a decade. For example, see National Intelligence Council, *Global Trends 2015: A Dialogue About the Future with Nongovernmental Experts* (Washington, DC: Central Intelligence Agency, 2000); and Amy B. Zegart, *Spying Blind: The CIA, the FBI, and the Origins of 9/11* (Princeton, NJ: Princeton University Press 2007).
32 James J. Wirtz, "Hiding in Plain Sight: Denial, Deception, and the Non-State Actor," *The SAIS Review of International Affairs* Vol. 28, No. 1 (2008), pp. 55–63.
33 Jennifer E. Sims and Burton Gerber (eds), *Transforming U.S. Intelligence* (Washington, DC: Georgetown University Press, 2005).
34 Director of National Intelligence Dennis C. Blair has indicated that he intends to intensify the adoption of such "mission management." See 2009 National Intelligence Strategy, available at www.dni.gov/files/documents/Newsroom/Reports%20and%20Pubs/2009_NIS.pdf.
35 Benjamin S. Lambeth, *The Transformation of American Airpower* (Ithaca, NY: Cornell University Press, 2000).

10
CONCLUSION

The study of intelligence failure, and the nearly synonymous phenomenon of surprise attack, are often treated as unfortunate aberrations in international relations. Failures of intelligence are blamed on the frailties and psychological limits of the human mind or the inability of organizations and policymakers to process, interpret and respond to accurate indications of future events. Decisions to launch a surprise attack often are depicted either as a reckless, desperate act or based upon a fundamental miscalculation of the military balance or the political commitment of potential adversaries. These situations are viewed as so unexpected and unprecedented, that analysts, policymakers and soldiers in the field are excused when they fail to "connect the dots" and are caught napping: entire military establishments constructed at great expense suffer a prompt defeat without ever really getting the opportunity to enter the fray. Scholars often submit that the lessons learned from postmortems of these intelligence failures and military defeats will at best be idiosyncratic, making it difficult to tailor reforms to meet future challenges.

By taking a *strategist's view* of intelligence failure and surprise attack, however, this volume depicts these phenomena in a different context. This strategic perspective emerges in the previous chapters in three ways. First, it suggests that intelligence failure and surprise attack are best understood as a phenomenon that manifests in a specific strategic setting in which the structure of a conflict produces fundamentally different perspectives on what can be achieved in war. Second, it depicts intelligence failure and surprise as a product of competing strategies, one intended to deter war, the other intended to circumvent deterrence. Third, it offers strategies that could mitigate the occurrence of intelligence failure, strategic surprise and the failure of deterrence. The remainder of the conclusion will explore each of these points in turn.

The strategic context of intelligence failure and surprise attack

The premise of this volume is that the structure of a conflict, which is shaped by the overall military balance between two actors in a nascent or enduring dispute, influences their risk acceptance when it comes to engaging in conflict and their preferences when it comes to selecting military strategies. When both parties perceive themselves to be evenly matched, they tend to take an "attritional" view of conflict. They tend to depict war's outcome as the product of a "force-on-force" engagement between relatively similar militaries, an attritional slugging match with many dangers and pitfalls that leaves few opportunities for easy victory. This shared attritional view of conflict leads to risk aversion. Under these circumstances, actors might be willing to engage in coercion or modest compellence strategies to test their opponent's political commitment to achieving or preserving some objective. Indeed, Thomas Schelling's famous "threat that leaves something to chance" comes to mind as one actor attempts to manipulate risk, by raising the prospect of inadvertent escalation, political miscalculation or accidental war to achieve their objectives short of open conflict.[1] War is a possibility under these circumstances, especially if one side believes that they have a superior strategy, doctrine, tactics or technology that will upset the military balance. Some untoward military incident also can prompt a spiral of escalation that can terminate in all-out conflict. Nevertheless, rarely does one side go "all in" by attempting to launch a strategic surprise attack against what it perceives to be an evenly matched opponent.

The best example of this type of phenomenon is the situation of Mutual Assured Destruction that emerged during the second half of the Cold War between the United States and the Soviet Union. Because both sides enjoyed a secure second-strike nuclear capability against their opponent, the strategic situation was defensive dominant: neither side could secure victory in an all-out military conflict, both were destined to end up in what can be characterized as a losing situation, or at least it would be difficult to discern a material difference between the victors and the vanquished. A shared "attritional" mindset thus dominated the perceptions of the parties involved: the likelihood of unprecedented losses, if not outright annihilation, generally shaped their attitudes towards the desirability of engaging in war. Since there was no way to guarantee that the outcome of a conflict, regardless of the operational brilliance of its opening gambit, would not be determined by a full-scale nuclear exchange, there was apparently a common estimate that surprise attack and intelligence failure simply served as an express train to Armageddon. In the view of some analysts, Mutual Assured Destruction produced a "nuclear revolution" leading to stability, specifically the absence of great power conflict, between the United States and the Soviet Union.[2]

The potential for conflict between evenly matched opponents tends to produce a commonality in their perception of the desirability of using war as an instrument to achieve their objectives. Both *share* an attritional perception of war, a perception that highlights the costs, not the opportunities, when it comes to the use of force to achieve their goals. This also leads to a shared risk aversion, which reduces the attraction of jumping headlong into war by using strategic surprise to present the opponent with a fait accompli. When both sides perceive a militarily balanced strategic setting, they are more likely to share an "attritional" mindset when they contemplate a potential conflict, producing a relatively high degree of risk aversion when it comes to their political and military interaction. This type of strategic setting fails to create the conditions needed for the occurrence of surprise attack and intelligence failure. Neither side perceives an incentive to launch a strategic surprise attack; thus, intelligence failure at the outset of war is also unlikely.

Ironically, intelligence failure and surprise become more likely as the military balance becomes increasingly skewed. Under these conditions, an asymmetric mindset emerges between the strong and the weak party in an enduring or nascent dispute. The stronger party retains an attritional view of war, believing that the outcome of war will be determined by a force-on-force contest in which the weaker party stands virtually no prospect of winning. For the stronger party, the prospect of deterrence remains robust because they perceive no realistic pathway to circumvent their superior military capabilities. Conflict, from the perspective of the stronger party, has nothing but a downside for the weaker party, while the stronger party rarely sees itself fettered in the exercise of its superior military capability. The weaker party, however, recognizes its inferior military position, but tends to focus on various constraints that in theory could limit the stronger party's use of its superior capabilities. Domestic weakness, alliance handicaps, competing interests, and a lack of political will are identified by the weaker party as constraints that will limit or even curtail the stronger party's response to surprise attack or the creation of a fait accompli. The constraints faced by the stronger party loom large in the minds of decision-makers leading a weaker challenger, increasing the salience and attraction of surprise as a preferred strategy.

As Michael Handel noted nearly forty years ago, these asymmetric perceptions set the stage for strategic surprise and intelligence failure. On the one hand, the weaker party becomes highly risk acceptant because they come to see their opponent as constrained. In their view, the stronger party might launch an all-out response to a surprise attack and a resulting fait accompli, but the chance that this worst-case scenario will come to pass is minimal given the constraints faced by their stronger opponent. The weak believe that they can sidestep the deterrent threats and superior military capability possessed by their stronger opponent while achieving their objectives. On the other hand, the stronger party believes that their overwhelming military capability is self-evident and that their deterrence strategy is robust. They believe that their weaker opponent is constrained by their military inferiority. In this situation, the stronger party encounters various idiosyncratic, psychological and organizational impediments that hamper its ability to respond to signals of impending attack. Signals suggesting an impending attack or some other type of fait accompli are considered too harebrained or reckless to be taken seriously; the stronger side's analysts and policymakers are unable to envision how others might believe that their ability to respond to strategic surprise is limited.

When the stronger party detects signals of some impending attack or event, they cannot be integrated into their prevailing cognitive schema, leaving intelligence analysts slow to recognize and policymakers reluctant to respond to the opponent's potential courses of actions that appear ex ante as highly implausible or downright self-destructive.

Thus, strategic surprise and intelligence failure occur in a specific strategic setting. Moreover, because strategic surprise and intelligence failure can only occur in a contest between at least two parties, it is important to specify the conditions under which these phenomena are likely to occur: they occur in conflicts between strong and weak actors in which an asymmetric view of not only the nature of conflict, but what can be achieved in war emerge. Because they recognize their military inferiority, the weak tend to privilege domestic political, economic, diplomatic and social constraints when they estimate their stronger opponent's response to surprise attack. Because they enjoy military superiority, the strong tend to highlight their opponent's military inferiority when developing intelligence estimates of future events. Under these circumstances intelligence failure becomes likely since an accurate estimate would not only have to overcome prevailing mindsets, but personal, organizational, policy and strategic assumptions and bureaucratic routines that govern entire intelligence and defense establishments. In theory, these handicaps can be overcome, but the risk paradox, identified by Handel, tends to hold sway, obscuring the significance of key signals and slowing policymakers' response to indications of impeding attack. Unfortunately, as one side begins to perceive incentives and opportunities to launch a strategic surprise attack, its opponent becomes increasingly likely to suffer a failure of intelligence that lays the groundwork for surprise attack to succeed.

Surprise, intelligence failure, and the interaction of competing strategies

The literature on surprise and intelligence failure pays little attention to the notion that these phenomena are produced when *competing strategies* interact to produce war. One strategy, deterrence, is embraced by the stronger party in the conflict. The strategy embraced by the weaker opponent, by contrast, is often described in a variety of ways—the gambit, reckless gamble, strategic mistake, strategic surprise attack, fait accompli, etc. Nevertheless, when one embraces the notion that competing strategies produce surprise attack and intelligence failure, the strategy of surprise attack appears useful because it quickly and efficiently destroys the strategy (specifically deterrence) embraced by the stronger opponent. In other words, strategic surprise attack is *strategic* because it completely unhinges the defense plans and ongoing military efforts of the stronger opponent.

In the competition between the strong and the weak that creates the psychological setting needed for surprise and intelligence failure to occur, the stronger opponent more often than not bases its defense strategy on the concept of deterrence. In other words, the stronger opponent does not necessarily embrace strategies of pre-emption or preventive war to preserve its security, but instead threatens retaliation against the weaker opponent in the event that the weaker opponent crosses some well-defined or, more often than not, somewhat obscure "red-line." The objective behind deterrence is to credibly threaten the use of superior military capability to preserve the peace or maintain the status quo. The goal of deterrence is to prevent war, not to specify in great detail the various operations needed to prosecute and prevail in war if deterrence fails. In fact, the exact nature of the potential military campaign in the aftermath of deterrence failure is sometimes only considered in general terms by the stronger party. If a deterrence strategy succeeds, war will not occur and military operations against the opponent will not be necessary. The objective behind deterrence is to preserve the peace, not prosecute some war. If war occurs, deterrence, the strategy developed at great expense by the stronger party, fails. Indeed, it fails completely at the outset of a war initiated by a surprise attack.

The strategy of surprise attack thus becomes an attractive strategy for the weaker opponent because it offers an opportunity to destroy the stronger opponent's deterrent strategy. Surprise attack immediately eliminates the ability of the stronger opponent to obtain or retain its primary strategic objective, preservation of the peace or the status quo. The eruption of hostilities creates an entirely new military and political setting, a setting that the stronger power hoped to avoid by making deterrent threats. By definition, the stronger power would now confront a host of questions and issues that it sought to avoid in the first place. For example, executing deterrent threats will only guarantee that war, the state of affairs it sought to avoid, will become a grim and possibly lengthy reality. Practical military and political difficulties created by the need to actually execute deterrent threats will also loom large, especially in light of the setbacks inflicted by the weaker opponent's opening gambit. Deterrent threats that seemed inherently credible and militarily effective in peacetime, will now appear to be difficult and costly to put into practice. Many will wonder if the effort is really worth the candle; after all it is one thing to threaten to use force to preserve the peace, it is quite another to act on those threats if deterrence should fail, especially if some fait accompli does not threaten vital national interests. Surprise attack and intelligence failure are strategically devastating because they force the stronger party to undergo a fundamental strategic reassessment once its preferred strategy has failed. Surprise attack can indeed inflict a military setback against a stronger opponent, but its impact on its strategy is devastating. Surprise attack holds out the prospect of altering the stronger party's estimate of the political desirability of actually using, not just threatening, the use of force.[3]

The fact that surprise attack destroys the stronger party's deterrent strategy also can explain why it is so closely linked to intelligence failure. Intelligence analysts would not only have to recognize that they are about to be attacked or suffer some undesirable fait accompli, they would also have to recognize that their deterrence strategy is about to fail catastrophically. They would have to recognize and convince policymakers that the opponent believes that they can unilaterally achieve some objective, while effectively sidestepping significant military opposition. Developing accurate estimates and politically compelling warning would have to entail acknowledgement of policy failure and the ineffectiveness of national defense strategy. The stronger party's analysts and policymakers also find it extraordinarily difficult to contemplate a future where their superior military capability will be rendered temporarily superfluous, leading to a breakdown of deterrence. They would have to recognize that their superior military capability has lost its effectiveness, at least temporarily. Surprise attack also shifts the onus of escalation onto the stronger party who would now have to choose to actually use, not just threaten the use, of force. And, as Schelling would suggest, forcing the onus of escalation onto one's opponent is a strategically superior position.

Thus, surprise attack can be depicted as a rational, albeit extraordinarily risky, strategy for the weaker party facing a superior opponent that embraces a deterrent strategy. Surprise attack destroys the opponent's strategy, alters the political and military setting from peace to war, and forces the stronger opponent to undertake a fundamental strategic reassessment at the most inopportune time. Strategic surprise not only allows the weaker party to achieve some fait accompli, it also delivers a sharp domestic and international political shock that might lead to the general acceptance of the new status quo. It breaks the weaker party out of the straightjacket created by the military superiority of its opponent. Surprise attack makes salient the constraints created by domestic politics, competing priorities and international opposition—constraints that just might make the stronger party reassess its overall stakes in a given dispute.

Countering surprise and avoiding intelligence failure: Possible strategies

The attraction to surprise as a strategy, and the looming possibility of intelligence failure, often produce tragic consequences in international relations. Stronger parties fail to deter weaker adversaries, while weaker adversaries initiate horrendous attritional engagements that often end catastrophically for them. Wars that the strong do not want to fight and the weak cannot expect to win are the outcome of surprise attack and intelligence failure.

It is not possible to alter the structural conditions that can lead to surprise attack and intelligence failure, i.e., simmering conflicts between strong and weak powers. More productive paths might focus on efforts to increase self-awareness of the cognitive biases that shape both strong and weak actors' perceptions of both parties' opportunities and constraints in the conflict or to take actions to manipulate the perceptions of the weaker party. For instance, the strong must recognize that employment of their superior military capability is not unfettered; they should recognize that they might even appear hamstrung by competing security demands, the opinions or vulnerability of allies, and social or domestic political considerations. Weaker parties tend to search for these "non-material" political, social or even "moral" weaknesses when it comes to painting a rosy picture of how the victim will respond to a strategic surprise attack. The weak acknowledge the superior strength of the stronger party, but they estimate that the stronger party will either choose not to respond massively or will be unable to bring their full strength to bear in the erupting conflict. The irony here is that surprise attacks are often brilliant and daring operational evolutions, but they support an overall strategy that does not reflect the best traditions of the military profession or the craft of politics. This strategic recklessness makes it hard for intelligence analysts to detect what is about to transpire and to communicate credible and actionable warnings to their political leadership. From the perspective of the stronger party, signals of impeding attack that are clear after the fact are difficult to discern ex ante because they cannot be fitted into a plausible scenario that ends in the military defeat of the stronger party.

What can the strong do to alter the "non-attritional" mindset and risk acceptance of the likes of Saddam Hussein, Osama bin Laden, or the clique of militarists that held sway in Japan in 1941? First, they must avoid a mistake commonly made by the strong when they suspect that their deterrence, or compellence strategies for that matter, appear to be losing their efficacy, i.e., engage in activities that are intended to highlight their military superiority over their weaker adversaries. When signs of trouble emerge, the strong often believe that the weaker adversary has somehow underestimated their military inferiority, which leads to actions that are intended to display or demonstrate their superior military capabilities. The movement of the Pacific Fleet to Pearl Harbor or the Johnson administration's coercive bombing campaign against North Vietnam were both designed to bring home to weaker adversaries their obvious military inferiority. In both instances, US policymakers seemed to believe that the governments in Tokyo and Hanoi suffered from some type of strategic "myopia"; they literally moved their superior military capabilities closer to the opponent to allow them to get a better look, so to speak, at what they were facing. These types of activities, however, fail to address the weaker party's perception that "non-material" factors will constrain the stronger party. Weaker parties recognize the military balance for what it is; they overestimate the impact of competing security demands, alliance handicaps and social or political considerations that face a stronger adversary. In effect, actions taken by the stronger party to increase its freedom of maneuver—settle other disputes, shore up alliances, or build political consensus at home or abroad—increase the credibility of deterrence strategies because they help eliminate or reduce potential constraints when it comes to executing deterrent threats, thereby undermining a fundamental perception that makes surprise attack attractive to the weaker party.

Second, despite their military superiority, the strong have to take steps to reduce their vulnerability to the weaker party's ongoing efforts to develop cunning military operations that manifest in surprise attack. Deterrence postures, force structures, doctrines and operational routines that remain static provide weaker parties with known challenges that can be subjected to a deliberate planning process that can unfold over months or even years. Change, especially if it occurs within a shorter cycle than the deliberate planning process undertaken by the weak, can greatly complicate the weaker party's efforts to sidestep the superior forces of the strong. To be successful, surprise attack depends on events unfolding within the finest of margins; anything that reduces the weaker opponent's confidence in its situational awareness and casts doubt on the stronger party's "day alert" or even "generated alert" posture should help to bolster deterrence.

Third, deterrence would be strengthened if the stronger party could take steps to more firmly place the onus of escalation onto the weaker party. In other words, deterrence strategies should not fail gracefully, so that strategic surprise produces little collateral damage or allows the attacker to focus on obtaining a specific objective. Instead, deterrence should fail deadly, producing a clear and foreseeable path to attritional warfare. Opportunities to launch focused and relatively bloodless attacks to achieve specific objectives only create incentives for the weaker party to gamble that the stronger party will not engage in sustained hostilities to reverse some fait accompli. Admittedly, it is difficult to say exactly what this type of deterrence posture would entail, but in theory it would involve actions to reduce the stronger party's degree of choice when it comes to responding to strategic surprise attack. Deterrent threats should appear more credible to the weaker party if it believes that hostilities will inevitably lead to an attritional engagement it cannot hope to win. Not only would such actions demonstrate the political commitment of the stronger party to defend the status quo ex ante, it would create an image of an automatic attritional response that might nullify the effects of various constraints that the weaker party hopes will temper the victim's reaction to strategic surprise attack.

What insight does this strategic perspective offer for intelligence analysts? Several recommendations emerge that are simple enough in theory, but remain extremely difficult to put into practice. They are difficult to realize because they require intelligence analysts to be aware of their own institutional, strategic and political context while remaining capable of stepping outside of that context to see the evolving situation from the weaker party's viewpoint. At a moment when deterrence matters most and security through the instrument of military superiority appears assured, they have to recognize the possibility of prompt strategic failure and communicate a credible warning and maybe even a course of action to an unreceptive audience.

The first step that analysts must take to achieve this type of analysis and warning is to overcome a mindset in which potential conflicts are depicted as force-on-force, attritional events that will inevitably culminate in victory for the stronger (their) side. Ironically, once analysts and policymakers believe (correctly) that a full-scale military clash will inevitably lead to the defeat of the weaker party, they find it difficult to perceive that the weaker opponent might still seek more limited objectives because of the likelihood that any conflict will escalate into a full-blown engagement that the weaker party cannot hope to win. Strategic surprise attack is not necessarily directed at achieving outright military victory in war, but is instead intended to destroy deterrence strategies, alter the status quo, shift the onus of escalation onto the stronger party and force the stronger party to reassess its strategic position. When Admiral Isoroku Yamamoto noted that the only way for Japan to win a war against the United States was to dictate terms in the White House, he was suggesting that was never going to happen.[4] Surprise attack creates a hope in the mind of the weaker opponent that valuable objectives can be achieved in a conflict with a much stronger opponent without overall victory in war and possibly even without a serious response or an existential defeat. Intelligence analysts must recognize that weaker opponents might gamble on using strategic surprise attack to achieve limited, albeit apparently unrealistic, objectives.

Second, intelligence analysts have to assume that weaker opponents are constantly searching for shortcomings both in the stronger party's deterrence strategy and in their military posture. Military superiority is not a panacea; it does not translate into a constant readiness to meet and repel attack everywhere. Technical, social and political change also is a fixture in world politics and if the pace of change outpaces the rate of organizational response, "niche" vulnerabilities can emerge in an otherwise robust defense posture, the type of vulnerabilities that attract the attention of the weaker party's defense planners. What emerges then is a need for analysts to conduct a sort of "net assessment" by comparing estimates of the opponent's course of action against realistic depictions of their own deterrent strategies and force postures. Given the organizational culture of the US intelligence community, however, undertaking this type of net assessment is highly problematic. Intelligence analysts and managers strive to remain aloof from direct involvement in policy formulation or political disputes, a position that stands in the way of gaining an intimate knowledge of potential weaknesses in current deterrence strategy, overall force posture and peacetime military operations. Nevertheless, signals of a weaker opponent's impending actions that appear bizarre or harebrained if viewed in isolation can take on far more alarming character if they appear to be directed against an emergent vulnerability in the stronger party's strategy or defenses. Net assessment is critical because it can highlight how existing organizational routines or planned responses to warning of enemy attack, which often increase policymakers' confidence that their overall defense posture is robust, would actually play into the hands of the attacker.

Third, intelligence analysts also have to understand that they must respond when the system is "blinking red." In other words, when unease spreads across the intelligence establishment about ongoing events, when seemingly bizarre assessments begin to surface about the opponent's future course of action, or when intelligence "dissenters," individuals who break with a consensus to sound increasingly shrill alarms, begin to make their opinions known, the time has come to reassess conventional wisdom and established policies. These types of developments actually constitute strategic warning of surprise attack because they demonstrate that signals about the opponent's intentions can no longer be accommodated into accepted assessments and that established policies or procedures can no longer respond to the developing situation. Indeed, analysts, intelligence managers and policymakers need to understand that time is actually running out when reports of unease, the opponent's bizarre behavior or vigorous analytic dissent reach senior policymakers.

Fourth, intelligence analysts must understand the dilemma faced by policymakers when it comes to responding to strategic warning. On the one hand, estimates of the opponent's future course of action are probabilistic; the costs and consequences of some prediction are not a forgone conclusion. On the other hand, the decision to respond to warning entails significant and certain costs. Policymakers thus confront a situation in which they are asked to bear certain costs to head off events that may, or may not, happen. Further complicating matters is the fact that policymakers prefer estimates that entail a high degree of certainty, but they also prefer that the courses of action they select will be certain to head off untoward events. Because intelligence analysts and managers cannot say ex ante that their estimates of the opponent's future are certain and that potential courses of action are guaranteed to prevent some untoward event from transpiring, policymakers tend to adopt a "wait and see" approach to unfolding events. Given the fact that surprise attacks depend on the finest of margins, however, limited responses that alter defense postures, especially if they are visible to the opponent, might be enough to derail initiatives that depend on events unfolding exactly as planned. Moreover, because limited responses might entail limited immediate costs, policymakers might find it easier to adopt modest changes in defense postures that are intended to reduce the likelihood of what appears ex ante to be a rather bizarre course of events. In that sense, anything that upset's the weaker party's planning process and finely tuned plans buys time for the stronger party to improve its situational awareness or maybe even ward off surprise attack.

Surprise attack, intelligence failure and the failure of deterrence occur in a specific international setting that can be easily recognized by intelligence analysts and policymakers alike. Recognition of this setting is not sufficient to prevent the occurrence of these phenomena, but it can serve as a warning to all concerned that despite outward appearances, peace is not assured. Conflicts between the strong and the weak entail particular risks.

Notes

1 Thomas Schelling, *The Strategy of Conflict* (Cambridge, MA: Harvard University Press, 1960).
2 Robert Jervis, *The Meaning of the Nuclear Revolution: Statecraft and the Prospect of Armageddon* (Ithaca, NY: Cornell University Press, 1989).
3 Colin Gray recently defined the term *strategy* as the art of using all the instruments at one's disposal to alter the political preferences of the opponent to suit one's interests. Colin Gray, *The Strategy Bridge: Theory for Practice* (Oxford: Oxford University Press, 2010). From this perspective, surprise attack alters the terms of the contest between weak and strong powers. The stronger power politically prefers to threaten the use of force to defend the status quo, but the weaker power is gambling on the possibility that it might not find it politically acceptable to actually use force to re-establish the *status quo anti bellum*.

4   Yamamoto offered the observation in January 1941 to an ultra-nationalist who was clamoring for war with the United States: "Should hostilities break out between Japan and the United States, it would not be enough that we take Guam and the Philippines, nor even Hawaii and San Francisco. To make victory certain, we would have to march into Washington and dictate the terms of peace in the White House. I wonder if our politicians, among whom armchair arguments about war are being glibly bandied about in the name of state politics, have confidence as to the final outcome and are prepared to make the necessary sacrifices," quoted in William Weir, *Fatal Victories* (New York: Pegasus Books, 2006), p. 203.

INDEX

10 Corps 32-3
9/11 Commission Report 118
ABM Treaty 108
Adler, Emanuel 93-4
Afghanistan 11, 13, 58, 61, 110, 131
Ahmad, Mahmud 33
Alfred P. Murrah Federal Building 59
all or nothing response 119-121
alliance handicaps 144, 148
Al-Qaeda 3, 5-6, 12-13, 18, 20, 51, 57-62, 75, 87, 106, 108, 110, 111n7, 118-119, 121-22
Arab Cooperation Council 76
Arab-Israeli War (1973) 4, 16, 49, 88, 110, 126, 129
Ardennes forest, 16-17, 27, 103
Army Republic of Vietnam (ARVN) 71
asymmetric attack 6, 10, 18, 29, 31, 103-05, 108-10
asymmetric warfare 86
Aum Shinrikyo 59
axis of evil 30, 106
Aziz, Tariq 78-9

Baghdad 76-7, 90-1
Baker, James 78-9
Balance of power paradox 66-7, 69, 75, 89-91, 95
Bastogne 138
Battle of Midway 12, 19-20, 113, 138

Bay of Pigs 34, 128
Bell, J. Bowyer 51-2, 54n13
Betts, Richard 5, 19, 139n8,
Big-unit War 70
Bipolarity 68-9, 72, 79
Blainey, Geoffrey 18, 84-5, 98n3
blinking red 118, 150
bolt out of the blue attack 56 58, 116
Border Security Force (BSF) 36
Budhwar, V. 37
Bundy, William P. 73
Bush, George H.W. 5, 75-6, 78-9, 87, 91
Bush, George W. 58, 61, 109

casualty averse America 16, 18, 97
Central Committee of the Vietnamese Worker's Party 71
Central Intelligence Agency (CIA) 4, 6, 15, 17, 19, 34, 59, 62
Cheema, Zafar Iqbal 34, 43n21
Chiang Kai-Shek 72
China 18, 29, 33, 35, 57, 61, 68, 72, 89, 96-97
Christensen, Thomas 18, 20, 96-7
Claude, Inis 69
Clausewitz, Carl von 10-12, 21n12, 46, 54n1, 104-05
Clinton, Bill 6
Cold War 2, 67, 74, 75, 89, 96-7, 116-119, 122, 128, 130, 143

combined arms operations 7, 124-8, 138, 139n2
communications intelligence (COMINT) 35-36
Congressional Research Service 58
Corona satellite 129
cry-wolf syndrome 3, 9, 21fn3
Cuba 15, 17, 33, 43n19, 48, 87, 98n12, 113, 123n1, 128, 132
Cuban Missile Crisis 17, 27, 96, 128-9

Daniel, Donald 49
Davis, Jack 123n8
day alert 95, 114-118, 121, 149
denial and deception 7, 9, 14-15, 31, 46-54, 54n1, 76, 116, 121-22, 124, 131, 135
Department of Homeland Security 135
deterrence failure 1-2, 7, 75, 84-6, 88-9, 90-5, 97, 146
deterrence trap 93
deterrent strategy 2, 7, 146-7
devil's advocate 107
Diem, Ngo Dinh 71
Directorate General of Military Intelligence (DGMI) 36, 39
Dobrynin, Anatoly, 17
Dras-Kargil Highway see National Highway 1A

Egypt. 4, 16, 49, 51, 54n9, 88, 129
electronic intelligence (ELINT) 36
Eskan Village 58
extended deterrence 85

false fronts 52
Federal Bureau of Investigation 59, 121, 130
Federal Emergency Management Agency 59
Ferris, John 49-50
Force Commander Northern Areas (FCNA) 32-3
Foreign Affairs 58
Fortmann, Michel 96
Fourth Generation Warfare 93
Freedman, Lawrence 76
Fulda Gap 116

Gauhar, Altaf 44fn24

generated alert 114-116, 118, 120, 149
Geneva Accords 71-71
geospatial intelligence (GEOINT) 124, 129, 131, 135, 139n3
Germany 30, 106, 88n17
Giap, Vo Nguyen 71, 74, 90-1
Gilgit 38-40, 45n47
Gilmore Commission 57
Glaspie, April 76
Golan Heights 49
gold-plating 4
Gomulka, Wladyslaw 43n19, 98n12
Gorbachev, Mikhail 78
group think 9

Hammes, Thomas 93
Handel, Michael 10-11, 13-14, 17, 19-20, 21n10, 21n12, 31, 86, 106, 144-5
Hanoi 70-2, 74, 79-80, 90-1
Hasan, Javed 33
Hawaii 12, 56, 59, 91, 110, 152n4
Hegel, G.W.F. 20
Heuer, Richards 52
Hiroshima 14
Hitler, Adolf 99fn17
Holocaust 4
human intelligence (HUMINT) 35-6, 38, 124, 132-3, 135-6
Hussein, Saddam 5, 30, 75-9, 84, 87, 90-91, 99n23, 138, 148

imagery intelligence (IMINT) 36, 139n3
India 27-30, 32-42, 42n2, 43n11, 43n14, 43n16, 44n22, 44n31, 44n32 45n48, 45n49, 45n50, 97, 99n21
indications and warning 7, 38, 113-120, 122, 135
information overload 3, 6
Intelligence Bureau (IB) 35-6, 39, 44n29
intelligence cycle 3, 5, 41, 122
intelligence dissenters, 19, 150
intelligence pipeline 5-6, 15, 19, 41, 56
Intelligence Reform and Terrorism Act of 2004 125
International Studies Quarterly 20
Iraq 4-5 11, 75-9, 87, 97, 94, 126; 2003 invasion 4, 109
Israel 4, 49, 54n9, 77, 88, 94, 129; Air Force 4, 49
Israeli issue, 76

Italy 30, 106

Jammu 27, 32, 40, 43n13
Japan 17-19, 30-32, 42n6, 48, 56-7, 60-2, 87-8, 91, 97, 103, 105-6, 111n7, 113, 127, 130, 148, 150, 152n4; Navy 19, 27, 59, 87, 110, 122
Jersey City 52
Johnson, Lyndon B. 70; administration 71-3, 79, 91, 148

kamikaze 60
Kargil 6, 27-9, 32-42, 43n2, 43n13, 43n16, 44n24, 44n31, 44n33, 44n34m
Kargil Review Committee 36-8, 42n2, 44n33, 44n34
Karsh, Efraim 76
Kashmir 27, 32, 34, 39, 40, 43n11, 43n13, 44n26, 44n32
Kennedy, John F. 43n19, 98n12; administration 96, 128, 132
Kent, Sherman 123n1
Kenya 58
Khan, Aziz 33, 41
Khan, Sahibzada Yakub 44n24
Khe Sanh 48, 127
Khobar Towers 57, 106
Khrushchev, Nikita 15, 33, 43n19, 87, 96, 98n12, 132
Knorr, Klaus 69
Kosovo 61, 75, 99n23
Kuwait 5, 75-80, 85, 87, 90-91

Ladakh region 29, 40
Lahore 39, 45n43, 48n43
Lahore initiative 30, 35, 40
Law Enforcement Sensitive (LES) Information 135
Lebow, Richard Ned 43n19, 81n12, 98n12
Leh 34, 37, 45n34
Levite, Ariel 22n26
Levy, Jack 65
Line of Control (LOC) 32, 34-5, 37-41, 44n31, 45n48
Little Round Top 138
Luttwak, Edward 11, 22n16, 22n17, 98n8

MAGIC 130
Malik, V.P. 45n48, 45n50
Manhattan 51, 56

McGarvey, Patrick 71
McNamara, Robert S. 73-4, 91
McNaughton, John 73
Mearsheimer, John 70
Measures and signals intelligence (MASINT) 124, 131-2, 135
Milosevic, Slobodan 85, 99n23
Minh, Ho Chi 71, 74, 91
mission-specific myopia 4
Missouri 20
Moscow 17, 69, 79, 90, 117
Mount Surabachi 138
Mumbai attacks 99n21
Musharraf, Perez 33, 43n21
Mushkoh 34, 36-7, 39
Mutual Assured Destruction 96, 143

Nagasaki 14
National Highway 1A 34, 39, 45n42
Nazi Germany 6, 91, 99n17; Ardennes offensive 16-17, 103
need to know basis 4
Neelum Valley 32
net assessment 100n31, 119, 150
New Delhi 30, 43n14
New York 18, 56
non-state actor 1, 6, 9, 18, 93, 113, 115, 117-22, 123n6, 134, 139
North Atlantic Treaty 65; Organization 85, 116
North Vietnam 15-16, 19, 67, 70-2, 74, 79, 90-1, 148
North Vietnamese Army (NVA) 48, 71, 74
Northern Light Infantry 27, 34
Nuclear Posture Review (2002) 108

On War 10
Open source intelligence (OSINT) 124, 133-5
Organization of Petroleum Exporting Countries (OPEC) 75
Osama bin Laden 6, 20, 51, 58, 61-2, 106, 148
Owl of Minerva 20

Pakistan 27-30, 32-42, 42n2, 43n11, 43n13, 43n14, 43n16, 44n22, 44n23, 44n24, 44fn26, 45n42, 43n43, 45n49, 45n50, 87, 99n21
Paul, T.V. 66

Pearl Harbor 2-3, 5-6, 12, 16-20, 27-8, 30-2, 48, 56-62, 87-8, 91, 97, 103-4, 108, 110, 111n7, 122, 127, 148
Penkovsky, Oleg 132
Pentagon 6, 11, 13, 56, 62, 118,
People's Army of Vietnam see North Vietnamese Army (NVA)
People's War 72
President's Daily Brief (PDB) 6
preventive war 109, 146
Prince Sultan Air Base 57

Rahman, Omar Abdel 51-52
Rana, Surinder 44n32
red lines 83, 86, 89, 97n1
red team 103-5, 107-111, 112n11
Research and Analysis Wing (R&AW) 35-6, 38-9
Revolution in Military Affairs (RMA) 96
Richardson, J.O. 99n16
Richelson, Jeffrey 131
risk paradox 10, 13-14, 17, 31 106, 145
Riyadh 57-8
Rodriguez, Jose 55n20
Roosevelt, F.D.R. 57, 99n16; administration 57, 88, 99, 110
Rusk, Dean 17
Rwanda 61

Saigon regime 15, 19, 70-2, 79
Salami tactics 89, 97n1
Schelling, Thomas 143, 147
September 11, 2001 terror attacks 3, 5-6, 11, 13, 18, 20, 21n13, 28, 51, 53, 56-62, 103, 108, 110, 118-19, 121-2, 125
Sharif, Nawaz 27, 33, 45n47
Shevardnaze, Eduard 77
Siachen 32, 34, 39, 87
SIGINT 3, 124, 130-1, 135-6
SIGMA I 73
Signals Intelligence see SIGINT
signal-to-noise ratio 9, 22n26
silver bullet 11, 127, 129
Singh, Jasit 40
Singh, Surinder 36-37, 44n34
Somalia 57, 106, 110
South Vietnam 15, 48, 70-74, 80, 90
Soviet Union 58, 67-8, 70, 72, 74, 76-7, 79, 89, 96, 99n23, 116, 123n2, 129, 143
special forces 12

Special National Intelligence Estimate (SNIE) 85-3-62 15, 17
special operations 10, 12, 60
Srinagar-Leh 40, 42
Stalin, Joseph 22n28
State Department 4
Stein, Janice Gross 43n19, 81n12, 98n12
Suez Canal 49

Taliban 13, 58, 61, 107, 126
Tanzania 58
Taylor, Maxwell 74, 91
Terrorism: Near Eastern Groups and State Sponsors 58
Tet offensive 15, 19, 48, 90, 110, 127
The Concept 4, 49
Theory of International Politics 67, 89
Type I error, 5
Type II error, 5

Ultra secret 3, 130
Ultra syndrome 3, 9, 21n3
United Nations (UN) 65, 77-8; Resolution 678 78
United States 2-3, 5, 12, 17-18, 29, 30, 33, 43n19, 48, 51, 53, 57-62, 67-8, 70-76, 78-80, 87, 89, 90-1, 94, 96-7, 98n12, 99n21, 105-7, 110, 111n7, 116, 123n2, 129, 134, 139, 143, 150, 152n4; Department of Defense 59, 62
United States Navy 12, 58-9, 88, 99n16, 108, 114, 138; Pacific Fleet 56, 87-8, 91, 99fn16, 148
unnecessary wars 2, 84
USS Arizona 52
USS Cole 58, 106

Vajpayee, A.B. 30
Viet Cong 15, 19, 48, 70-1, 91
von Hlatky, Stefanie 96

Waltz, Kenneth 67-9, 89-90
War on Terrorism 62
Washington, D.C. 18, 57-8, 62, 69, 79, 87, 91, 96, 98n12, 128, 152n4
weak-state optimism 86, 94
Whaley, Barton 49, 51-2
Winter Air Surveillance Operations (WASO) 37
Wohlstetter, Roberta, 22n26, 31

Wolfers, Arnold 69, 80n10, 81n13
World Trade Center 3, 6, 12-13, 20, 51, 56, 62, 87, 103, 106, 118
World War II 3, 99n17, 105, 107, 125, 129-30, 138

Yamamoto, Isoroku 150, 153n4
Yom Kippur War see Arab-Israeli War (1973)

Zia-ul-Haq, Muhammad 44n24